M000308005

A STUDENTS' TEXT-BOOK
OF ASTROLOGY

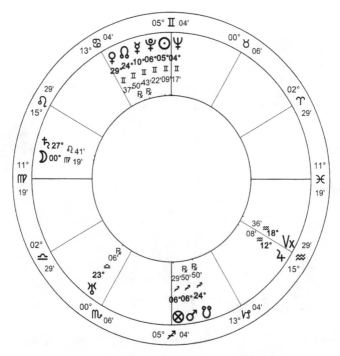

Born May 26, 1890, 12:04 pm GMT, Birmingham, UK.
Died, December 31, 1942, London

Other books by Vivian Robson:
Astrology and Sex
A Beginner's Guide to Practical Astrology
Electional Astrology
The Fixed Stars and Constellations in Astrology
The Radix System
Your Affinity
Alan Leo's Dictionary of Astrology (*as editor*)

THE VIVIAN ROBSON MEMORIAL EDITION OF

A STUDENTS' TEXT-BOOK

OF

ASTROLOGY

BY

VIVIAN E. ROBSON, B. Sc.

MARYLAND
ASTROLOGY CLASSICS
207 VICTORY LANE, BEL AIR MD 21014

On the cover:
Brompton Cemetery, London, 1981. Photograph by David R. Roell.
Vivian Robson is not buried here.

Vivian Erwood Robson (1890-1942) Curator Turned Astrologer, by Hugh
S. Torrens. Copyright 1989 by Hugh S. Torrens, used by permission of
the author. Grateful thanks to Prof. Torrens for his help, and for sup-
pling Vivian Robson's Death Certificate.

Grateful thanks to Mr. Philip Graves for his tireless assistance.
And thanks to the British Museum, and the Geological Society.

ISBN: 978 1 933303 37 6

THE VIVIAN ROBSON MEMORIAL EDITION
of
A Student's Text-Book of Astrology
is
Copyright © 2010 by William R. Roell
All rights reserved

A Student's Text-Book of Astrology
was first published in 1922

Published by
Astrology Classics
the publication division of
The Astrology Center of America
207 Victory Lane, Bel Air MD 21014
on line at www.**AstroAmerica.com**

PREFACE

For many years there has been a demand for an up-to-date, concise, and comprehensive text book of Astrology that is complete in itself and does away with the necessity of purchasing one or more additional volumes, and it is primarily to meet this need that the present work has been undertaken.

The method of arrangement that has finally been adopted is in some respects new, inasmuch as it has been my endeavour to make each chapter complete in itself and so dispense with the usual annoying necessity of turning back to the introductory chapters in order to find the influence of the planets and signs on the particular matter under consideration. Each chapter is, therefore, arranged so as to include the general rules applicable to that section, the specific effects of planets and signs, and a number of special rules or aphorisms. By including the latter I am aware that I lay myself open to the charge of treating the subject in too cut-and-dried a manner, but I have endeavoured to correct any such view of astrology itself in the chapter on general principles of judgment, and moreover, many of the rules are of such value that it seemed a pity to omit them, especially as accuracy and definition of judgment are the qualities most needed in present day astrological practice.

A good deal of hitherto unpublished material will be found scattered throughout the book, and as much detail in every case as could be conveniently compressed in a manner consistent with clearness. Had space been no object I should have endeavoured to have illustrated each important statement by an example nativity, but this would have expanded the work to an unmanageable size, and was found to be impracticable.

In conclusion I take this opportunity of expressing my thanks to many friends and pupils for their helpful interest and suggestions, and in particular to Mr. Clifford Bax, without whose kindly offices the work would never have been produced ; to my colleague, Miss J. Harrap, who read and criticised most of the manuscript ; and to my wife who undertook the laborious task of typing the whole work.

VIVIAN E. ROBSON.

48, Flanders Mansions,
   Bedford Park, London, W. 4.
      6th June, 1922.

NOTE TO SECOND EDITION

A few trivial errors and omissions have been rectified in this edition, and the tables of Standard and Summer Time have been improved by the addition of further information. No other changes have been made.

CONTENTS

SECTION I.
GENERAL PRINCIPLES AND THE CASTING OF A HOROSCOPE

SECTION II.
THE JUDGMENT OF A HOROSCOPE

VII

SECTION III
DIRECTIONS AND RECTIFICATION

APPENDIX

The Vivian Robson Memorial:

Vivian Erwood Robson (1890-1942)

SECTION I

GENERAL PRINCIPLES OF ASTROLOGY AND THE
CASTING OF A HOROSCOPE

CHAPTER I

THE FUNDAMENTAL PRINCIPLES OF ASTROLOGY

1. DEFINITION. The science of Astrology is concerned with the effects of planetary positions upon the earth and its inhabitants. The exact nature of such a connection is a matter of speculation, though its reality may be proved experimentally, and we are not in a position to say, with any degree of certainty, whether the planets actually *influence* Mundane affairs or whether they are merely signals and pointers that denote certain causes without necessarily originating them. It should be remembered, therefore, that when we speak of the influence of a planet we are using a convenient phrase to denote the obvious connection of planet and effect without concerning ourselves as to its theoretical justification.

2. FACTORS EMPLOYED. Astronomy is the foundation of astrology, and a horoscope is simply an accurate diagram representing the positions of the heavenly bodies in relation to the earth at any given moment. The actual factors employed are the Sun, Moon, and planets, the Signs of the Zodiac, and the position or orientation of the earth. In certain cases these are supplemented by fixed stars, eclipses, comets, and other celestial phenomena, but such aids

3

are secondary, and except in the case of eclipses are rarely used.

3. THE SOLAR SYSTEM. For all practical purposes the factors employed in astrology are limited to the Solar System. The central, and by far the largest body of the system, is the Sun, round which revolve the planets and their satellites, the nearest to the Sun being Mercury, the next Venus, then the Earth with its satellite, the Moon, and then Mars, the Asteroids, Jupiter Saturn, Uranus, and lastly Neptune, which is the most distant. Each of these bodies has its own characteristic nature and produces or signalises definite effects, and all are of considerable astrological importance, with the exception of the Asteroids, whose influence has not yet been properly investigated, and which are rarely included in a horoscope.

From time to time misconceptions have arisen here owing to the terminology adopted by astrologers, and some explanation is necessary. The astrologer knows quite well that the Sun is to all intents and purposes stationary, and that the earth moves round it, and also that the Moon is merely a satellite, but he often finds it convenient to refer to the Sun and Moon as planets, and to speak of the Sun's movement when he really means its apparent change of position due to the Earth's movement. It should, therefore, be understood that such remarks are used merely for convenience and refer to *apparent* phenomena. For practical astrological purposes the earth is taken as the main body and all the positions used are those that appear to be held by the planets *as seen from the Earth*, or in other words they are *geocentric*

n the centre of the Earth) and not
ic (seen from the centre of the Sun)
are used in Astronomical works. This
has ⌐ n used as an argument against astrology,
but a little thought will show that it is really
of no weight. We are concerned with the effects
of the planets on ourselves and on the earth,
and therefore, while using the true positions in
space of the planets we measure the angles
between them and note the positions they
occupy relative to ourselves rather than to the
Sun.

4. ORBITAL REVOLUTION. All the planets perform two movements simultaneously, viz : revolution round the Sun and rotation upon their
own axes, but except in the case of the Earth
we are concerned only with their revolution.
The path, or *orbit*, of every planet is an ellipse
nearly approaching a circle, of which the Sun
occupies one of the fixed points or *foci*. No
two bodies perform a complete revolution in
the same time, and while it takes the earth
one year to return to the same point in space,
Neptune requires almost 165 years. Therefore
it is only after millions of years that the planets
all return to any given position with respect
to each other, and except in the case of people
born at the same time and place no two horoscopes can ever be exactly alike. Owing to these
differences in speed there is a continual ka-
leidoscopic change taking place in the heavens
as seen from the earth, one planet overtaking
and passing another, and then apparently slowing
down, stopping and beginning to move backwards for a time. This apparent backward motion
is known as *retrogradation* and is merely an

illusion caused by the combined motions of the planet and the earth and their position relative to the Sun. The most familiar example of a similar illusion is furnished by two railway trains moving side by side. From the point of view of a man seated in the slower train he is stationary while the overtaking train is moving forwards. If, however, his train gradually increases in speed, the other will appear to him to be slowing down, to stop, and finally to move backwards as his train gradually draws ahead. The illustration is not quite parallel but will no doubt serve to indicate the principle involved. It is sufficient here to emphasise the fact that no planet ever really moves backwards, and that retrogradation is only apparent. Any given planet, however, moves more quickly at certain points of its orbit than at others, the Earth's speed varying from about 59 minutes of space to 61 minutes a day, and this fact becomes of importance when dealing with the question of time.

5. THE ZODIAC. The path of the Earth round the Sun is called the *ecliptic*, and it is observed that all the planets' orbits lie nearly in the same plane, and are included in a belt of about 9 degrees on either side of the ecliptic. This belt is termed the *Zodiac* and is divided equally into 12 sections of 30 degrees each, which are called *signs* and are given distinctive names. The Zodiac is a circle and therefore has no real beginning, but an arbitrary point is taken as its commencement and is termed *the first point of Aries* or 0° Aries, and is used as the standard for all measurements. This point is that at which the Sun passes from south to north decli-

nation and is one of the two points where a line from the centre of the earth to the Sun cuts the Earth's equator, which happens on about March 21st and September 21st each year, the former being the date when the Sun is in 0° Aries. This circle of the Zodiac is used in Astrology to define the positions of the planets, and they are measured in signs, degrees, minutes and seconds from 0° Aries and in degrees, minutes and seconds above (north)or below (south) the ecliptic line. The distance from Aries is termed celestial *longitude*, and that above or below the ecliptic, celestial *latitude*. At the same time another system of measurement is used which has reference to the Earth's equator or to its projection in space. The same point of intersection between the equator and ecliptic, 0° Aries, is used as the starting point, but the measurement is taken along the equator and north or south of it instead of along the ecliptic, the longitudinal distance being measured in degrees from 0° to 360° or in hours from 0 to 24 and termed *Right Ascension*, and the distance north or south, *declination*. All these standards are used in Astrology, the most usual, however, being longitude and declination.

One other point needs mention and that is the exact nature of the Zodiac. There are really two zodiacs, namely, the zodiac of constellations and the zodiac of signs, the former consisting of 12 actual unequal constellations along the line of the ecliptic, bearing the same names as the signs, and the latter being an imaginary circle or belt equally divided into 12 parts. *It is the latter, or zodiac of signs, that is used in astrology, and the constellation zodiac may be disregarded.* Originally the two coincided, but owing to a phenomenon known as the Precession of the Equinoxes the point 0° Aries is gradually passing backwards through the constellations at the rate of about 50 seconds per annum, and now falls on or about 10° Pisces of the constellations.

6. ROTATION. The earth performs one complete rotation upon its own axis from west to east in 24 hours, and the effect of this movement is to make Sun, Moon, planets, and stars appear to rise in the east, pass across the sky, and set in the west. In other words each sign and degree of the zodiac rises, culminates, and sets once in 24 hours, and it is on account of this that the *time* of birth is of such great importance in astrology, as it enables us to fix the exact position of the earth in relation to the other bodies and points in space. One complete rotation of the earth is called a *day* but it is necessary to distinguish between three kinds of day, viz:— Sidereal, Solar or Apparent, and Mean.

(*a*) *Sidereal Day.* Suppose a star is exactly overhead at a given time. The Sidereal Day is the time taken by the earth to rotate through one complete circle so that the star again occupies the same position, or in other words it is the time elapsing between two successive passages of a given star over a fixed point. The Sidereal Day is about 4 minutes shorter than the day registered by the clock.

(*b*) *Solar or Apparent Day.* Instead of a star the Sun is used as the standard and the Solar Day is the time elapsing between two successive passages of the Sun over a fixed point, and is

8

about 4 minutes longer than the Sidereal Day. The reason for this is that the earth moves about one degree during the day so that at the end of one complete rotation the Sun appears to have advanced one degree, and the earth has to rotate through this extra distance, which takes it about 4 minutes, in order to bring the Sun back to the same place. The Solar Day is not in general use as it is variable in length. The earth moves at a variable speed, according to its place in its orbit, and therefore the Sun appears to move either more or less than one degree a day, which will, therefore, be more or less than 4 minutes in excess of the fixed and unvariable Sidereal Day.

(c) *Mean Day.* As the Solar Day varies in this manner the *average* length of all the days in a year is used in practice and is called the Mean Day. All our civil time is *Mean* Time, which may or may not coincide with Solar Time, there being at times a discrepancy of as much as 16 minutes. All astronomical and astrological tables are computed for Mean Time, and all births are registered in Mean Time also, except in the very rare cases where a Sun-dial is used. Then the apparent Time given by the Sun-dial must be converted into Mean Time by adding or subtracting the difference (called the Equation of Time) which is given for every day of the year in Whitaker's Almanac, but this is of extremely rare occurrence and cases will probably never be encountered by the student.

The two standards of time used in astrology are the Mean and Sidereal, and as the Mean Day is $3^m 56^s.56$ longer than the Sidereal, Mean

A STUDENTS' TEXT-BOOK OF ASTROLOGY

Time may be at once converted into Sidereal Time by the addition of 3ᵐ 56ˢ.56 per diem or 9ˢ.86 per hour. There is a column in the Ephemeris headed "Sidereal Time" which gives the Sidereal Time at noon on the day in question. A clock registering Sidereal Time is in every Observatory and is set at 0ʰ 0ᵐ 0ˢ when 0° Aries is immediately overhead or "on the mid-heaven". One degree passes across the mid-heaven in about 4 minutes and, therefore, the Sidereal Time at noon on any day shows what degree is on the mid-heaven at that moment, and by adding the time elapsed between noon and birth we obtain the Sidereal Time at birth and know from that the degree on the mid-heaven at that particular moment. To avoid calculation the Sidereal Time corresponding to any mid-heaven degree is tabulated in the "Tables of Houses" which also show the degree rising and those upon other important points. Thus we know exactly where a vertical line drawn from the earth is "pointing" in space and being given the longitudes of the planets we can insert them in a diagram in their proper positions relative to the earth.

7. TIME. The subject of time standards is of the greatest astrological importance. The Ephemeris is computed to Greenwich Mean Time (abbreviated G.M.T.) and it is essential to know in what standard of time a birth is registered in order to be able to find the corresponding G.M.T. and also the Local Mean Time (abbreviated L.M.T.)

(a) *Local Mean Time.* Local noon is the moment measured in Mean Time at which the Sun is on the mid-heaven of any particular place. In the following remarks *Mean* Time must be always understood as we are no longer concerned with Solar Time.

When it is noon at Greenwich the Sun is overhead, but at New York it will not long have risen, and noon there will not occur for approximately another 5 hours, the *Local* Time at New York being about 7 a.m. or more exactly 7. 4 a.m. Therefore noon at Greenwich is equivalent to 7.4 a.m. at New York.

We have already seen that in casting a horoscope the planets must be arranged according to the way the earth is pointing, and it follows that when we are finding the degree on the mid-heaven we must use Local Time or our positions will be wrong. On the other hand, however, the Sun occupies the same degree and minute of longitude at Greenwich noon as it does at 7.4 a.m. at New York, and as the planetary positions in the Ephemeris are all computed for G.M.T. we must find the G.M.T. corresponding to our Local Time when calculating their exact longitudes.

The Local Mean Time of any place depends entirely upon its longitude east or west of Greenwich. The earth rotates at the rate of one degree in every 4 minutes and therefore the Local Time of a place 1° West of Greenwich will be 4 minutes earlier than the G.M.T. *To find the difference in time between Greenwich and any given place* convert the longitude of the place into time at the rate of 1 hour for each 15°, 4 minutes for each degree, and 4 seconds for each minute. The easiest method is to call the degrees of space minutes of time, and the minutes of space seconds of time, and multiply by 4.

Thus New York is 74° 0' West of Greenwich. Call this 74^m 0^s and multiply by 4. The result is 296^m 0^s or 4^h 56^m 0^s. If the place is West of Greenwich subtract the result from G.M.T. to obtain L.M.T. and if east add it.

(b) *Standard Time.* It is not convenient in practice for every place to use its own Local Time and definite standards have been adopted to cover large areas. Thus the whole belt of country lying between 67°W30' and 82°W30' uses a standard time that is 5 hours slow of Greenwich. This is nearly correct for New York but not for many other places in the area as it is a purely artificial time. In dealing with such cases as these where a birth is registered in Standard Time it is only necessary to add or subtract the Standard to obtain the correct G.M.T., and from that we can at once arrive at the true Local Time by applying the longitude in time to the G.M.T. Thus suppose a birth took place at Pittsburg, Long. 80°W0' at 2.15 p.m. Standard Time. The standard in use is 5 hours slow of Greenwich, and the G.M.T. will, therefore, be 2^h 15^m plus 5^h = 7^h 15^m p.m. The longitude in time of Pittsburg is 5^h 20^m 0^s which must be subtracted from the G.M.T. to obtain L.M.T. Thus 7^h 15^m minus 5^h 20^m = 1^h 55^m p.m. The result is, therefore, that birth took place at 1.55 p.m. L.M.T. corresponding to 7.15 p.m. G.M.T. A Table is included in the Appendix showing the standards at present in use and where possible the dates upon which they were adopted.

(c) *Summer Time.* Summer Time is a variety of Standard Time in which one hour is added to the G.M.T. or to the Standard Time of the place during certain months of the year, so that all birth time then registered must have one hour subtracted from them to convert them into the time normally used at the place. There is much confusion in the dates that have been adopted by various countries, and in many cases, partly owing to the War, our knowledge is not exact, but a Table is given in the Appendix showing so far as possible the dates during which Summer Time has been used since its adoption in 1916.

(*d*) *The Calendar*. The Calendar now in universal use is the Gregorian, or New Style, which has replaced the Julian or Old Style. It is important when calculating horoscopes for ancient times or for modern Russian dates to know in what style the date is recorded, and a Table is therefore included in the Appendix showing the dates on which the various countries adopted New Style, and also the number of days difference between Old Style and New Style in various centuries. The question is entirely one of chronology and a detailed explanation of the differences in style is therefore unnecessary.

CHAPTER II

THE ALPHABET OF ASTROLOGY.

1. THE PLANETS. There are 9 heavenly bodies that are employed in astrology, their names and symbols being as follows :

Sun	☉	Jupiter	♃
Moon	☽	Saturn	♄
Mercury	☿	Uranus	♅
Venus	♀	Neptune	♆
Mars	♂		

Each of these bodies is a centre of force and exerts its own particular kind of influence affecting us according to its position in the horoscope and the sign and house through which the influence is transmitted. The general nature of each planet is as follows:—

Sun. Hot, dry, positive, electric, masculine, vitalising, strong, sanguine and inflammatory. It is never retrograde.

Moon. Cold, moist, phlegmatic, negative, magnetic, feminine, fruitful, changeable, wandering and sympathetic. Its nature is convertible as it partakes largely of the nature of the planet most strongly aspecting it. The Moon is a collector and absorber of influence, and carries the influence of one body to another. It is never retrograde, but was considered so by the ancients when its motion was less than the mean value of 13° 11′ a day.

Mercury. Cold, nervous, changeable, active, excitable, and busy. Its influence is convertible, and it takes on that of the planet in strongest aspect with it, becoming masculine or feminine and benefic or malefic according to the aspecting planet.

Venus. Warm, temperate, moist, fruitful, negative, magnetic, graceful, joyful and pleasure-giving. She was called the Lesser Fortune by the ancients, and her influence is favourable, tending to peace, harmony, justice and love.

Mars. Hot, dry, barren, inflammatory, positive, electric, energetic, warlike and quarrelsome. It was called the Lesser Infortune and is usually unfavourable, tending to accidents, wars, quarrels, fires and passions.

Jupiter. Warm, moist, fruitful, positive and electric. It was called the Greater Fortune and its influence is benevolent, charitable, jovial and expansive.

Saturn. Cold, dry, barren, melancholy, negative and magnetic. It is the Greater Infortune and its influence is separative, secretive, apprehensive, suspicious, selfish, cold and chaste.

Uranus. Cold, dry, barren, positive and electric. It is eccentric, explosive, spasmodic, original, erratic, separative and tends to accentuate the will and individuality.

Neptune. Warm, moist, fruitful, negative and magnetic. Its influence is chaotic, dreamy, fanciful, psychic, spiritual, deceptive and tends to sacrifice or self-suppresion.

These influences are general and are exerted in every department of life, being modified by signs and houses, and their application in particular cases will be explained later. The use of the terms "benefic" and "malefic" is a convenience. The nature of a planet is neither good nor bad, and the question of fortunate or unfortunate influences depends upon the planet's position and aspects in the horoscope. It is important to remember that a malefic will produce good if well aspected, and a benefic will prove unfortunate if badly aspected. There is, however, probably more sympathy between conditions of life here and the nature of the benefic planets, for while a badly aspected malefic will produce serious evils, a benefic in a similar condition will not be so strongly and violently evil.

Each planet moves through the zodiac in the order of the signs, passing from Aries to Taurus, and so on to Pisces, from which it again passes into Aries, and its position is denoted by the degree it occupies in any particular sign. At various times all the planets, with the exception of the Sun and Moon, appear to move backwards through the zodiac, i.e. from Aries to Pisces to Aquarius, and so on, after which they bcome stationary and again move forwards. A planet thus moving backwards is called *Retrograde* (symbol ℞), and when moving forward *Direct* (symbol D). The point at which it is stationary passing from direct to retrograde is called its *First Station* and that at which it again becomes direct is called its *Second Station*. A retrograde planet is weaker than one that is direct and usually promises more evil or good than it performs. Retrogradation weakens both good and evil planets

alike, and does *not* make a malefic more evil,
as is sometimes stated. A planet that is stationary is always of very great importance and its
influence in a map is thereby greatly accentuated.
When within 8° 30′ of the Sun a planet is said
to be "combust", and this was considered a
weak and unfortunate position by the ancients,
though less harmful to Mercury than to the
other bodies.

2. THE SIGNS OF THE ZODIAC. The circle of
the zodiac is divided into 12 equal parts of
30° in extent, each of which is called a "Sign",
The signs are divided into two groups termed
Northern and Southern, and as they form a
circle the first six are always opposite the last
six. The names and symbols should be learnt
in order, and it is necessary to know at a glance
the sign opposite any given one. The Latin
and English names of the signs, together with
their symbols are as follows :—

Northern.				*Southern.*	
1. Aries, The Ram,	♈	opposite to	7.	Libra, The Balance,	♎
2. Taurus, The Bull,	♉	,, ,,	8.	Scorpio, The Scorpion,	♏
3. Gemini, The Twins,	♊	,, ,,	9.	Sagittarius, The Archer,	♐
4. Cancer, The Crab,	♋	,, ,,	10.	Capricorn, The Goat,	♑
5. Leo, The Lion,	♌	,, ,,	11.	Aquarius, The Waterman,	♒
6. Virgo, The Virgin,	♍	,, ,,	12.	Pisces, The Fishes,	♓

There are many divisions and classifications
of the signs which will be dealt with where
necessary, but the following classifications are
important and should be memorised. It is not
necessary to enter into a description of the
influences of signs and divisions at present, as they
will be fully treated in the chapters on Judgment.

17

(a) *Triplicities.*

Fiery Signs	♈	♌	♐
Earthy Signs	♉	♍	♑
Airy Signs	♊	♎	♒
Watery Signs	♋	♏	♓

(b) *Quadruplicities.*

Cardinal or Moveable Signs	♈	♋	♎	♑
Fixed Signs	♉	♌	♏	♒
Mutable, Common or Flexed Signs	♊	♍	♐	♓

(c) *Positive and Negative Signs.* The signs are alternately positive and negative, the odd signs ♈ ♊ ♌ ♎ ♐ ♒ being positive and masculine, and the even signs ♉ ♋ ♍ ♏ ♑ ♓ negative and feminine.

(d) *Decanates.* Each sign of 30° is sub-divided into three parts of 10° each, called Decanates. The first decanate of a sign is under the sub-rulership of the sign itself, the second is sub-ruled by the following sign of the same triplicity, and the third is ruled by the remaining sign of that triplicity. Thus 0° to 10° ♈ is sub-ruled by ♈, 10° to 20° ♈ is sub-ruled by ♌, which is the sign following ♈ in the fiery triplicity, and 20° to 30° ♈ is sub-ruled by ♐. Similarly, 0° to 10° ♍ is under ♍, 10° to 20° ♍ is under ♑, and 20° to 30° ♍ is under ♉.

3. RELATION OF SIGNS AND PLANETS. Definite relationships exist between the planets and signs of the zodiac. A given planet does not act with equal power through all signs, as in some cases the two influences are sympathetic and in others antagonistic, so that the influence of the planet is more favourable and less disturbed in some signs than in others. There are four

chief kinds of relationship that are of particular importance, namely, House, Detriment, Exaltation and Fall.

(*a*) *House.* Each planet is said to be the *ruler* of two signs, with the exception of the Sun and Moon, which rule one each, such signs being the zodiacal *houses* of the planet. In each case one sign is odd or positive and the other even or negative, the former being termed the *day* house, and the latter the *night* house. In present day astrological practice this distinction is usually ignored, but the ancients set some store by it and considered the day house to have chief power in a day horoscope, and the night house in a night horoscope. A planet in its own house is in its most powerful position and tends to operate more strongly and favourably than when otherwise placed. Afflictions to such a body are not so serious, while good aspects act more powerfully.

(*b*) *Detriment.* A planet is in its detriment when in one of the signs opposite to those it rules. This is its worst position and its influence is then rendered weaker for good and more powerful for evil.

(*c*) *Exaltation.* Each planet is said to be exalted when it is in a certain sign of the zodiac, and it is then rendered more powerful for good though not to quite so great an extent as when in one of its houses. Unlike house and detriment a planet has only one sign of exaltation, and the ancients held it to be exalted only when in a particular degree of that sign. This point, however, is now ignored, and a planet is considered to be exalted when in any part of the sign. For the sake of completeness the Table below indicates the exact degree of exaltation which was assigned to each body.

(*d*) *Fall.* The fall of a planet is the sign (and degree) opposite to its exaltation. This is a weak position that renders the planet less powerful for good and more powerful for evil. It is held to be less serious than the detriment, but too much importance should not be attached to this comparison, as in many cases a planet in its fall seems to act more unfavourably than when in detriment. This is particularly the case with ♂ which is usually more evil in ♋ than in ♉ or ♎.

These four positions are termed *essential dignities and debilities,* in contradistinction to the *accidental* dignities and debilities which will be noted later, the house and exaltation being the chief dignities, and the detriment and fall the chief debilities.

The planets ♅ and ♇ have been discovered so recently that some doubt exists as to their houses and exaltations ♒ is usually assigned to ♅ as its house, but ♏ has also been suggested, while in the case of ♇, ♓ is almost always said to be its house, its exaltation being ♐ or ♑ In these cases the house rulership of ♒ will be shared by ♄ and ♅, and of ♓ by ♃ and ♇, and in reading a horoscope this should be borne in mind. At our present stage of knowledge it is not safe to assume, for example, that ♇ entirely replaces ♃ as ruler of ♓, and both bodies should be considered.

The following Table shows at a glance the above relationship of signs and planets :—

THE ALPHABET

Sign	House of	Detriment of	Exaltation of	Fall of
♈	♂	♀	☉ 19°	♄ 21°
♉	♀	♂	☽ 3°	♅ ?
♊	☿	♃	—	—
♋	☽	♄	♃ 15°	♂ 28°
♌	☉	♄ or ♅	—	—
♍	☿	♃ or ♆	☿ 15°	♀ 27°
♎	♀	♂	♄ 21°	☉ 19°
♏	♂	♀	♅ ?	☽ 3°
♐	♃	☿	—	—
♑	♄	☽	♂ 28°	♃ 15°
♒	♄ or ♅	☉	—	—
♓	♃ or ♆	☿	♀ 27°	☿ 15°

4. ASPECTS. The aspects are certain distances between the planets measured in degrees of the zodiac. It is found that when planets are a certain number of degrees apart they affect one another either favourably or unfavourably, according to the distance separating them. Thus a distance of 90° is always exceedingly adverse and planets so situated are inharmonious and spoil each other's effect.

As already mentioned the zodiac is divided into 12 signs (12ˢ) each of 30 degrees (30°) in extent. Each degree is divided into 60 minutes (60′) and each minute into 60 seconds (60″). Thus from ♈ 0° to ♉ 0° is one sign or 30°; from ♈ 12° to ♋ 12° is 3ˢ or 90°; from ♉ 25° 42′ 36″ to ♍ 14° 39′ 20″ is 108° 56′ 44″ and so on. The distances between planets are measured in this manner, and it is customary always to use the shortest distance as all the aspects are contained in the semicircle of 180°. Thus ♉ 0° to ♐ 0°

is either 240° or 120° according to whether we count from ♉ or from ♐, and we therefore use 120° as that is less than 180°.

Only certain distances are of influence and it is to these that the name *aspects* is given. Each aspect possesses its own influence which is exerted irrespective of the planets concerned. Thus the square or 90° is evil in all cases, even between benefic planets, while the trine or 120° is favourable even between malefics. In other words good aspects always produce good results even from bad planets, while bad aspects produce evil even from good planets.

The following Table shows the names, symbols and nature of the aspects, together with the number of degrees constituting them, and also their „orbs" which will be explained later.

Name of Aspect	Symbol	Number of signs apart	Number of Degrees Apart	Nature	Orb
Parallel	∥ or P	—	—	Variable	1°
Conjunction	☌	0	0	Variable	8°
Semi-sextile	⊻	1	30	Weakly good	2°
Semi-square	∠	1½	45	Weakly bad	4°
Sextile	✳	2	60	Good	7°
Square	□	3	90	Bad	8°
Trine	△	4	120	Very good	8°
Sesquiquadrate	⊡	4½	135	Weakly bad	4°
Quincunx	⊼	5	150	Weakly bad	2°
Opposition	☍	6	180	Very bad	8°

(a) *Effect.* The *Parallel* is strictly a position and not an aspect. It occurs when two planets occupy the same degree of *declination* no matter

22

whether both planets are in north declination, both in south, or one in north and the other in south. Like the *conjunction* this aspect is variable, that is to say it is favourable between good planets and unfavourable between evil ones. Thus ♀ ♂ or P ♃ is always favourable, while ♂ ♂ or P ♄ is always unfavourable, and similarly the ♂ or P between ♀ and ♄ is also unfavourable as ♄ spoils the influence of ♀.

The ♂ and P are both of very great strength and together with the ☍ take precedence over all the other aspects. The action of the P is similar to the ♂ if the bodies are in no other aspect but if on the other hand they are already in some aspect the P strengthens it, so that a P between two bodies already in □ acts in terms of the □ and renders it stronger than it otherwise would be.

Planets in ♂ tend to act alternately and it should be remembered that they do not altogether blend although they are both acting through the same part of the zodiac. There is usually a more or less rapid change from one body to another. Thus ♀♂♂ generally causes the native to change quickly from anger to smiles and vice versa, though it also gives energy to the feelings and some softness to the passions. In a ♂ both bodies are always active and it is a mistake to imagine that one is cancelled out. The relative strength, however, is not equal and depends largely upon the sign occupied, for ♀ ♂ ♂ in ♎ is much more favourable to ♀, which rules ♎, than to ♂, while the reverse would be the case with ♀ ♂ ♂ in ♈.

A ♂ is usually rather difficult to interpret especially when three or more bodies are con-

cerned and it tends to limit the native owing to
the presence of several planets in one sign, for
the various energies and experiences of the
planets are all exerted or received through one
channel.

Another position linking up two planets is
that known as *mutual reception*, which occurs
when each body is in a sign ruled by the other,
as for example ♃ in ♈ and ♂ in ♐. This is
also said to cause the two planets concerned
to act as if in conjunction.

The *opposition* is usually classed as the worst
aspect of all, but this is often not so as it frequently acts as a complementary aspect and
loses much of its evil nature. Furthermore with
an ☍ it is often possible to incline the balance
to one side or the other, whereas in the case of
the square this is not possible and the latter
may usually be taken as the worse affliction.
In the matter of character the □ is always
more evil than the ☍ and exercises a more
distorting influence as it causes a twist in the
nature, whilst the ☍ gives more "cussedness"
and sets the native in opposition to others.

With regard to the other aspects in the list,
the ✶ is sometimes said to be of more purely
material benefit than the △, but this is doubtful.

There are two ancient rules connected with
the aspects that have fallen into disuse which
may be stated as follows:—

1. Three planets in trine to one another from
the corners of an equilateral triangle are said
to be in *grand trine* and to exert a very evil
influence.

2. In signs of long ascension (♋ to♐) a ✶ is
equivalent to a □, and a □ to a △, while in

signs of short ascension (♑ to ♊) a □ is equivalent to a ⚹, and a △ to a □.

Both these rules are extremely doubtful but as they have not been investigated it seems desirable to mention their existence.

The list of aspects given above is not complete and numerous others have from time to time been suggested. They are, however, all very weak and may safely be ignored. The chief ones are the Vigintile 18°, Quindecile 24°, Decile 36°, Quintile 72°, Tredecile 108°, and Biquintile 144°. The foregoing aspects were first suggested by Kepler, but since then others have been put forward and a great number were introduced by the late George Wilde, which, however, were never properly proved and have not been accepted.

(b) *Orbs*. Planets are in aspect with one another when within a few degrees of the exact distance constituting the aspect. The number of degrees that can be allowed in this way is known as the *orb* of the aspect, and the approximate values are shown in the Table on p. 22. Thus the orb of a square is about 8°, and this means that two planets are in □ when distant from each other from 82° to 98°. The influence of the □ first appears when the bodies are 82° apart, gradually reaches a maximum at 90°, and then decreases until the effect disappears at about 98°, These orbs are all approximate and must not be taken as hard and fast dividing lines. For example, the orb of the conjunction is given in the Table as 8°, and this may be followed in general cases, but when the aspect is formed between the Sun or Moon and another planet 10° may be allowed, and between the Sun and Moon themselves it may be extended to 12°.

This is a larger variation than is allowable in the cases of the other aspects, and with these it will be advisable to keep to the values shown in the Table. The orbs of the aspects are, however, subject to modification by the planets concerned, and may sometimes be extended when several planets enter into the configuration. Thus, suppose ♂ to be in ♈ 10°, and ♀ in ♈ 20°. As they stand they are beyond the orb for a ☌, but if at the same time another body, say ♃, were in ♌ 15°, it would be in △ to both and would act as a medium in bringing them into ☌.

Exact aspects were at one time called *partile* and aspects within orbs *platic*, but these terms are rarely used nowadays. Another distinction that is sometimes met with is in the direction from which an aspect is cast, a *dexter* aspect being one thrown forward in the zodiac, and a *sinister* aspect one thrown backwards. The latter is said to be stronger for good or evil than the former.

When a quickly moving planet is going towards an aspect with a more slowly moving one by overtaking it it is said to be *applying* to the aspect, and to be *separating* from it after completion. The ☽ is the most quickly moving body and applies to all the rest. The order of speed of the others being ☿ ♀ ☉ ♂ ♃ ♄ ♅ and ♆, so that ♂ applies only to ♃ ♄ ♅ and ♆, whilst ♆ cannot apply to any. A separating aspect is said to be stronger than an applying one since its effects have already manifested and are in being, whilst those of an applying aspect have not yet fully materialised.

(*c*) *Measurement of aspects.*

1. Never use an aspectarian but always work out the aspects independently. In a short time

one can see them without calculation if this is done, but the use of an aspectarian or similar mechanical device destroys this power.

2. Start with the ☉ and note the number of degrees between it and the ☽. Then take ☉ to ☿, ☉ to ♀, ☉ to ♂, and so on in order. Next take ☽ to ☿, ☽ to ♀, etc., then ☿ to ♀, ☿ to ♂, and so on until all have been examined. A definite order should always be followed and the most convenient is ☉ ☽ ☿ ♀ ♂ ♃ ♄ ♅ ♆. Write down the symbol of each aspect as it is noted in tabular form as in the diagram at the foot of the map on p. 50.

3. Note that planets in or near the same degree of signs are always in aspect.

4. To any given planet's longitude add 15° (or subtract 15° if preferred) and note planets in the same degrees of different signs. Such may be in ∠ or ⚼ but the result must be checked as they may be at distances of 75°, 105°, or 165°, which are not aspects.

5. Signs of the same triplicity are in trine, and signs of the same quadruplicity are in square or opposition.

5. MUNDANE HOUSES. The usual forms of horoscope diagrams are as follows:—

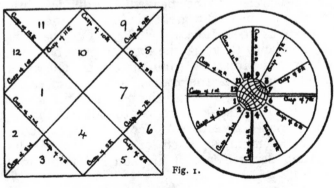

Fig. 1.

The square form was in use in most of the older books but the circular map has almost entirely replaced it and beyond understanding the square map the student should not concern himself with it as the circular diagram is much easier to follow.

The map is drawn from the point of view of an observer facing towards the south. The small central circle represents the earth. The South point or Midheaven (often called Medium Coeli, and abbreviated M.C.) is immediately overhead and is the point reached by the Sun at noon. The North point (called Imum Coeli and abbreviated I.C.) is underfoot, while the East point or Ascendant, where the planets rise, is on the left hand, and the West point or Descendant, where they set, is on the right. By the rotation of the earth in a direction opposite to the hands of a watch the planets all appear to rise on the eastern horizon and set on the western, the horizontal line in the map representing the horizon, and the vertical line the meridian. One such rotation takes place in 24 hours, and is quite distinct from the contrary movement of the planets in their passage through the signs.

The circle of the heavens is divided into twelve segments by great circles, and these are known as the *Mundane Houses*. For the sake of simplicity they may be thought of as bounded by spokes projecting from the earth. The outer circle represents the zodiac, and as the earth, with its spokes, rotates, the points of the zodiac cut by each spoke, are continually changing, about one degree passing across the M.C. spoke every 4 minutes. Each of these houses rules certain departments of life and is known by a number as shown in the diagram. The 1st, 10th, 7th, and 4th houses are termed *angular* or *angles*, and are of the greatest strength and importance.

The 2nd, 11th, 8th and 5th are termed *succeedent* and come next in importance.

The 3rd, 12th, 9th and 6th are termed *cadent*, and are the weakest.

In a purely general way planets in angles have most influence on the external world, those in succeedent houses on the emotions, and those in cadent on the mind, but this is not exclusively so for all houses affect all states of existence, though to a different extent.

The beginning point of each house is called the *cusp*, and is indicated in the diagram. The cusp is the strongest point of the house and planets on cusps are stronger and more important than when they are well within the house. Each house also has its orb, and a planet exerts an influence on a house when outside it but within 5° of its cusp. Frequently such a position as this blends the influence of both houses, and the planet has some effect upon each.

The various matters ruled by each house are given in the following list and should be thoroughly memorised.

First House. The "native" or subject of the horoscope, his personal appearance, body, outlook on life, etc. It rules the head and corresponds to the sign Aries

Second House. Money and possessions. Rules the throat and corresponds to Taurus.

Third House. Short journeys, letters, writings, papers, brothers and sisters, contemporary relatives, neighbours, and the lower mind. Rules the arms and shoulders and corresponds to Gemini.

Fourth House. The home, early life and also the end of life, the grave, houses and land, mines, places under the earth, the inner aspirations, and basis of character, and one of the parents. Opinions differ as to which parent is represented by this house, the western astrologers assigning it to the father, and the eastern astrologers to the mother. It has also been suggested that the fourth house represents that parent of opposite sex to the native, or alternatively the parent who has least influence over the native. Rules the breast and stomach, and corresponds to Cancer.

Fifth House. Pleasures, love affairs outside marriage, places of amusement, such as theatres, etc., holidays, speculation, children and schools. Rules the heart and back, and corresponds to Leo.

Sixth House. Health and sickness, servants, employees, aunts and uncles on the side of the parent represented by the fourth house, food and clothing, small animals, and the subconscious mind. Rules the intestines and corresponds to Virgo.

Seventh House. Marriage, the wife or husband, partners, contracts, and open enemies. Rules the reins and kidneys, and corresponds to Libra.

Eighth House. Death, loss, decay, wills, legacies, and money of marriage or business partner. Rules the generative and excretory systems, and corresponds to Scorpio.

Ninth House. Long journeys and voyages, publications, the Church and clergy, religion, the higher mind, dreams, the law and legal affairs. Rules the hips and thighs, and corresponds to Sagittarius.

Tenth House. Employers, superiors, business, profession or occupation, the outer aspirations, and honour and credit. To this house is assigned one of the parents, the opposite one to that ruled by the fourth house. Rules the knees, and corresponds to Capricorn.

Eleventh House. Friends, associates, companions, hopes and wishes, and income from business. Rules the legs and ankles and corresponds to Aquarius.

Twelfth House Self-undoing, confinement, prisons, hospitals, asylums, exile, secret enemies, sleep, aunts and uncles on the side of the parent ruled by the 10th house, and large animals. Rules the feet and corresponds to Pisces.

It will be noted that each house corresponds to a sign, as the first house to Aries, and so on. This correspondence is important and always holds good no matter what sign may actually occupy the cusp.

Houses below the horizon are more obscure than those above, as will be seen by comparing the rulerships of opposite houses. Thus the third house rules short journeys and the ninth long ones ; the fourth the home and inner life, the tenth business and the outer life, and so on.

In every respect the houses are similar to the signs and share the positive and negative, and other qualities, associated with the signs to which they correspond. Their influence, however, is more personal than that of the signs on account of the fact that all the planets pass through all the houses once a day, whereas they may stay in one sign for years The effect of any planet in a house is entirely different from its effect in any other house, and it is therefore essential to know the *time* of birth and also the place, in order to ascertain the house position of the planets.

6. THE RELATION OF HOUSES AND PLANETS. The planets are more favourable in certain houses than in others, just as in the case of the signs, and these positions are termed *accidental* dignities and debilities. Since each house always corresponds to a particular sign a planet is favourable in the houses corresponding to its signs·of house or exaltation and unfavourable in those corresponding to its detriment and fall. Thus ♄ is favourable in the 10th house, which corresponds to ♑ and also in the seventh which corresponds to ♎, its exaltation. Apart from this the planets are said to "joy" in certain houses, and the older astrologers gave the following list :— ☉ in 10th, ☽ in 3rd, ☿ in 1st, ♀ in 5th, ♂ in 6th, ♃ in 11th and ♄ in 12th. These, however, are not important and are usually ignored at the present time.

7. SENSITIVE POINTS. (See Appendix)
This section may be omitted by the beginner.
In addition to the factors already mentioned there are certain sensitive points in a horoscope.

(*a*) *The Moon's Nodes.* These are the points at which the Moon's orbit cuts the ecliptic. The position of the North node or Dragon's Head (symbol ☊) is given in the ephemeris, and the South node or Dragon's Tail (symbol ☋) is always exactly opposite or 180° from it. These points are said to have an influence, according to house and sign position, and to affect a planet by conjunction though not by aspect. The Head is of a benefic nature and is said to be exalted in ♊ 3°, while the Tail is malefic and is exalted in ♐ 3°. Any influence possessed by these points is probably due to the fact that they mark the approximate position of eclipses that fell during ante-natal existance.

(b) *The Part of Fortune or Fortuna* This is found by adding the longitude of the ☽ to the longitude of the Ascendant, and from the sum subtracting the longitude of the ☉.

Example. Given Asc. ♊ 5° 49', ☉ ♋ 13° 21', ☽ ♐ 8° 27'. Required the longitude of Fortuna.

Expressing these quantities in signs we have the ascendant in 2ˢ 5° 49', i.e. it has passed through two complete signs, viz, ♈ and ♉, and is in 5° 49' of the next.

Then,	Asc.	2ˢ	5°	49'
+	☽	8	8	27
		10	14	16
—	☉	3	13	21
		7	0	55

Thus, Fortuna is in ♏ 0° 55'.

Twelve signs may be added, if required, to allow of subtraction or deducted if the sum exceeds that amount.

The use of this point will be shown later.

8 SUMMARY. We have now completed a survey of the elements which build up a horoscope. We have planets, signs, houses, and aspects, each exerting its own influence, and the task before the astrologer is to combine their effects into a coherent whole in accordance with certain guiding rules.

It is difficult to assign any order of importance to the factors employed as all are equally necessary, but some help may be found in the

Astrology C

following idea. A planet is universal and shines through a particular sign for a longer or shorter period. Therefore all people born in that period will have that planet in the same sign, and in some cases this will mark a generation. The ray from these again passes through a particular house which adds its own colouring and gives a more personal effect, since the house positions change so rapidly. Therefore we may conclude that in general house positions are more personal and of greater significance in small matters and environment than planets and signs, while signs are of greater effect on character. This rule is largely true but must not be followed too closely as every point is of importance and all the factors work together.

CHAPTER III

CASTING THE HOROSCOPE.

The data necessary in order to be able to cast a horoscope are the time, date, and place of birth. The actual time of day is a very important consideration as that alone can determine the degrees of the zodiac upon the cusps of the houses and consequently the house positions of the planets. In a general delineation of a horoscope an error of a quarter of an hour or so is usually allowable, but in certain systems of directing, or estimating the times of future happenings, an error of 4 minutes will throw events out a whole year. It is possible to "rectify" a birth time, but this is a tedious process and is frequently uncertain unless the time is known approximately. When stating the time of birth it is convenient to write midnight as 0.0 a.m. of the following day and noon as 0.0 p.m. This will save the confusion that frequently arises, especially in births taking place near midnight. It may always be taken for granted that a birth time is recorded in the standard in use at the birthplace unless otherwise stated.

The date of birth is needed in order to find the positions of the planets at the time, and the latitude and longitude of the place are necessary to fix the local and Greenwich times of birth and to determine the cusps of the houses which vary according to latitude.

These are the only essential data, but before the horoscope can be cast it is absolutely necessary to obtain an *Ephemeris* for the year of birth and *Tables of Houses* for the latitude of the place.

An Ephemeris is a small paper-covered publication containing the Sidereal Time and the longitudes, latitudes, and declinations of the planets for Greenwich noon on every day of the year. *Raphael's Ephemeris* is that most commonly used and may be obtained for any year from 1800, the price being 1/- per year. Tables of Houses contain the signs and degrees upon the cusps of the houses for given Sidereal Times. They are calculated for various latitudes and do not change from year to year as do the Ephemerides. Raphael publishes a shilling book of 18 Tables serving for all places from 50° to 59°, and also a five shilling set covering all latitudes from 0° to 60°.[1]

The casting of a horoscope falls naturally into two divisions, namely, (1) finding the cusps of the houses, which must be done for Local Time, and (2) finding the planets places, which must be done for Greenwich Time. A map form should be obtained or the diagram should be drawn as in fig. 1, and the following rules, which cover all possible cases, should be applied in the order given :—

---

[1] *These publications and other astrological requisites may be obtained from Mr. J. M. Watkins, 21, Cecil Court, Charing Cross Road, W. C.*

CASTING THE HOROSCOPE

A. — TO CALCULATE THE CUSPS OF THE HOUSES

I. For north latitudes.

1. Consider whether the given time of birth be Standard Time, Local Mean Time, Summer Time or Greenwich Time.

2. Convert the given time into *Local Mean Time* as follows:—

(*a*) If given in Local Mean Time retain it unchanged.

(*b*) If given in Standard Time find the standard in use at the birth place from the Table in the Appendix. If the place is west of Greenwich add the standard to the given time, and if east of Greenwich subtract it. The result is the Greenwich Mean Time (G.M.T.) of birth.

(*c*) If given in Summer Time subtract one hour to obtain G.M.T. or Standard Time in the case of a foreign birth.

(*d*) If given in Greenwich Mean Time or converted into that by rules 2 (*b*) or 2 (*c*).

(I) Convert the *longitude* of the birthplace into time. For this purpose 15° of longitude = 1 hour of time, 1° = 4 minutes, and 1′ = 4 seconds. The easiest method is to call the degrees of longitude minutes of time, and the minutes of longitude seconds of time, and multiply them by 4.

(II) If the birthplace is west of Greenwich subtract the longitude in time from the G.M.T. of birth and if east of Greenwich add it. The result is the Local Mean Time of birth.

3. Extract from the Ephemeris the Sidereal Time at Greenwich for the noon previous to birth.

4. Find the longitude of the birthplace in time as explained in rule 2 (*d*) (I). For every hour

allow 9.86 seconds (or approximately 10 seconds) and proportionately for the minutes and seconds. A Table for this correction will be found on p.243

5. If the birthplace is west of Greenwich add this correction to the Sidereal Time found in rule 3, and if east of Greenwich subtract it. The result is the Sidereal Time at the birthplace for the noon previous to birth. (This rule and the last may be omitted in English births).

6. Find the number of hours, minutes, and seconds that elapsed between the noon previous to birth and the actual Local Mean Time of birth. Thus 2.30 p.m. is $2^h 30^m$, and 2.30 a.m. is $14^h 30^m$.

7. Add to the time elapsed a correction at the rate of 9.86 seconds per hour (see Table on p.243.)

8. Add the total result obtained in rule 7 to the Sidereal Time obtained in rule 5. The result is the Sidereal Time at birth. If the Sidereal Time so obtained exceeds 24 hours, subtract 24 hours and use the remainder.

9. Turn to the Tables of House for the latitude of the birthplace. If approximate results only are required find the nearest Sidereal Time in the Tables to that obtained in rule 8 and write on the map the signs and degrees on the cusps of the 10th, 11th, 12th, 1st, 2nd, and 3rd houses corresponding to that time.

10. If accurate results are required it is usual to calculate the cusps of the 10th and 1st houses to minutes as follows:— Extract from the Tables the nearest Sidereal Times greater and less than that obtained in rule 8. Subtract the lesser from the greater and reduce the difference to seconds. Call this *a*. Subtract the lesser Sidereal Time in the Tables from that found by rule 8,

and reduce this difference also to seconds. Call this b. Then for the 10th house $\frac{b \times 60}{a}$ = the number of minutes to be added to the degree on the tenth cusp corresponding to the lesser Sidereal Time in the Tables. (The degree on the 10th in the Tables is exact, and 0' is implied, as for example 10 ♉ means 10° 0' ♉).

For the ascendant, subtract the degrees and minutes on the cusp corresponding to the lesser Sidereal Time in the Table from those corresponding to the greater and reduce the difference to minutes. Call this c. Then $\frac{b \times c}{a}$ = the number of minutes to be added to the degree and minute on the cusp of the ascendant corresponding to the lesser Sidereal Time in the Tables. In the case of the other cusps take the degrees corresponding to the nearest Sidereal Time in the Tables.

11. Write these signs and degrees on the cusps indicated by the number at the heads of the columns and complete the circle by writing in the same degrees of the opposite signs on the opposite cusps and inserting intercepted signs, if any.

II. FOR SOUTH LATITUDES.

A. Follow rules 1 to 8 of the previous section.

B. To the Sidereal Time so found add 12 hours (subtracting 24 hours from the sum if it exceeds that amount).

C. Use the Table of Houses for the same latitude North as the birthplace is South. Thus for 40° S. use the Table for 40° N.

D. Take the Sidereal Time found in B and follow rules 9 to 10 of the previous section, but

write on the map the *opposite signs* to those given in the Tables, retaining the same degrees. Thus if the Tables give 24 ♊ on a cusp write down 24 ♐.
E. Complete the map as in rule 11 above.

B. — TO CALCULATE THE PLANETS' PLACES

1. Convert the given time of birth into *Greenwich Mean Time* as follows :—

(*a*) If given in Greenwich Mean Time retain it.

(*b*) If given in Summer Time subtract one hour to obtain Greenwich Mean Time or Standard Time if foreign.

(*c*) If given in Standard Time, add the standard to the given time if the place is west of Greenwich, and subtract it if east. The result is the Greenwich Mean Time.

(*d*) If given in Local Mean Time add longitude in time if place is west of Greenwich, and subtract it if east. The result is the G.M.T.

2. Extract from the Ephemeris the longitudes of the planets on the noon previous to birth and on the noon after. Subtract the lesser longitude from the greater in each case, thus obtaining the distance each moves in 24 hours.

3. Find the time elapsing between birth and the *nearest* noon.

4. Find the Diurnal Proportional Logarithm of this time from the Table on the last page of the Ephemeris.

5. Add to this the Prop. Log. of the planet's daily motion as found in rule 2.

6. Find from the Table the number of degrees and minutes to which the sum corresponds.

7. If in rule 3 the nearest noon was before birth (i.e. a p.m. birth) add the degrees and

minutes obtained in rule 6 to the longitude of the planet on the previous noon.

If the nearest noon was after birth (i.e. an a.m. birth) subtract them from the longitude on the noon after birth. The result is the longitude of the planet at birth.

Note:— If a planet is Retrograde reverse rule 7 and subtract for p.m., or add for a.m.

8. Insert the planets in their proper places in the map.

9. Repeat rules 2 to 7 using the Declinations instead of the longitudes. If the Declination is decreasing it must be treated similarly to a Retrograde planet.

10. The latitudes are obtained in a similar way but are not needed for general work.

The above rules have been given in as concise a form as possible in order that reference to them by the more advanced student may not be hampered by a mass of explanation. For the benefit of the beginner they will now be exemplified, and as an example we will choose a birth in England, as that will be of most service to the student. Having once mastered the principles involved he will have no difficulty in erecting a horoscope for any time and place by means of the above rules.

Example, Birth, 3rd April, 1922, 7.30 *a.m. Summer Time, Bristol, Lat.* 51° N. 27', *Long.* 2° W 36'.

Birth is in Summer Time and this is converted into G.M.T. according to rule 2 (*c*) by subtracting 1 hour, giving the true G.M.T of birth as 6.30 a.m.

By rule 2 (*d*) (I) the longitude of the birthplace, 2° W 36' is converted into time as follows :—

$$2^0 \ 0' = 2 \times 4 \text{ minutes} \qquad\qquad = 8^m \ 0^s$$
$$0^0 \ 36' = 36 \times 4 \text{ seconds} = 144^s = 2 \quad 24$$
Therefore $2^0 \ 36' \qquad\qquad\qquad = \qquad\qquad\overline{10^m \ 24^s}$

Bristol is west of Greenwich and therefore by rule 2 (*d*) (ii) the longitude in time must be subtracted from the G.M.T. to obtain the Local Mean Time, thus :—

Greenwich Mean Time $= 6^h \ 30^m \ 0^s$ a.m.
Subtract Long. in time $\qquad 10 \quad 24$
Local Mean Time $\qquad = \overline{6 \quad 19 \quad 36}$ a.m.

Turning to the Ephemeris for 1922 and opening it at April we find a column on the lefthand side headed "Sidereal Time" and in which the Sidereal Time is given for noon each day. Take out the Sidereal Time for the noon *previous* to birth, which in this case is the 2nd April. It will be found to be $0^h \ 40^m \ 11^s$. (Rule 3).

As the birth is in England rules 4 and 5 may be omitted as the resulting correction is too trifling to be of any account.

By rule 6. The local time elapsed from the previous noon is $18^h \ 19^m \ 36^s$.

By rule 7. The correction for this is found from the Table on p. 243 as follows:—

Correction for $18^h = 2^m \ 57^s.42$
,,   ,, $19^m = \qquad 3 .12$
,, $36^s = \qquad 0 .10$
$\qquad\qquad\qquad\qquad \overline{3 \quad 0 .64}$

Call this $3^m \ 1^s$ and add it to the time elapsed.
Time elapsed $\qquad\qquad\qquad = 18^h \ 19^m \ 36^s$
Plus correction $\qquad\qquad\qquad\qquad 3 \quad 1$
$\qquad\qquad\qquad\qquad\qquad \overline{18 \quad 22 \quad 37}$

By rule 8. Add to S.T. at previous noon $\qquad\qquad\qquad\qquad\qquad 0 \quad 40 \quad 11$
S.T. at moment of birth $\qquad = \overline{19 \quad 2 \quad 48}$

CASTING THE HOROSCOPE

The Tables of Houses for the nearest latitude are those for London, Lat. 51° N 32'. Turn to these and look down the columns headed "Sidereal Time" to find the nearest tabulated time to 19ʰ 2ᵐ 48ˢ . To the right of the column containing Sidereal Time are six columns each of which is headed by a number. This number refers to a house and the six columns give the degrees on the cusps of the 10th, 11th, 12th, 1st, 2nd and 3rd houses. Immediately below the house number is the sign that occupies the cusp and the rest of the column shows the degree corresponding to the given Sidereal Time.

The Sidereal Time in our example, 19ʰ 2ᵐ 48ˢ, falls between 19ʰ 0ᵐ 50ˢ and 19ʰ 5ᵐ 8ˢ in the Tables, and is nearer to the former. If an approximate result only is required we may copy down the signs and degrees on the cusps exactly as given in the Tables opposite to 19ʰ 0ᵐ 58ˢ, thus :—

10	11	12	Ascen.	2	3
♐ 14	♒ 4	♓ 5	4 ♉ 24	♊ 6	♊ 26

It will be noted that in some cases the sign at the top of a column gives place to another in the column itself, and when this occurs it is the latter that must always be used, so that it is necessary to run the eye up the column to see if any such change has taken place. In the example this has happened in columns 11, 12 Ascen, and 2, the signs at the top of the other two columns being unchanged.

To obtain greater accuracy follow rule 10, thus:—

Greater S.T. in Tables 19ʰ 5ᵐ 58ˢ
Lesser   „   „   „   19   0   50

Difference   5   8 $=$ 308ˢ $= a$

Given S.T.   19   2   48
Subtract lesser S.T.   19   0   50

1   58 $=$ 118ˢ $= b$

Then $\dfrac{b \times 60}{a} = \dfrac{118 \times 60}{308} = \dfrac{7080}{308} = 23'$ to the nearest minute.

This must be added to the degree corresponding to the lesser Sidereal Time and the result becomes ♐ 14° 23'.

For the Ascendant we have:—
Cusp corresponding to greater S.T. 6° ♉ 30'
     „   „   „ lesser   „   4   24

2   6 $=$ 126' $= c.$

Then $\dfrac{b \times c}{a} = \dfrac{118 \times 126}{308} = \dfrac{14868}{308} = 48'$ to the nearest minute.

Therefore the exact Ascendant becomes 4° ♉ 24' plus 0° 48' $=$ 5° ♉ 12'.

We now have the following values corresponding to our Sidereal Time of birth:—

10	11	12	Ascen.	2	3
14 ♐ 23	♒ 4	♓ 5	5 ♉ 12	♊ 6	♊ 26

These signs and degrees should be written down on the cusps of the houses in the blank map as shown in fig. 2.

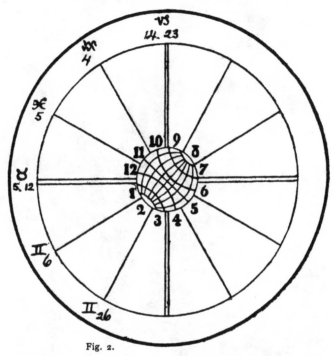

Fig. 2.

The cusps of the remaining houses bear the *same* degree of the *opposite* signs in each case, so that the cusp of the fifth house will be ♌ 4, of the sixth ♍ 5, and so on. When these have been written in, the map must be looked over to see that no signs are omitted. It will be found in the present case that the signs ♊ and ♐ occur on two houses in each case, and that ♈ and ♎ do not appear at all. When this happens the omitted signs must be placed in the circle between the cusps in the position they occupy according to the order of the signs, and if this is done in the example the map will appear as in fig. 3.

45

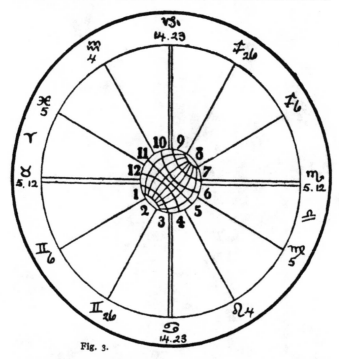

Fig. 3.

Such omitted signs are called "intercepted" and
the phenomenon is due to the obliquity of the
ecliptic and the latitude of the place. In the
example map the second house contains only
20° of the zodiac, viz., from ♊ 6° to ♊ 26°, while
the 12th contains just over 60°, viz., 25° of ♓,
all of ♈, and just over 5° of ♉. The zodiac may
be thought of as an elastic band that appears
to be stretched in some places and compressed
in others, though of course it is really a regular
circle viewed obliquely. The degrees shown in
the map are the points where the house cusps
cut the zodiac, and the other degrees that are not
marked fall within the houses, the signs and

46

degrees always retaining their correct order and always passing round the map in an anticlockwise direction.

Having now completed the cusps it only remains to find the planets' positions. For this we use the Greenwich Mean Time of birth, which we found to be 6.30 a.m. of the 3rd April. For the longitudes we need the columns in the Ephemeris headed "Long". with the planets' symbol above. The longitudes there given for noon on 2nd and 3rd April, which are the noons immediately preceding and following birth, are as follows:—

	☉	☽	☿	♀	♂
2 Apr.	11 ♈ 57 51	8 ♊ 15 57	21 ♓ 44	24 ♈ 52	18 ♐ 37
	♃	♄	♅	♆	
	14 ♎ 16 ℞	3 ♎ 39 ℞	11 ♓ 24	13 ♌ 18 ℞	
3 Apr.	☉ 12 56 59	☽ 21 16 54	☿ 23 22	♀ 26 6	♂ 18 57
	♃ 14 8	♄ 3 34	♅ 11 27	♆ 13 18	

A retrograde planet is denoted by the symbol ℞, and it remains retrograde until the symbol D (direct) occurs. The ☉ and ☽ are given to seconds and their positions may be found by proportion or by logarithms to the nearest minute.

The *nearest* noon is that of 3rd April, and the time elapsed from birth to that noon, as required in rule 3, in 5ʰ 30ᵐ (i.e. 12ʰ less 6ʰ 30ᵐ = 5ʰ 30ᵐ).

The prop. log. of this time, as given in the Table on the last page of the Ephemeris is .6398.

Beginning with the ☉, we find that its motion from noon on the 2nd to noon on the 3rd was 0° 59′ 8″. To find how much it moved in 5ʰ 30ᵐ add the prop. log. of 0° 59′ to the prop. log. of 5ʰ 30ᵐ.

$$
\begin{array}{lll}
\text{Prop. Log. of } 5^{\text{h}}\,30^{\text{m}} & = & .6398 \\
\text{,, \quad ,, \quad ,, } 0°\,59' & = & 1.3875 \\
\hline
 & & 2.0273
\end{array}
$$

This is the prop. log. of 0° 14′ to the nearest minute, and by rule 7 it must be subtracted from the Sun's longitude at noon on the 3rd.

Long. ☉ noon 3 Apr. (to nearest
minute) = 12° ♈ 57′
less 0 14
Sun's long at birth = 12° 43

The ☽ moves 13° 0′ 57″ or 13° 1′ between the two noons.

Then Prop. Log. of 5ʰ 30ᵐ = .6398
,, ,, ,, 13° 1′ = .2657
Moon's motion = .9055 = 2° 59′
Long. ☽ at noon 3rd = 21° ♊ 17′
less 2 59
Long. ☽ at birth = 18 18

If the Moon's longitude is required to seconds it is advisable to take a proportion between the times of noon and mid-night instead of from noon to noon as its motion is irregular.

The above process must be repeated with all the planets, remembering that in the case of retrograde planets the result must be added instead of subtracted. This is the case with ♃, ♄, and ♅.

The positions thus obtained are as follows:—

☉	☽	☿	♀	♂
12 ♈ 43	18 ♊ 18	23 ♓ 0	25 ♈ 49	18 ♐ 52
♃	♄	♅	♆	
14 ♎ 10 ℞	3 ♎ 35 ℞	11 ♓ 26	13 ♌ 18 ℞	

Having thus obtained the planets' longitudes it is necessary to repeat the process to find their declinations, which are as follows:—

☉	☽	☿	♀	♂
5 N 2	17 N 57	5 S 0	9 N 15	22 S 38
♃	♄	♅	♆	
4 S 7	1 N 0	7 S 58	16 N 57	

The student should check these results.

For ordinary purposes the latitudes of the planets are not required, but if needed they may be calculated in the same way. If desired the nodes and Fortuna may also be computed.

It now remains only to place the planets in the map in their correct positions and to calculate the aspects. In inserting the planets it is advisable to write each body close to the cusp bearing the same sign and parallel with it, and also to arrange them in numerical order, according to their degrees, care being taken to place them on the proper side of the cusp. Planets in intercepted signs should be written parallel to the rim of the map.

The casting of the horoscope is now complete and the finished map, together with the aspects, is shown in fig. 4.

49

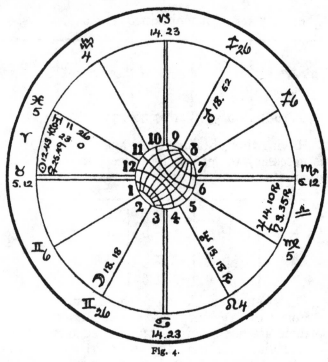

Fig. 4.

Planet	Lat.	Decl.		☉	☽	☿	♀	♂	♃	♄	♅	♆
Sun	5 N 2		☉		✳	P		△	⚹P	☍	∨	△
Moon	17 N 57		☽			□	✳	☍	△		□	✳P
Mercury	5 S 0		☿					□	P			
Venus	9 N 15		♀					△				
Mars	22 S 38		♂						✳		□	△
Jupiter	4 S 7		♃									✳
Saturn	1 N 0		♄									
Uranus	7 S 58		♅									
Neptune	16 N 57		♆									
Ascdt.			ASC.									
M. C.			M.C.									

50

SECTION II

THE JUDGMENT OF A HOROSCOPE

CHAPTER I

GENERAL PRINCIPLES OF JUDGMENT.

The art of judging a horoscope is usually divided into two branches, analysis and synthesis. The former process consists in splitting up the map into its component parts and thereby ascertaining the exact influence of each position and aspect, whilst the latter is concerned with the building up of all these isolated pieces of information into one coordinated whole.

Astrology, like everything else, requires the exercise of a great deal of common sense, and it is necessary to realise at the outset that the horoscope is a *person* and not a set of disconnected planetary influences. Always remember that there is something that links up these scattered and contradictory fragments into a connected and coherent whole, and blends contradictions in such a way as to form a definite character or individual. The art of judging a map lies in the ability to make it live. Anyone can copy the effects of aspects or positions from a book, but this is not judgment and the result is a very wooden and artificial reading that is devoid of individuality, and describes a puppet rather than a human being. The astrologer must, so far as possible, identify himself with the horoscope, and having at hand a full analysis of the map and a knowledge of the strength and weakness of

53

its parts, he must put himself in the native's place and decide how he himself would act and feel if under the same influences. Remember that contradictions do not cancel out but always exist side by side. In every horoscope there are innumerable conflicting tendencies, not one of which should be ignored. They are all in the character, though some are strong and others weak, and the whole aim of a good synthesis is to estimate correctly the relative strength and prominence of contradictions so as to present a living picture of the native. Do not get carried away by one position or over-emphasise hastily. This is a very common fault among astrologers and is partly due to the rather dogmatic rules that have to be laid down. It is impossible in any one book to do more than give the influence exerted by a single position, and no account can be taken of modifying factors. In most cases, therefore, such statements of influence should be received cautiously and not be emphasised unless the rest of the map is in agreement. To a certain extent the same remarks apply to aphorisms a great number of which will be found in the following pages. These are extremely useful in judging details as they are positions that have been found to occur in a number of maps, all of which show the same peculiarity. Some caution is needed in dealing with them, however, and they must not be taken as hard and fast rules that admit of no exceptions, for the general nature of the map may be entirely contradictory, in which case the aphorism would be much modified or even contradicted.

The most difficult element of judgment lies in estimating the degree of mental, moral, or spiritual development of the native whose map is being studied. No rules can be given for this, for it is either beyond the horoscope or we have not yet discovered the key, and intuition is the only guide unless we know the native's status in life. Every planet and sign acts on all planes of existence and must be interpreted accordingly. Every planet is the centre of a radiating force which is absorbed by all the beings in the universe in proportion to their capacity and in accordance with their development, or in other words the planetary force flows through them along the line of least resistance. Therefore if once the development of the person is known we can interpret all influences in terms of that development, and if it is unknown the best we can do is to interpret in terms of the present day average development.

The following general hints on judgment will be found of great service and importance:—

1. When judging any particular matter consider to which house it belongs, such as wealth to the 2nd, sickness to the 6th, and so on, and note if there be any planets in that house and the sign in which they are situated. Blend the influence of the planet with that of the house and sign, remembering that each sign corresponds to one of the houses, as for example ♌, being the fifth sign, corresponds to the 5th house and has the same meanings. Thus ♂ in the 2nd would mean a tendency to extravagance since ♂ is outgoing and expansive in its nature. If it were in the sign ♌ expenditure would be lavish, with a tendency to display, since this is the nature of the sign, and would be concerned with amusements, pleasures or speculation for the same reason.

55

Note the aspects to the planet. A malefic well aspected will produce beneficial results, whilst a benefic will be weak or adverse if ill-aspected. The planets throwing good aspects promise benefit through the matters ruled by them and by the houses and signs containing them and the houses which they rule, and the afflicting planets denote the sources and nature of loss or evil. The houses ruled by an aspecting planet afford a useful key to interpretation. Thus if ♃ is in ♌ in the 2nd house, ♐ on the 6th, and ♓ on the 9th, a great deal of money (♃ in 2nd) will be obtained through speculation, etc. (fifth sign ♌), through Jupiterian people and occupations, and also through matters such as health or travel, ruled by the 6th and 9th houses, since these are the houses ruled by ♃, If ♄ were to cast a favourable aspect from the 12th there would be gain through investment and Saturnian affairs and secretly, or in some other manner denoted by the 12th, and also through marriage and legacy, as Saturn's signs ♑ and ♒ occupy the cusps of the 7th and 8th houses which rule these matters respectively.

2. If the house is unoccupied note the aspects to the degree on its cusp and also the position and aspects of the ruler of the sign on its cusp in exactly the same way and treat it as you would a planet *in* the house.

In a case such as this the house containing that ruler is of considerable importance, thus, if ♌ were on the cusp of the 2nd, that house unoccupied, and the ☉ in the 7th, financial affairs would be greatly bound up with 7th house matters such as marriage and partnership. In general the house and sign position of the ruler of any house is important in the affairs of that house, and a rising planet near the Ascendant always brings into prominence the affairs of the houses it rules. Therefore, when judging the influences of a planet in a house always note which houses it rules as these will strongly implicated.

3. The *dispositor* of a planet is also of importance. The dispositor of any planet is that body which rules the sign containing it. Thus the dispositor of ♄ in ♎ is ♀ which rules the sign ♎.

4. The nature of the sign on the cusp influences the affairs of the house. Thus the cardinal and watery sign ♋ on the cusp of the 9th is an indication of voyages which will be upheld or contradicted by other factors in the map.

5. Houses containing intercepted signs are always important as the house contains part of three signs and therefore its affairs are complicated. In general the sign on the cusp indicates the earlier experiences in matters ruled by the house, and the other signs the later. This idea may also be used in connection with transitory matters related to the house. Thus if the latter degrees of a cardinal sign are on a cusp and the house also contains part of the following fixed sign it usually happens that any event denoted by that house starts off under the cardinal influence and later on is affected by the fixed sign, so that there will be an energetic and impulsive beginning followed by a slower period of greater tenacity and purpose.

6. Planets are not equal in strength in any one map. A planet in elevation or in an angle, or in a favourable sign or house, or very strongly aspected, is stronger for good than another not so placed. Of the houses the angles come first

in importance, then the succeedents, and then
the cadents, and in the case of the signs the order
of importance is first cardinal, then fixed, and
then mutable. A planet in its own sign or exaltation is stronger and more powerful for good
than when in other signs, whilst a planet in fall
or detriment is stronger for evil. A retrograde
planet usually denotes hindrances in matters
signified by it and much of its good or evil does
not materialise. This position does not, however,
make it more malefic as has sometimes been
erroneously stated. A stationary planet is always
very important as its influence is thereby intensified.

7. The planet ruling the rising sign, i.e. the
sign on the cusp of the 1st house, is called the
Lord or Ruler of the Ascendant, and is always
of great importance. In a general way it typifies
the native himself, and is frequently said to be
the ruler of the horoscope, but it need not necessarily be so if there is another body that is
exceedingly strong by sign, position, and aspect.
Always try to determine which planet is strongest
in the map as that body will have great influence
over everything. Such a planet should be in an
angle and strong by sign and aspect. Strength
is increased by elevation, and the most elevated
planet in the map is always important, as also
is a rising planet, and one with a large number
of aspects. In the mere matter of strength the
nature of the aspects involved is not of conse-
quence, and the strongest planet will often be
more evil than good.

8. In general cardinal signs and angles tend to
act more markedly on the physical plane and
in events, fixed signs and succeedent houses on

the emotional plane, and mutable signs and cadent houses on the mind, but these distinctions are merely general as all the signs and houses act on all planes.

9. Note that characteristics shown by planets in angles or cardinal signs will always be marked, whereas those denoted by planets in obscure positions will operate more internally and will not be so noticeable outside. Planets in the 4th, 6th, 8th, or 12th usually denote inner or concealed characteristics. Thus the lord of the 5th afflicted in the 12th will give secrecy and concealment in love affairs, and in many cases such matters will play a part never appreciated by others.

10. Remember that the planets act through the signs and that these in turn act through the houses, so that sign influence has a deeper significance than house influence, and denotes a more lasting effect or tendency. Thus a planet in a favourable sign and an unfavourable house is some indication of a well developed character struggling in a bad environment.

11. In judging a map for any particular department of life remember that every planet, sign and aspect has some bearing on the matter. Thus, marriage is primarily denoted by the luminaries (i.e. the Sun and the Moon), the 7th house, ♀, and ♂, but every position can be interpreted in the light of marriage just as it can in that of finance or health. All you have to do is to read the symbols in the map in a different language, for they are universal and apply to the *whole* of the life in all its branches.

12. The aspects to any planet indicate the assistance or hindrance that it receives. Every

planet is a significator of something in the life indicated by the houses containing or ruled by it, and the planets aspecting it show the people and things that help or hinder the affairs of which it is significator. An unaspected planet denotes that the matters ruled by it will be isolated and uninfluenced by others. If the ruler of the Ascendant is unaspected the native will always be left to his own resources and receive little, or no, assistance from others.

13. There is usually a link between the two houses ruled by one planet, and it is found that the native of any sign responds greatly to the house occupied by the other sign ruled by the lord of the Ascendant. Thus, natives of ♍ are greatly occupied with work and professional matters, since ♊, the other sign ruled by ☿, is on the 10th house.

14. When judging of any matter always look for several indications. No important characteristic is ever indicated by one position alone, and the more important the matter the greater number of testimonies will there be found.

15. Obtain a general idea of the native's character before making a detailed judgment in order to be able to see matters in the right proportion. In a strongly Saturnian map an aspect from Mars will not have the same effect as in a martial map. If there are strong indications of caution an influence tending to hastiness or impetuosity will be much modified, and similarly there will be only moderate caution if the general nature of the map is impulsive.

16. Contradictory tendencies exist side by side and operate alternately. Thus, ☽ □ ♄ and ☽ △ ♃ denote meanness and generosity respec-

tively. If ♄ is elevated and stronger than ♃, the prevailing tendency will be towards carefulness, but the trine to ♃ will operate at times in generosity, and in all probability the native will be generous at heart but unable to avoid saving or possibly will not possess the money necessary to practise generosity. The position of ♃ and the houses ruled by it would show the directions in which money was spent. In all cases such as this interpret in terms of the general character. Had ♃ been the stronger, then generosity would have been the prevailing tendency with periods of carefulness or impecuniosity. In all cases the strength of the planet will show the dominating influence.

17. A useful method of obtaining a complete analysis of a horoscope and one that may be recommended to the beginner, is as follows :— Take a number of sheets of paper and head them Character and Mind, Money, Health, etc., allowing a separate sheet of paper to each department of life. On every sheet note each planet, sign position, house position, and aspect that has any bearing on the matter and write against each its influence. Having completed the sheets go over them one by one and balance up the conflicting statement by considering the relative strength and weakness of the planets, signs, houses, and aspects concerned, and the number of separate testimonies pointing one way. Then write out the judgment giving prominence to the strong characteristics, indicating the less conspicuous tendencies underlying the character, and omitting the weak antagonistic influences that are at variance with the rest of the map. Practice in this method gives thoroughness and impresses

the nature of the influences on the student's mind making it increasingly easy for him to write a complete delineation without reference to any book and developing his power of independent judgment. On no account should any statement taken from this or any other book be written down as it stands in a final judgment without a careful balancing of indications.

18. Always use common sense and try to think out what will be the natural effect of a position. Do not make the mistake of thinking a rule or aphorism infallible, but use it merely as a useful guide or pointer to be accepted or rejected according to whether it is upheld or dismissed by other indications. There is no hard and fast rule in the whole of astrology except in its mathematics.

CHAPTER II

INFANT MORTALITY AND LENGTH OF LIFE

The first and most important consideration when dealing with the horoscope of an infant is that of its chances of survival, for it is obviously futile to delineate a map when the native has little, or no, chance of life.

The vital spots in any horoscope are the ☉, ☽, and the degree rising on the cusp of the Asc., which should be treated as a planet and consideration given to the aspects it receives. One of these points is chosen according to certain rules, as that which has chief influence over life, and acts as significator of the length of life, this body or point being known as the *Hyleg*, or Giver of Life. The function of the Hyleg is to indicate the approximate length of life by means of its strength or weakness, and severe afflictions to the Hyleg must occur for death to ensue. The rules by which it is chosen are as follows:—

1. The "hylegiacal places" are from 25° below the Asc., to 5° above (measured by oblique ascension), the upper half of the 11th house, all the 10th and 9th houses, and from 25° above the cusp of the 7th house to 5° below.

The 8th and 12th houses, and all below the earth, except those portions of the 1st and 7th already indicated, can never be hylegiacal.

2. If the Sun occupies a hylegiacal place it must always be chosen as Hyleg.

3. If the Moon occupies a hylegiacal place when the Sun does not, it then becomes Hyleg.

4. If neither the Sun nor the Moon is in a hylegiacal place the Ascendant must be chosen.

These are the generally accepted rules, but it must be admitted that the question of Hyleg is still a somewhat open one. It has been suggested that the Hyleg may change as the horoscope progresses and another body passes into a hylegiacal place, but much research still remains to be done upon this matter.

The length of life is estimated by the proportion of good and bad aspects received by the Hyleg. If this body is free from affliction and supported by favourable aspects, a long life may be predicted while if it receives only bad aspects the life will be short. In practise it is advisable to study all three vital points and not to predict a very early death unless all these points are badly afflicted and there is little or no assistance from the benefics.

Aspects to the Hyleg and the other vital points from ♀ and ♃ are the most desirable, but may be weakened if these bodies are weak by sign or position and if they also happen to rule the 6th, 8th or 12th houses. Any aspects from the ☉ and ♂ give vitality, but the unfavourable ones dispose to fevers and accidents. Good aspects from ♄ and ♅ prolong the life in old age but have little effect in youth, especially in the case of ♅, which appears to have little effect upon the life as its afflictions rarely kill by themselves. Aspects from ♆ also seem to have little vitalising

64

effect, and those from ☿ are variable being favourable or the reverse according to whether the strongest aspect to ☿ is favourable or otherwise, as in all cases ☿ is negative and takes on itself the nature of the nearest aspecting planet considered together with the aspect.

The vitalising effect of the signs when rising or containing the ☉ or ☽, is as follows:—

1. ♈, ♌, ♎, and ♐ are very strong and give great power of resisting disease. They will prolong life even in a severely afflicted map, and in ordinary cases give a considerable length of life.

2. ♉, ♊, ♍, ♏, and ♒ are moderately strong and in ordinary cases promise a fair length of life. ♉ and ♏ are critical in infancy but increase in strength later in life. ♒ is often rather frail and is the weakest of this group. ♊ and ♍ are wiry rather than strong.

3. ♋, ♑, and ♓ are the weakest of all and if at all afflicted give much difficulty in rearing. ♑, however, often gives a long life if the native survives infancy as it becomes increasingly strong as old age is reached.

In judging the length of life either of an infant or adult consider the signs and houses occupied by the ☉, ☽, and ruler of the Ascendant, and also the rising sign and aspects to the cusp of the 1st house. If the majority of these are in vital signs, strong by house, and well aspected, a long life may be predicted, but if weak and greatly afflicted, especially by the rulers of the 4th, 6th, 8th and 12th houses, and little or no help is obtained from the benefics, or they are weak by sign, life will not be sustained. The point which is Hyleg needs special consideration. It is said that the Kabalists erect a map for the seventh hour after birth in order to judge whether the child will live. The following are particular rules:—

1. If the ☉ or ☽ be in an angle, and one of the malefics be in conjunction with it, or else distant from both ☉ and ☽ so as to from the apex of two equal sides of a triangle of which the ☉ and ☽ form the other apices, and at the same time no benefic planet assists and the dispositors of the ☉ and ☽ are also weak or afflicted by the malefics, the child then born will immediately die.

2. If the ☉, ☽, and Asc., are all afflicted by the malefics, especially from angles, and no assistance is given by ♀ or ♃ the child will die in infancy. Note that angular afflictions are always the most serious, and that favourable aspects from the benefics will be rendered of little efficacy if these bodies are very weak.

3. If the ☉ and ☽ are in opposition, and at the same time are both in square to two malefics also in opposition, the child will be stillborn or will die at once. If, however, in such a case the ☉ and ☽ are separating, and ♃ and ♀ precede them, the child will live for a short time.

4. Afflictions from an elevated planet are worse than from one not so placed, and are much more difficult to overcome.

5. In general ♂ afflicts the ☽ more than it does the ☉ as they are of different natures, and similarly ♄ afflicts the ☉ more than it does the ☽ for the same reason.

6. ☊ in conjunction with a malefic in the 4th, or the luminaries besieged by (i.e. in between) malefics often kills at birth or just after.

7. The conjunction of ♃ or ♂ to the Hyleg preserves life, but if the ☉ is Hyleg the effect is less, as some of the benefic influence is destroyed,

and if ♃ or ♂ rule the 4th, 6th, 8th or 12th, their influence is greatly lessened.

8. Other positions unfavourable for length of life are :—(a) Malefics in the Asc. ; (b) ruler of Asc., combust, cadent, retrograde or in the 8th ; (c) ☉ or ☽ in 6th, 8th or 12th, or afflicted from these houses or by their rulers ; (d) ☉ ☌ or ☍ ☽, especially if it is at the same time an eclipse.

9. Afflictions to the ☽, whether it be Hyleg or not, are of primary importance in the case of an infant, and the last and next aspects of the ☽ should be considered. If in a severely afflicted map it separates from a benefic and applies to a malefic the evil is strengthened, but if from a malefic to a benefic there is more hope of improvement.

CHAPTER III

PERSONAL APPEARANCE AND PHYSICAL PECULIARITIES.

Personal appearance is one of the most difficult matters to judge from a horoscope as it is modified by many factors.

The following are the most important general rules :—

1. The personal appearance is denoted primarily by the rising sign or Ascendant and is modified by the sign containing the ruler of the Ascendant. The rising decanate should also be observed as that often exercises a slight modifying effect.

2. Rising planets modify the typical appearance of the sign, and a planet on or very near to the Ascendant is always of great importance.

3. Planets exactly aspecting the Ascendant are important and introduce modifications in accordance with their own natures and sign positions.

4. A sign containing 3 or more planets usually influences the appearance.

In judging of appearance in practice look first to the rising sign and rising planet (if any) then to the ruler of the Ascendant, and lastly to planets aspecting the Ascendant. The typical appearance given by each sign when alone is as follows:—

ARIES. *Body.* Medium height or over ; lean ;

spare; wiry; long neck; strong, thick shoulders; fingers often short and thick. *Head* round, short, held erectly. *Face* long, with high cheek bones and broad temples, tapering to a narrow chin ; often with mark or scar ; upper lip often long ; sometimes lips project and underlip is thick and hanging. *Hair* red, sandy, brown, or sometimes very dark, and either wiry and straight or crisp and curly ; recedes on temples ; frequently parted in the middle ; often stands up like horns on each side of the forehead. *Eyes* grey or greyish brown, occasionally blue, with alert sharp and piercing look ; sometimes large and prominent. Eyebrows dark and bushy. *Nose* thin and aquiline or long and close to the face with a slight rise in the middle. *Teeth* white and strong, wide apart and usually large and prominent, often projecting. *Complexion* usually pale but sometimes ruddy. *Peculiarities.* Often like a ram or sheep in appearance ; tend to butt sideways with the head when excited ; habit of craning the neck ; strong voice, and sharp and direct speech, often using slang ; hasty handwriting ; energetic walk ; rush at things.

TAURUS. *Body.* Medium, height or under; thickset and squarely built ; short and strong neck ; strong shoulders, often stooping ; strong broad and plump hands and feet ; women frequently handsome. *Head* round or square, broad, and well set into shoulders. *Face* square ; full forehead; full lips, often well shaped ; wide mouth; heavy jaw and chin. Some types have thinner lips and a flat space between nose and upper lip. Features sometimes flattened. *Hair* dark and usually curling or wavy ; often very plentiful ; does not readily turn grey. *Eyes* brown or dark, large, round, sometimes prominent, and often slow moving and mild. Eyelids heavy and often partly lowered, giving sleepy look. Eyelashes long, dark and curling. *Nose* well shaped, often making straight line with the brow; nostrils usually thick. *Complexion* creamy white but sometimes coarse or swarthy; thick skin. *Peculiarities*. Often like a bull in appearance; hairy body and hands; very fond of good living and coarsen in age; deep musical voice and often sing; sometimes wear muttonchop whiskers; walk with small steps holding body still and set.

GEMINI. *Body.* Tall, upright, thin and slender; long arms and legs; narrow chest; often sloping shoulders; usually long, slender and artistic fingers, but sometimes hands and feet are short and fleshy; neck long and thin; women often short. *Head* long and narrow. *Face* long; wide and intellectual forehead; long chin; wide thin lips; small ears. *Hair* usually straight, soft and brown, sometimes black. *Eyes* hazel, usually bright, fine and expressive; quick sight; cruel glint in eyes when angry. *Nose* either long and straight, or resembles a bird's beak, being thin, aquiline, and cut straight across at the end. *Complexion* clear and pale, skin rather yellowish. *Peculiarities :* often like a bird or monkey; often perky and hopping about like a sparrow; voice high pitched, and speech quick, sometimes cackling; walk quick and energetic; long strides, swinging arms, and head projecting; often fanciful in clothes; restless, hands and feet never still; women fond of changing furniture.

CANCER. A very variable sign, much modified by the sign containing the Moon. *Body.* Two types, one tall and slim, and the other short, squat, and fleshy. Latter is more typical. Body is usually rounded and often has a top-heavy appearance and a watery or puffy look ; wide and full chest and bust ; slender arms ; short, fleshy and small hands and feet. *Head* round with low broad forehead. *Face* long and narrow or round ; often double chin and pendulous cheeks ; large mouth. *Hair* brown, light, golden brown or colourless ; men usually dark. *Eyes* grey, light blue or colourless, usually large and watery ; eyelids often baggy, eyebrows sometimes meet over nose. *Nose* short, small and round, tip prominent or bending over with a caught-up look at the nostrils. *Teeth* poor and often distorted or overcrowded. *Complexion* pale or muddled. *Peculiarities :* pleasant voice, talkative but also reserved ; laborious, rolling or swaying walk, often giving the impression at a distance that the toes are turned inwards and that one foot is placed slightly in front of the other ; often sit with feet turned inwards towards each other, or legs twisted round the chair rails ; sometimes tend to move sideways like a crab ; often wear moustache with points turned upwards ; handwriting irregular with hooked letters,; lower type, such as washer-women often stand with arms folded and a hand on each elbow.

Leo. *Body.* Medium height or tall ; fine figure; squarish body ; strong broad shoulders ; dignified appearance ; large bones and muscles ; long, strong and straight back ; hands large and brown, finger nails with large moons. *Head* large, round and domed, held erectly. *Face* round or oval; high forehead ; strong chin ; curved cheek bones ; large mouth, often with down drooping corners ; lips held well together. *Hair* light, yellow, tawny, flaxen, or light brown, usually wavy. Some types have very plentiful hair like a mane, and others incline to baldness on the top. *Eyes* often yellowish or sherry coloured, sometimes blue or grey ; sometimes full and staring ; but often partly covered, though always intent looking and not sleepy ; occasionally a habit of looking sideways ; eyelids and eyebrows set close together. Certain types have weak sight or a slight cast in one eye and wear pince-nez, usually of the rimless make. *Nose* small and straight like that of a lion or cat, rather spread at the nostrils. *Teeth* large, strong and yellowish white. *Complexion* florid or ruddy. *Peculiarities :* often like a lion ; very erect and dignified walk but buoyant step ; good dancers ; sometimes purr when pleased ; large appetite ; fond of brown clothes and boots; strong and powerful voice.

VIRGO. *Body*. Medium height, slender, usually spare, and neat, compact and refined in appearance ; shoulders often wide. *Head* well developed but not large. *Face* round; high forehead; often serene and pure expression with delicate and finely formed features, but sometimes with sharp and pointed features ; lips usually thin but sometimes full, and occasionally the lower lip slightly projects. *Hair* dark to light brown, generally swept back and falling over the ears ; inclined to baldness on top. *Eyes* dark, hazel, or grey, large, sharp and bright ; sometimes set too closely together in lower types, giving a foxy and cunning look. *Nose* straight, with very thin and mobile nostrils. *Complexion* pale or dark, skin usually more olive than white. *Peculiarities:* often like a fox ; active walk ; often lame ; quiet voice, but sometimes shrill when excited ; dress neatly and quietly ; handwriting very neat, careful and small.

LIBRA. *Body.* Tall, slender and slight in build but tending to become stout in later life ; often very beautiful ; hands and feet small but broad and plump ; fingers short with good nails. *Head* small, round and shapely, usually held on one side. *Face* oval or round, lips well curved and delicately marked ; chin well shaped, small and round ; expression often plaintive or dissatisfied. *Hair* usually brown but sometimes flaxen or black, smooth, fine, and often parted in the middle. *Eyes* blue or deep brown, often sharp and penetrating. *Nose* well formed, long and straight, making a straight line with the brow, but in some types upturned ; sometimes the nose appears to be abruptly cut off at the end, and the nostrils are wide. *Teeth* good, small, and even. *Complexion* often very good with fair, delicate and fine skin, but sometimes indifferent and inclined to be ruddy and pimply. *Peculiarities :* very graceful movements ; soft voice, but often with an undertone of petulancy and dissatisfaction ; walk with a springing up-and-down movement ; handwriting large, rounded and artistic.

SCORPIO. *Body.* Medium height or under ; thickset ; powerful ; strongly made ; square type of body with tendency to stoutness, but taller types have gracefully curving back at the waist ; full muscular throat ; strong bony hand with square tipped fingers. *Head* squarish. *Face* broad, often square ; large mouth ; square jaw ; prominent brows with sharp facial angles ; often Jewish type of face. *Hair* dark, wavy or curly, often coarse, crinkled, thick on the temples, and low on the forehead ; sometimes shows several tones of colour. *Eyes* dark, with a very intense gaze ; often beady ; eyebrows have a ruffled look. *Nose* often aquiline, but sometimes flattened and broad at the base. *Teeth* well shaped and strong. *Complexion* usually dark, swarthy, or dusky ; skin often dirty looking and lacking colour in the cheeks. *Peculiarities.* Often like a scorpion, serpent or eagle ; good fighters ; speech very intense and dramatic, making secrets or mysteries of trivialities ; voice sometimes shrill and penetrating ; tragic manner ; sometimes wear side-whiskers ; women often strikingly handsome ; sinuous movements ; walk with the head erect and still, but twisting the body from side to side ; handwriting often spiky.

SAGITTARIUS. *Body.* Tall, slim and well made ; strong, aristocratic, athletic looking and active ; sometimes stooping ; long hands and feet, and legs often disproportionately long ; very long neck ; broad shoulders. *Head* broad. *Face* sometimes oval, but usually long, narrow, and of even width ; broad rounded forehead ; strong chin, often dimpled. *Hair* brown, nut brown, or chestnut, often with a twist in it ; growing off the forehead and thinning at the temples. *Eyes* grey, blue, or brown, often rather prominent ; bright, clear, honest looking, and expressive, often twinkling ; eyebrows well marked; eyelids often appear to be stretched wide open in the middle ; eyes often slant downwards slightly towards the cheekbone. *Nose* long, thin, and usually straight, lying fairly close to the face, but sometimes aquiline. *Teeth* long, strong, and often projecting. *Complexion* fresh, ruddy or sunburnt and healthy looking. *Peculiarities:* often like a horse ; very restless ; great talkers, but often tend to stammer or have a slight impediment in speech ; fond of walking, and take long strides, head thrown back and arms swinging ; particular over dress, but often careless in handling clothes ; fond of checks, women affect tailor-made costumes.

CAPRICORN. *Body*. Medium height or under ; spare and bony; thin and wiry; often ill-formed; weak chest; sloping shoulders ; long thin scraggy neck ; weak limbs, and often weak at the knees ; bony hands. *Head* often small. *Face* thin and hard set, often with melancholy expression ; prominent, clearly defined, but often irregular features; thin, firm lips; prominent, narrow, pointed and bony chin, sometimes lantern-jawed ; browbones prominent ; ears sometimes project and are deficient in the lobes. *Hair* dark or black, thin, lank, and usually scanty. *Eyes* dark, usually deeply set. *Nose* long, often bent inwards at the tip ; prominent ; often strongly aquiline producing nutcracker appearance in age. *Teeth* often bad. *Complexion* dark or swarthy, often with coarse skin. *Peculiarities*. Often like a goat, camel, or elephant ; awkward, jerky, but energetic walk, sometimes holding head down, and often appearing as if they would fall to pieces ; angular movements ; often deformed ; frequently hurting their knees ; usually grave and serious, and often look worried ; strong voice, but inclined to be harsh and rasping, and sometimes cracks unexpectedly ; thin beard, if any ; angular and cramped type of handwriting ; dry and businesslike form of expression.

AQUARIUS. *Body*. Medium height or over, rarely short ; full rounded figure, often squarely built and tending to stoutness. *Head* often droops slightly. *Face* oval, or long and fleshy ; straight features but sometimes rugged ; often good looking ; well developed chin ; large mouth showing all the teeth when laughing ; sometimes ethereal appearance ; often with enquiring expression. *Hair* pale brown, flaxen, silky, and slightly curling ; sometimes falls in heavy clump over one side of the brow. *Eyes* blue or hazel, deep set and wide apart, with rather far-away expression ; sometimes hypnotic. *Nose* straight, but often very slightly aquiline. *Teeth* often poor. *Complexion* beautiful and clear, refined delicate skin. *Peculiariteis.* Fascinating ; very pleasant, soft and refined voice ; seldom laugh ; excellent speakers ; very quiet and retiring ; often brisk walk.

PISCES. *Body.* Medium height or under ; bulky and fleshy ; weak bones ; narrow chest ; often large, thick and rounded shoulders, and curved spine ; short legs ; small and plump hands and feet, latter often ill-made. *Head* large and wide, ill-made, and often drooping forward. *Face* round and fleshy; large mouth; full lips; tendency to double chin ; low and wide forehead ; very changing expression. *Hair* dark, soft, fine and plentiful. *Eyes* blue, sometimes dark ; full, watery, often weak looking, and sometimes filmy. *Nose* short and wide. *Teeth* small and shell-like, or uneven and overcrowded ; easily decay. *Complexion* sometimes beautiful, pale, and delicate, but often chalky and flabby ; clear skin ; colour easily comes and goes in cheeks. *Peculiarities.* Often rather fish-like ; flabby handshake ; stooping, rolling, lurching, and clumsy walk, head held down ; often with moustache of the walrus type or drooping at the corners ; uncontrollable laughter.

The planets when rising and near the Ascendant modify the above types very considerably. In general the effect of a rising planet upon appearance is to give some of the characteristics of the signs it rules. Thus the ☉ rising imparts some of the charccteristics of ♌ and in certain cases the native may easily be mistaken for this sign. Similarly the ☽ rising tends to give a ♋ appearance. In the case of the planets, however, the matter is rather more complicated as the appearance is usually more like one of the planet's signs than the other. Thus, ♀ rising sometimes resembles ♉ and at other times ♎, and it is not easy to say which sign will be the one impressed upon the native. The general modifying effect of each of the planets when rising, or strongly aspecting the Ascendant is as follows :—

The Sun. Adds dignity and gives a fresh complexion, full stature, large head, round face, light or yellowish hair, growing thin, and blue or grey eyes.

The Moon. Renders the body short and often squat, tending to plumpness, and gives a broad chest, face and forehead, fleshy hands and feet, brown hair, grey, soft and limpid eyes, one often slightly larger than the other, and a pale complexion.

Mercury. Adds tallness and length to the body and limbs, and gives thin nose and lips, dark hair and eyes, olive complexion, and a quick, talkative and active manner.

Venus. Adds plumpness, and gives a short body with short fleshy hands, small feet, round cheeks, red lips, well shaped mouth, smiling face, often dimpled, light brown and smooth hair, blue or brown eyes, clear complexion, and a musical voice.

Mars. Gives medium height and a strong and muscular body with large bones and broad shoulders. The face is round, with sloping forehead, prominent brows, aquiline nose, and often a mark or scar on the face. The hair is often red or light, crisp and curly, but sometimes black. The eyes are hazel, sharp and piercing, and the complexion fresh or ruddy.

Jupiter. Adds bulk and robustness to the body. tending to stoutness in later life. The bearing is dignified, and the face oval, with high forehead, arched brows, full beard, brown or chestnut hair, blue or brown eyes, and a fresh or sanguine complexion.

Saturn. Gives leanness, with a thin sometimes melancholy face, large ears, long nose, heavy brows, dark or black hair, dark, small and deep-set eyes, bad teeth, pale or sallow complexion, and a downward look when walking.

Uranus. Adds height and spareness, giving a wiry, muscular, and rugged appearance. The features are strongly marked, and the face is often good looking, with dark hair and eyes, and a pale complexion.

Neptune. Gives medium height and thinness, sometimes inclined to softness and plumpness. The face is long and thin, nervous looking as if strained or startled, often prematurely wrinkled, and with light, soft and silky hair, blue eyes, usually very sleepy or dreamy looking, a clear complexion, and a light coloured skin.

By means of the above descriptions we are able to obtain a good general idea of the native's personal appearance, but for a more detailed judgment of his peculiarities and defects the following special rules will be found necessary .—

(a) *Stature.* Tallness and shortness are very difficult to judge accurately, and the typical stature given by the signs is frequently modified. The chief factors in determining this question are the rising sign, its ruler, the ☽, and the planet in strongest aspect with the ☽ or ruler. In general the natives of ♊, ♌, ♐, and ♒ are tall, and those of ♉, ♋, ♑, and ♓ are short, the other signs disposing to an average height, but it is not safe to rely too much upon this alone. Some special rules are as follows :—

1. Planets aspecting a significator usually give taller bodies when rising than when setting.

2. The ☽ gives a shorter body when decreasing in light (i.e. passing from the ☍ of the ☉ to the ☌) than when increasing (i.e. passing from ☌ to ☍).

3. An earthy sign rising and the ☉, ☽, and ruler of the Ascendant in earthy signs gives a very short body. The same is the case if the majority of planets are in earthy signs and aspecting the ☽ and Ascendant.

4. If the ☽ is in the Ascendant in ♓ and ♃ is in ♋, especially in the 6th house, the native will be very short or a dwarf.

5. ♑ or ♒ rising, with ☿ and ♀ ☌ or ☍ ♄ causes a dwarfed body.

6. The ☽ and ruler of the Ascendant without latitude and in the ends of signs causes shortness.

7. The Ascendant in the beginning of a sign and its ruler in elevation dispose to tallness.

8. ☿ or ♀ in house or exaltation and aspecting the Ascendant give tallness, and the contrary

when in fall or detriment, ♄, ♃ or ♂ in fall or detriment, and at the same time retrograde, tend to shortness.

(b) *Corporature.* This is judged chiefly from the rising sign, its ruler, rising planets, and the ☽.

1. The watery signs rising or strongly occupied usually give stoutness, and excessive stoutness is usually caused by the prominence of these signs and the planets ☽, ♃ and ♆.

2. According to Ptolemy the ruler of the Ascendant without latitude gives thinness, and with latitude stoutness, South latitude increasing the activity and North latitude decreasing it.

3. ☉ ♂ ☽ makes the native ill-coloured and lean.

(c) *Hair.* The rising sign and the planets aspecting it show the colour of the hair.

1. ♂ exactly rising or in strong close aspect to the Ascendant gives red hair, while ♄ similarly placed gives black.

2. The mutable signs and especially ♊ and ♐ affect the hair most strongly, and ♐ or ♓ rising, with ♃ in houses 1, 2, 3, 7, 8 or 9 often produce premature baldness. The same may happen if ♄ rules the Ascendant and is similarly placed.

3. ♂ elevated above and afflicting ♀, especially from ♊, ♐, or ♒ causes the hair to fall out. The same frequently happens when ♂ afflicts ☿.

(d) *Eyes.* The colour of the eyes is shown by the rising sign and planets as previously indicated in the general descriptions. To these it may be added that ♀, ♂ or ☍ ♃ frequently gives deep blue or violet eyes.

The ☉ rules the right eye of a man and the left eye of a woman, while the ☽ rules the left eye of a man and the right eye of a woman. As a rule these bodies will be found afflicted in cases of defective eyesight.

The following are special rules :—

1. Defective sight or sore eyes are caused by afflictions to the ☉ or ☽ in or from ♈ and ♎. The same is caused by ☉ ☍ ☽ in these signs.

2. The ☉ in ♒ badly afflicted by ♄ often causes total blindness.

3. Certain fixed stars, nebulae, and clusters, are most usually involved in cases of blindness or defective eyesight, the most important being situated as follows :— Pleiades in ♉ 28° 51′, Praesaepe in ♌ 6° 9′, the Aselli in ♌ 6° 24′ and ♌ 7° 34′, and Antares in ♐ 8° 37′. The longitudes of these bodies increase at the rate of 50″.25 per annum the above positions being for 1st January, 1918.

If the ☉ or ☽ are in any of these places and either afflicting each other alone or afflicted by the malefics, or if the malefics afflict them from these places, blindness or defective sight results, one or both eyes being affected, according to whether one or both luminaries are afflicted. Affliction from ♄ gives danger from cold or cataract, from ♂ by fire, battle or accident, from ♅ by explosions or electricity and from ♃ by excess of light. The favourable aspects from the benefics show the amount of help and relief that may be obtained. One of the worst positions is when the ☽ is in the 7th house, the malefics in the 1st, and the ☉ also in an angle.

4. The ☽ in ☌ with the ☉ near Cingula Orionis (in about ♊ 24) causes blindness at least in one eye.

5. The ☉ or ☽ afflicted in the Milky Way (from about 21 ♊ to 5 ♋ and from about 16 ♐ to 7 ♑) often causes blindness.

6. ☉ ☍ ☽ free from affliction and not in angles causes a squint.

7. The following postions have some effect in causing blindness or defective sight. (*i*) ☉ ☌ ♂ in the 8th and ☽ ☍ ♄ from ♊, ♍, ♎, ♐ or ♒ (*ii*) ☽ ☌ ♄ in ♋ or ♑ in □ or ☍ to ♂; (*iii*) ☽ in 4th □ ♄ ♂ and ☉ in 8th ; (*iv*) ☽ in M.C., ☉ in Asc., and ♄ in 9th.

(*e*) *Ears.* Defective hearing is usually caused by afflictions to ☿. The following positions denote a tendency to deafness :—

1. ☿ afflicted by ♄, and especially when ☿ rules the 6th.

2. ☿ ruling 12th or 6th and afflicted in one of these houses or ☌ ☉.

3. ☿ ☌ ☉ afflicted by a malefic ruling 6th.

4. ☿ in ♑ afflicted by the malefics.

(*f*) *Speech.* Defective speech is usually denoted by afflictions to ☿, and generally involves the mute signs ♋, ♏, and ♓.

1. ☿ in one of the mute signs and afflicted by a malefic causes an impediment in the speech, especially when ☿ rules, or is in, the 6th.

2. ☿ ☌ ☉ and ♄ in an angle hinder speech, and the same effect is caused by ☿ in the first six degrees of ♏, ☍ ☽, and also by ☿ ☌ ☋ in the 6th, 8th, or 12th.

3. ♄ rising in a mute sign or in ♈, ♉, ♌, or ♑, often causes an impediment.

4. ♂ afflicting ☿ causes quick speech.

5. ♊, ♍, ♎, ♐ or ♒ on the Asc. and ☿ unafflicted gives free and graceful speech.

(*g*) *Teeth.*

1. ♂ in the Asc. in ♋, ♏, or ♓, causes loss of teeth.

2. ♄ ☌ ☉ in a watery sign, especially if in

the Asc. or 6th, causes much suffering from toothache.

3. ♄ in Asc. or 7th, except in ♐ and ♒, denotes trouble with teeth, and in earthy signs, except ♐, gives weak, distorted, and easily decaying teeth. If in an airy sign there may be much toothache but the teeth are seldom lost; and if in a fiery sign the teeth rot without much pain.

(*h*) *Deformity*. Deformity is caused by severe afflictions, especially in earthy signs and in angles, or in the 6th and 12th houses. The luminaries are frequently cadent and in no aspect to the Asc. whilst malefics occupy the angles. The signs ♈, ♉, ♋, ♌, ♏, ♐, and ♓ are most frequently concerned in such cases either as rising signs or containing the afflicting or afflicted planets. Afflictions from ♂ cause deformity through fire or wounds; those from ♄ through falls; and those from ♅ from explosions. When acting from birth, however, ♅ usually causes some inversion of the parts affected. Afflictions in mutable signs affect the legs and arms; in fixed signs the body; and in cardinal signs, the head.

1. ♐, ♒, or ♓ rising and containing the ☉ or ☽ and afflicted often produce lameness.

2. ☽ near ☊ or ☋ afflicted by malefics from angles makes a hunchback or deformed person.

3. ☽ ☌ ♂ and ☊ or ☋ in 12th and ♃ ☌ ☉ in 4th makes a hunchback.

4. ♄ afflicting Asc. or ☽ and the lord of the Asc. afflicting the dispositor of the ☽ usually denotes deformity or mutilation.

5. The ☽ in the Asc. with ☿ and ♄, afflicted by ♂ often causes hermaphroditism or sexual imperfections.

6. Other positions causing deformity are (i) malefics in angles, especially in the M.C. or Asc. and afflicting the rising degree ; (ii) ☉ and ☽ in 6th, 8th, or 12th, and their dispositors afflicted by malefics ; (iii) malefics in angles ruling 6th, 8th, and 12th, and afflicting the ☽ or lord of the Asc.

7. According to Ptolemy the new or full Moon nearest before birth should be examined, together with the dispositors of the luminaries. If at birth the ☽, ☿, and the dispositors of the birth luminaries, or most of these bodies, are in no aspect to the luminaries or their dispositors at the lunation, the birth will be monstrous, and if the luminaries at birth are in the bestial signs ♈, ♉, ♌, ♐, and ♑, it will not be human. The nature and disposition of the creature may be judged by the nature of the aspecting planets.

CHAPTER IV

CHARACTER AND MIND

CHARACTER. The most important significators of character are the ☉, ☽, the rising sign, and its ruler, but all the planets have some effect, expecially if they aspect the significators. The rising sign describes the native's outlook on the world and the side of his character that is most in evidence, the ☽ describes his personal attributes, and the ☉, the deeper and inner side of his character. If the ☉ is stronger than the ☽ the inner character will be stronger than the personality and vice-versa. If the Asc. is strong and the ☉ is weak the native will not have the inner strength to carry through what he begins, but if the Asc. is weak and the ☉ strong he will make resolutions and plans that he will not be able to carry out.

The signs containing the majority of the planets indicate the general type of character. Cardinal signs denote activity, energy, ardour, ambition, love of fame, restlessness. Fixed signs denote firmness, stubbornness, will power, plodding, organising, patience, conservatism. Mutable signs denote intellect, vacillation, indecision, nervousness, worry, duality, adaptability, cunning, Fiery signs give energy, activity, intellect, ardour, inspiration; earthy signs are practical, concrete, suspicious, plodding, worldly; airy signs

85

mental, idealistic, nervous, intellectual; and watery signs emotional, imaginative, changeable, and psychic; there is sometimes a tendency to drink of debauchery, especially if ♀ or ☿ be afflicted here.

The general type so indicated will be modified by the sign positions and aspects of the significators, good aspects giving the more favourable characteristics of the aspecting planets, and bad aspects the more unfavourable.

Mind. The chief significators of mind are the ☽, ☿ and planets in, or the ruler of, the 3rd house. In addition planets in the mutable signs and cadent houses also influence the mind. ☿ rules the pure intellect; the ☽, the brain and concrete mind; the 3rd house, the lower mind; the 9th the higher mind, philosophy, and dreams; the 6th the sub-conscious mind; and the 12th, the hidden, inner, and unconscious mind, and occultism.

The signs and aspects of the significators denote the mental characteristics. If ☿ and the ☽ are unconnected, not aspecting the Asc., and afflicted by the malefics, especially if mutable signs are involved, there is great danger of mental instability or madness, ♄ indicating melancholia, ♃ and ♂ religious mania, ♂ alone madness, and so on. The more aspects there are to ☿ the better, even if many are bad ones, as an unaspected ☿ tends to lack of balance. About the worst affliction to ☿ is from ♅, as this causes twisted, inverted, erratic, and eccentric ideas, and insanity, or at least liability to nervous breakdown. Other positions indicative of a tendency to insanity are ☿ afflicted by ♂ in a day map, or by ♄ in a night map; ♄ afflicting the Asc. by night, or ♂ by day, especially if in a watery sign ; ☽ ☌ ☉ in a sign ruled by ♄, or ☽ ☍ ☉ in one ruled by ♂. Good aspects from ♃ or ♀ will avert the greatest danger and judgment must be formed by comparing the strength of the afflicting planets with that of the planets casting good aspects.

The general type of character given by each of the signs when rising or containing the planets is as follows :

ARIES. Frank, outspoken, impulsive, brave, reckless, generous but selfish, extravagant, quarrelsome, destructive, ambitious, pioneering, jealous, independent, aggressive, clever, ingenious, shrewd, changeable, exaggerating, fond of politics, often bigoted, monopolise conversation, fight for rights, do not like to hear their faults. ♆, imaginative, poetical, scheming. ♅ abrupt, inventive. ♄, industrious, touchy, deceptive. ♃, enthusiastic, hopeful, judicious. ♂, positive, idealistic, argumentative, irritable. ☉, self confident, commanding, rash, independent. ♀, idealistic, ardent, demonstrative. ☿, quick, fluent, impulsive, exaggerative, clever, quarrelsome, greedy. ☽, enthusiastic, irritable, penetrative, disobedient, unconventional.

TAURUS. Dogmatic, obstinate, strong willed, self-possessed, slow to anger and forgiveness, resentful, selfish, strong passions, violent if roused, patient, plodding, careful and exact, fond of ease, and good living, proud, sensuous, magnetic, very reserved, loyal, domineering, strong sense of humour, strong opinions, good memory, fond of science or agriculture. ♆ artistic, musical. ♅, determined, considerate, occult. ♄, economical, diplomatic, fond of solitude, sullen. ♃, peaceful, dignified, just, compassionate.

G   87

nate. ♂, fearless, acquisitive, reserved, proud.
☉, over confident, autocratic, warm hearted,
meditative, ♀, strong and deep feelings, voluptuous, kind. ☿, practical, stubborn, cheerful,
strong likes and dislikes. ☽, quiet, persistent,
hopeful, conservative.

GEMINI. Flexible, irritable, worrying, self-
contained, nervous, vacillating, see both sides
to every question, versatile, changeable, clever,
inventive, original, fond of knowledge for its own
sake, always want to know why, subtle, brilliant
wit, fond of puns, puzzles, and conjuring tricks,
sceptical, schemers, capable of pure abstract
thought, mathematical, coldly scientific and
dispassionate, may be dishonest. ♃, humorous,
poetic, ♅, curious, inventive, occult. ♄, scientific, subtle, observers, self deceived. ♃, fond
of detail, refined, literary. ♂, acute, cunning,
clever, severe. ☉, ambitious, studious, refined,
thoughtful. ♀, considerate, sympathetic. ☿,
shrewd, scientific, clever, unbiased. ☽, secretive
ingenious, subtle, fond of intrigue.

CANCER. Quiet, reserved, quick temper, im-
patient, autocratic, very imaginative, fond of
sensation, fond of dramatising their own actions,
sentimental, very emotional, capricious, sensitive,
irritable, adaptable, very sympathetic with suffering, jealous, usually narrow minded, resent
criticism, often very depressed and gloomy,
tenacious and never let go unless frightened
unexpectedly. ♃, wayward, emotionally changeable. ♅, eccentric, restless, fanciful. ♄,
peevish, discontented, remorseful. ♃, kind,
popular, enterprising, ♂, ambitious, industrious,
unruly, domesticated, peevish. ☉, conscien-
tious, easy going, fond of pleasure. ♀, economical,

fickle. ☿, discreet, tactful, changeable. ☽, fond of ease and comfort, homely, emotional, changeable, sensitive, easily influenced.

LEO. Open, frank, ambitious, confident, scorns meanness, somewhat reserved and never tells all, lordly, generous, quick tempered, optimistic, fixed and dogmatic opinions, fond of poetry and drama, brave when necessary but often relies on display. Fond of show, fond of sunshine, fond of glittering things, brass, etc., and rich colours, always right, fond of giving advice. ♆, romantic. ♅, independent, fond of freedom. ♄, ambitious, determined, cautious. ♃, proud, loyal, magnanimous. ♂, commanding, argumentative, generous, fearless, impulsive. ☉, just, honourable, generous, ambitious. ♀, romantic, ardent, extravagant, fond of display and popularity. ☿, bombastic, large views, dogmatic, positive. ☽, dignified, enthusiastic, ambitious, artistic, fond of luxury and show.

VIRGO. Cool, practical, discriminating, very critical, often destructively so, impassive, faddy over little things, very inquisitive, modest, retiring, faithful, intellectual, strong opinions, fond of art, literature, science and mathematics, fond of collecting, good memory and reasoning power, not very original, slow to anger and forgiveness, quiet, persuasive, very good at detail work, fond of gardening, reading, cookery, needlework, etc., often servile to rich or distinguished people, fond of telling people their faults, worry over little things but brave in emergency, insist on respect, often rather old maidish. ♆, sensitive, retiring, mysterious. ♅, economical, antiquated, eccentric. ♄, cautious, bashful, melancholy, studious, captious. ♃, prudent, covetous, dictatorial, deceitful, fond of service, ♂, shrewd, affable, irritable, deceitful. ☉, ingenious, industrious, modest, small self confidence. ♀, chaste, or given to intrigue. ☿, intellectual, ingenious, critical, scientific, mysterious, sceptical. ☽, quiet, analytical, psychic.

LIBRA. Gentle, sensitive, inventive, artistic, imaginative, idealistic, honest, lazy, too easy going, fickle, very persuasive, indecisive, easily led by flattery, greatly influenced by surroundings, strong sense of justice, cheerful and melancholy by turns, very fond of pleasure and company, worry over trifles, horror of physical injuries or suffering, usually selfish and rather shallow. ♅, poetical, visionary. ♇, romantic. ♄, improvident, opinionated, scientific. ♃, compassionate, considerate, courteous, great love of justice. ♂, refined, captivating, courteous, idealistic. ☉, affectionate, sociable, imaginative, artistic. ♀, helpful to others, simple affections, equable. ☿, dispassionate, refined, broad mind. ☽, accomplished, kind, popular.

SCORPIO. Very strong character, great will power, quarrelsome, destructive, sarcastic, tremendous pride and self satisfaction, often claim to be much more advanced than others, persistent, follow one line until finished and then readily change, dramatic, sensational, impressive, fiery temper, brusque, ambitious, great magnetism, fertile imagination, very fond of secrets, mysteries, and occult matters, penetrating mind, fixed opinions, fond of occult or chemical research ♅, mysterious, proud, ♇, artful, secretive, superstitious. ♄, avaricious, jealous, comtemptuous, passionate, violent. ♃, haughty, overbearing, pride of birth. ♂, quick, acute, designing, passionate, tricky. ☉, firm, unbending, proud, passionate, contentious. ♀, jealous, seductive, character reader. ☿, keen, critical, curious, suspicious, fond of secrets. ☽, firm, abrupt, revengeful, selfish, conservative.

SAGITTARIUS. Frank, honest, open, impetuous, good natured, intuitive, sporting, strong sense of justice, irritable, generous, optimistic, independent, clever, versatile, quick, fond of prediction, fond of religious and philosophical subjects, fond of outdoor exercise, sport, and horses, apt to make shrewd shots and guesses, fond of giving advice. ♅, inspirational, utopian ideas. ♆, rebellious, turbulent, over generous. ♄, honest, trustworthy, sensitive. ♃, refined, kind, couteous, humane, fond of gambling and speculation ♂, impulsive, rash, rebellious, talkative, generous. ☉, generous, proud, sincere, restless, love of show and luxury. ♀, light hearted, susceptible, fond of pleasure. ☿, inspirational, passionate, talkative, rebellious, rash. ☽, energetic, restless, kind, sincere, fond of change and sport.

CAPRICORN. Ambitious, quiet, calculating, practical, scientific, melancholy, malicious, sometimes fond of service, diplomatic, suspicious, love of power, reticent, unrelenting, cautious, prudent, persistent, selfish, lustful, economical, often mean. ♅, crafty, subtle, designing, selfish. ♆, acquisitive, restless, romantic. ♄, apprehensive, suspicious, discontented, treacherous. ♃, autocratic, severe, orthodox, ♂, brave, enterprising, tactful, industrious. ☉, subtle, reserved, serious, conservative, conventional, self controlled. ♀, fickle, irresolute, restricted and ambitious affections. ☿, tactful, suspicious, patient, critical, discontented, scientific, irritable. ☽, fond of show or fame, selfish, covetous, very economical, cold, calculating.

AQUARIUS. Artistic, idealistic, humane, strong will, frank, open, cheerful, genial, timid, scientific, interested in life rather than form, fixed and strong opinions, good judges of human nature influence over animals, often break promises, ask advice and do not follow it. ♅, humanitarian, broad minded. ♆, eccentric, impressionable, scientific, ♄, observant, thoughtful, slow in speech and action. ♃, humane, cheerful, broad and tolerant mind, more philosophical than religious. ♂, nervous, clever, hospitable. ☉, obedient, cheerful, idealistic, democratic, prudent. ♀, faithful, obliging, chaste, romantic, effeminate, timid. ☿, eloquent, observant, humane, refined, intuitive. ☽, tolerant, inoffensive, sociable, political and scientific, fantastic imagination.

PISCES. Kind, romantic, vacillating, very imaginative, psychic, rather muddled, fond of good living, generous, emotional, very talkative, fond of animals, fond of sensationalism. ♅, sympathetic, peculiar ideas. ♆, fanciful, despondent. ♄, indecisive, lack of hope and courage, sensitive. ♃, hospitable, philantropic. ♂, satirical, humane, receptive, passionate, timid and bold alternately. ☉, hospitable, restless, changeable, lack of initiative, arrogant. ♀, hospitable, sympathetic, impressionable, philanthropic, obstinate. ☿, superficial, imitative, too receptive, muddled, little depth. ☽, dreamy, inconstant, quiet, easy going, restless, retiring, easily discouraged, lacks common sense or humour, intemperate.

The general influence of the planets is as follows

SUN. Dignified, proud, confident, honourable, arrogant, egotistical.

MOON. Ambitious, changeable, receptive, imaginative, romantic, sentimental, fond of novelty, Rising in ♈ and afflicting ☿, liar. Afflicted by ♀, untidy, and slovenly.

MERCURY. Active, energetic, clever, quick, alert, nimble, cunning, talkative. Takes on nature of planet in nearest aspect. Aspecting ☽, good at languages. Afflicted by ♂, quick mind but contentious and sarcastic. If in ♓ angular and afflicted by ♂ or ☉, fanatic. In good aspect with ♃, good judgment. If afflicted by ♃, hyprocrisy and deceit. If ☌ ♄, depth of mind. If ☍ ☽ in angles stupid. If retrograde or combust in ♉ or ♐ in 6th, 8th or 12th, not aspecting ☽ or lord of Asc., simple and rude mind.

VENUS. Artistic, affectionate, sociable, quiet, tender, refined, fond of pleasure, scents and ornaments. Afflicted by ♂, ardent and extravagant passions. Afflicted by ♄, sorrowful.

MARS. Courageous, confident, assertive, active, energetic, consequential, aggressive, destructive, proud, passionate, extravagant. Afflicted by ♄ or ♅, ungovernable temper. If rising in ♍, insufferable conceit.

JUPITER. Dignified, proud, jovial, philanthropic, kind, sympathetic, generous. If afflicted, hypocrisy, and pride of the nature of the planet afflicting. Afflicted by ♂ boasting and religious enthusiasm; by ♄, grasping, and unsympathetic. If in ♐ with ♍ rising, pretentious mind.

SATURN. Economical, cautious, diplomatic, suspicious, reserved, cold, selfish, just, ascetic, harsh, severe, industrious, thoughtful, melancholy apprehensive, steadfast. In 3rd, melancholia, morbidity, insanity. If ☌ ☽ in earthy signs, very melancholy. Afflicted by ♃, hypocrisy;

by ♂, violent ; by ♀, depraved; by ☿, dishonest; by♂ and ☿, enthusiast or fanatic; by the luminaries, discontented.

URANUS. Original, inventive, erratic, eccentric, genius, brusque, assertive, independent, romantic, fond of occultism, electricity, aviation, or antiquarianism.

NEPTUNE. Psychic, fantastic, aesthetic, very musical, fond of stringed instruments, dreamy, voluptuous, mystical, mediumistic, neurotic, self indulgent, peculiar and chaotic ideas.

CHAPTER V

HEALTH AND ACCIDENTS

The most important factors in the judgment
of health are the Sun, Moon, and Ascendant,
and the planets in, or the ruler of, the 6th house,
but any strong bad aspect renders those parts
of the body sensitive that are ruled by the signs
in which the aspect falls. The ⊙ and ☽ are
general significators of the life, the ⊙ ruling the
radical constitution, and the ☽ the functional
disorders and sympathetic system, and any
afflictions to these or to the Ascendant, which
rules the body, tend to disturb the health. The
seriousness of such a disturbance must be judged
by the strength or otherwise of the sign and house
positions of the bodies concerned, the strength
of the afflicting aspect, and the amount of help
received from ♀ and ♃. In general, afflictions
to the ⊙ are worse than those to the ☽ as they
denote defects in the radical constitution and
give less promise of relief, but afflictions to the
☽ are always serious in the case of women just
as are those of the ⊙ to men.

The relative power possessed by each of the
signs of withstanding disease has already been
given and should always be taken into consideration.

Each sign of the zodiac rules various parts of
the body and when rising, or on the cusp of the

6th, or containing afflicted or afflicting planets, causes those parts of the body to become sensitive and easily subject to disorder. The following list indicates the parts of the body ruled by each sign, the types of disease associated with them, and remarks on certain less obvious effects of planets afflicted therein :—

ARIES. *Rules* head, face, brain. *Ailments.* Head, stomach and kidney troubles, disorders of eyes and brain, fevers, neuralgia. *Remarks.* Planets here frequently cause peculiar internal diseases. ♂ inflammatory and mental complaints, pains in eyes and bowels. ☽ insomnia, especially if ♂ ♃

TAURUS. *Rules* Cerebellum, neck, throat, larynx, lips, ears. *Ailments.* Throat and heart troubles, diphtheria, quinsy, diabetes, piles, fistulas, apoplexy, disorders arising from over-feeding. *Remarks.* Nervous over health. Planets here often cause illness through foreign travel. ♄ danger of contagious diseases and from over-feeding. ♂ or ♄ rising in this sign gives fits in dentition.

GEMINI. *Rules* shoulders, arms, hands, lungs breath, blood. *Ailments.* Mind and nerve disorders, mental overstrain, worry, consumption, bronchitis, asthma. blood troubles. *Remarks.* Mind affects health. Planets here frequently give illness arising through the profession. ♅ spasmodic asthma.

CANCER. *Rules* breast, chest, stomach, digestive organs, ribs, elbows. *Ailments.* Gastric troubles, dropsy, scrofula, rheumatism, cancer, dipsomania, hypochondriasis. *Remarks.* ♄ here, pyorrhoea, also danger from impure magnetism. ♂ gastric troubles and weak sight, but sometimes power of resisting disease.

HEALTH AND ACCIDENTS

LEO. *Rules* spine, back, heart, wrists, forearm. *Ailments.* Heart troubles, palpitation, syncope, spinal meningitis, lumbago, violent sickness. *Remarks.* ♄ here, danger of overwork and from infection. ♂ peculiar ailments, pains in eyes and stomach, inflammatory and tumorous complaints. This sign rising and ☉ afflicted in the 5th is a sure indication of heart trouble.

VIRGO. *Rules* abdomen, umbilicus, bowels ,intestines, lower spine, fingers. *Ailments.* Bowel disorders, colic, dysentery, diarrhoea, constipation, dyspepsia, debility, worry. *Remarks.* Worry over health. ♄ here, sickness in early life, headaches, and mental diseases. ♂ danger from bad food, but sometimes power to resist disease through hygiene. ☽ danger to eyes.

LIBRA. *Rules* kidneys, lumbar region, skin. *Ailments.* Skin and kidney disorders, diabetes, Bright's disease, nephritis, lumbago, eczema, blood disorders. *Remarks.* ♄ here, locomotor ataxia, and danger of contagious diseases.

SCORPIO. *Rules* urinary and generative organs, nose, anus, bladder, appendix, pelvis. *Ailments.* Piles, ruptures, fistulas, venereal diseases, heart, throat and blood disorders, infectious diseases, and ailments arising from excess. *Remarks.* ♄ here, liable to epidemic complaints. ♃ gout, bloodpoisoning, hereditary diseases. ♀ venereal diseases, heart trouble at end of life.

SAGITTARIUS. *Rules.* hips, thighs, nerves, arteries. *Ailments.* Rheumatism, sciatica, gout, blood trouble, ailments affecting lungs and nerves. *Remarks.* ♄ here, danger of nervous breakdown at end of life. ♂ danger from operations or medical errors.

CAPRICORN. *Rules* knees, hands, bones, joints,

97

teeth. *Ailments*. Rheumatism, skin diseases, eczema, leprosy, impetigo, urticaria, colds and chills, ailments affecting the knees. *Remarks*. ♄ here, chronic illnesses, ♂ acute diseases. ☉ heart disease. ☽ biliousness, melancholia, hypochondriasis, chest and throat troubles.

AQUARIUS. *Rules* legs, ankles, blood, circulation. *Ailments*. Nerve and blood disorders, anæmia, cramp, sprained and broken legs and ankles. *Remarks*. Planets here may give avoidance of illness by the study of hygiene, food reform, or temperance. ♀ or ☽ varicose veins. ♂ acute diseases, weakness or pains in legs.

PISCES. *Rules* feet, toes, lymphatic system. *Ailments*. Bowel disorders, gout, colds, dropsy, tumours, infectious diseases, ailments arising from excess. *Remarks*. ♂ here, consumptive tendencies. ♀ tender feet, sickness after marriage. ☉ dropsy and diabetes.

The positions given in the above remarks are intended to be merely supplementary, for as a general rule an afflicting planet disturbs those parts of the body ruled by the sign concerned and causes illnesses of its own nature affecting those parts.

It is found that afflictions in any sign affect those signs in opposition or in square to it. This is known as polarity and is very important in practice. Thus, kidney diseases (♎) will affect the eyes (♈); internal troubles (♏) will affect the blood (♒) and the heart (♌), and so on. In general the quadruplicities and triplicities have each a group influence as follows :— *Cardinal*. Head, stomach, kidneys, skin, *Fixed*. Blood, throat, heart, urino-genital organs. *Mutable*. Nerves, lungs, bowels, digestion. *Fire*. Head, heart, hips. *Earth*. Throat, bowels, digestion, knees, skin. *Air*. Lungs, kidneys, blood, nerves, *Water*. Stomach, urino-genital organs, feet. Thus an affliction in any sign is liable to cause a sympathetic disturbance of the organs ruled by the other signs of the same triplicity or quadruplicity, but the maximum effect is exerted by the afflicted sign itself.

The parts of the body and diseases ruled by the planets are as follows:—

SUN. *Rules* heart, back, vitality, blood, brain, right eye of a man, and left eye of a woman. *Ailments*. If afflicting Asc., or ☽, or itself afflicted, debility, fevers, sunstroke.

MOON. *Rules* breast, stomach, saliva, fluidic and lymphatic systems, left eye of a man and right eye of a woman. *Ailments*. If afflicting Asc., or ☉, or itself afflicted, functional disorders, chills, colds, dropsy. If in 6th, fanciful over food or too fond of liquids ; sometimes gives meningitis

MERCURY. *Rules* brain, mind, lungs, tongue, speech, hands, arms, nerves, hair. *Ailments*. Nerve disorders headaches, neuralgia, insomnia, giddiness, nervous breakdown, lung diseases. If in 6th causes faddiness over food or interest in hygiene.

VENUS. *Rules*. throat, chin, eustachian tubes, complexion, cheeks, umbilicus, reins, ovaries, veins, internal generative organs. *Ailments*. Kidney troubles, venereal diseases, and ailments affecting the throat, heartburn, tonsilitis, cysts, and ailments arising from indiscretion in diet. If in 6th often gives careful nursing.

MARS. *Rules* nose, forehead, bile, gall, muscles and sinews, external generative system. *Ailments*. Fevers, infectious and inflammatory diseases, sharp and sudden diseases, operations, shingles, fistulas, ailments affecting the nose, ruptured bloodvessels. If in 6th some tendency to illness through over-eating, also sudden diseases. If in 12th extreme and sudden weakness.

JUPITER. *Rules* blood, semen, liver, arteries, pleura, absorptive system, right ear. *Ailments*. Blood disorders, accumulations of fluid, liver disorders, pleurisy, boils, abscesses, quinsy, apoplexy, and ailments arising from surfeit and indiscretions in diet.

SATURN. *Rules* bones, joints, teeth, spleen, secretive system, left ear. *Ailments*. Colds, chills, dull aches, rheumatism, chronic and lingering diseases. If in 6th gives danger through fasting or ascetic habits, and of chronic diseases. If in 12th, liable to gout.

URANUS. *Rules* nerves, membranes of the brain and spinal cord. *Ailments*. Obscure and incurable diseases, cramp, ruptures, sudden and spasmodic ailments, nervous breakdowns, paralysis.

NEPTUNE. *Rules* brain, and telepathic organs. *Ailments*. Obscure and incurable diseases, obsession and psychic ailments, vague and irrational fears, and the various "phobias", worry, ailments arising through drug taking, excessive smoking or tea and coffee drinking.

The exact nature of an illness is shown by the combined influence of the planet and sign. Thus ♄ is weakening and obstructive and ♒ rules the blood, so that ♄ in ♒ tends to anaemia or bad circulation. Similarly ♃ in ♒ causes blood impurities arising through excess, and so on. These effects take place when the planet afflicts the luminaries in or from these signs, or is afflicted in the 6th.

HEALTH AND ACCIDENTS

In judging of health :—

1. Note the rising sign, its afflictions, and the ruler. The sign will give the ailments to which the native is subject considered in connection with the afflicting planet, and also the organs most likely to be affected.

2. Observe the ☉ and ☽ and note the signs containing them and the afflicting planets and their signs. If they are free from affliction, well placed and aspected, the health will be good. In general afflictions to the ☉ indicate lasting and hereditary diseases, and those to the ☽ the ailments arising from time to time and more easily cured.

3. Note the sign on the 6th, and to a lesser extent those on the 4th and 8th as these indicate sensitive parts of the body. Planets in these houses and especially in the 6th and 12th will disturb the health if afflicted and affect the parts ruled by the signs containing them.

4. Note any strong afflicted or afflicting positions anywhere, as these will also mark sensitive points.

5. Observe the help given by good aspects from ♀ and ♃. These afford relief but cannot assist very much if weak by sign, house, or aspect. If very strong they will save the life and often ward off illness also. Good aspects from these planets indicate not only the prospects of recovery but also the sources of help. Any good aspect to an afflicted significator affords relief through its house and sign position ; thus if lord of the 12th or in the 12th there will be benefit from hospital treatment, if in 6th from nursing, if in 3rd from relatives and neighbours, and so on.

6. The relative preponderance of sickness and

health must be judged by the relative strength of the afflictions and good aspects to the significators of health. ♀ or ♃ in the 6th exert a protective influence on the health but if afflicted cause troubles according to their natures. In general the health is good if the luminaries are strong and well aspected; lord of 6th fortunate; luminaries well aspected by planets in 6th; and lords of 1st and 6th in good aspect (not ♂).

7. The house position of the ruler of the 6th often shows the source of illness but the houses ruled by the afflicting planets must also be considered. In general the effect of the ruler of the 6th in the houses is as follows:— 1st. Much ill-health, often caused through the native's own fault. The same effect follows if the lord of Asc., is in 6th, 2nd. Loss of money or expenditure on health. 3rd. Illnesses on journeys. 4th. Hereditary illnesses. 5th. Illness through pleasures. 6th. Through work. 7th. Through marriage or women. 8th. Bad health and often near death. 9th. Illness abroad or on voyages. 10th Through business or by promotion. 11th. Through disappointments, 12th. Much confinement.

8. The houses correspond to the signs, and a malefic in say the 2nd may affect the health not only through the sign containing it but also through ♉, the sign normally corresponding to the 2nd house. To determine whether house or sign will be affected note the condition of the house corresponding to the sign and of the sign corresponding to the house. Thus ♄ in ♊ in 2nd may affect lungs (♊) or throat (2nd house corresponding to ♉). To determine which will suffer note whether there are afflictions to the

3rd house (corresponding to ♊) or to ♉ (corresponding to 2nd house). If ♉ is afflicted judge that the throat will suffer, but if the 3rd house is worse look to the lungs. If judgment cannot be formed in this way note also the condition of the planetary rulers.

9. The house positions of the luminaries and ruler are important and if these bodies are in the 4th, 6th, 8th, or 12th they denote poor health throughout life. The same effect frequently follows if they are in conjunction with the rulers of these houses. Afflictions from these rulers or planets in these houses are worse than from other bodies or positions.

10. The house and sign position of the afflicting planet shows not only the general part of the body affected but also the particular spot. The beginning of a sign rules the upper parts of the organs subject to it, the intermediate degrees rule the middle, and the end of the sign rules the lower parts. Furthermore the odd signs and houses rule the left side in a man and the right in a woman, while the even signs and houses rule the right side of a man and the left of a woman.

The following are the chief aphorisms relating to health :—

A. GENERAL.

1. The Asc. and all planets in signs of one triplicity cause continual trouble from ailments pertaining to that triplicity.

2. Lords of Asc. or of sign intercepted in 1st, afflicted by malefics in 6th or 12th denotes general ill-health.

3. ☉ or ☽ afflicted in 6th or 7th denotes much illness, and the health is weakened if ☉ afflicts ☽

4. ☉ ☌ ☽ makes the native infirm and tends to weak mental balance or peculiar diseases.

5. Lord of Asc. applying to a bad aspect of lord of 6th indicates that the native is negligent of his health.

6. Malefics rising cause accidents or acute and painful illnesses ; if setting long and tedious diseases.

7. Benefics oriental or angular and aspecting ☽ indicate that diseases will be curable. If ♃ it will be by medicine, and if ♀ they will cure themselves. If the benefics be cadent or occidental the disease will be wholly incurable.

8. If the benefics are in no aspect to the ☉ and ☽, and the malefics are in angles the diseases will be incurable, and even if the benefics assist, a cure will not be effected if the malefics are strong and elevated above them.

9. Malefics rising before the ☉ or after the ☽ cause diseases and their effects are increased if ☿ is with them.

10. When ♄ is instrumental in causing disease it frequently indicates a tendency to complain, and if ☿ is also afflicting the native may talk much about his illness or even parade it for profit or beg from door to door.

11. ♂ in any aspect with ☉ gives great vitality, but if afflicting, danger of accidents and fevers.

12. ♂ elevated above ♄ makes the native sickly and a weakling, but if ♄ is elevated above ♂ he is strong.

13. ☽ □ or ☍ ♄ or with ☋ in 1st or 2nd shows the whole life to be infirm.

14. The ☽ afflicted in ♈, ♉, or ♊ disposes to cancer and facial eruptions ; in ♋, ♌, or ♍

ringworm, tetters, and shingles; in ♎, ♏, or ♐, scurvy and a variety of leprosy; and in ♑, ♒, or ♓, boils, pimples, and scabbed lips.

15. Malefics angular in ♋, ♑, or ♓, and rising after the ☽ or before the ☉ cause scurvy and scrofula.

16. ☿ afflicted by ♄ or ♂, or in square to the ☽ from 1st or 7th causes ailments affecting the head, and if both malefics are concerned it often causes apoplexy.

17. ☽ P ♄ or ♂ causes diseases affecting the head, which will be very severe if ☿ is at the same time afflicted by ♄ or ♂.

B. SPECIAL.

1. CONSUMPTION. (*a*) Many afflictions from mutable signs dispose to consumption. If ♄ is the afflicting planet the disease will be slow, but if ♂, rapid.

(*b*) ♄ elevated near M.C. and □ or ☍ ☉ tends to consumption, especially if in mutable signs.

(*c*) ♄ ☌ ☊ especially in an angle and in square to the ☽ in a cadent house.

(*d*) ☉ and ☿ afflicted in ♓ in 6th with ♍ rising tends to consumption.

2. CANCER. The astrological indications are not yet certain. As a rule the ☽ is badly afflicted and there are afflictions from ♃, ♄ or ♅, and the signs, ♈, ♉, ♋, ♎, and ♑. ♄ in ♋ often indicates the death of a parent, usually the father, from cancer.

3. EPILEPSY. (*a*) ☿ and ☽ not aspecting each other, or when in ♓ and ♑ or in 6th, 8th, or 12th, and neither aspecting Asc.

(*b*) ♄ by night and ♂ by day strong in an angle and afflicting both ☿ and ☽.

(c) ♄ by day and ♂ by night disposing of ☿ and ☽.

(d) ♅ in a watery sign on Asc. and afflicting, causes epilepsy or water on the brain. Other positions causing epilepsy are ☽ in Asc. ☍ ☿ and ♄; ♄ ☍ ♂ in angles; ☽ ☌ ☉ and ♂ in 4th in square or opposition to ♄; ☉ and ♀ in Asc. ☍ ♄; luminaries afflicted by ☿ and ♂. Malefics angular rising after ☽ or before ☉ and in ♊ or ♐ also cause epilepsy, but if in the very end of the sign they are said to produce gout, cramp, and rheumatism. In nearly all cases of epilepsy the Asc. is heavily afflicted.

4. GOUT. (a) Both luminaries afflicted in watery signs.

(b) Luminaries in conjunction with or opposition to malefics in ♈, ♉, ♋, ♏, ♐, ♒, or ♓, the luminaries or malefics having house or exaltation in 1st or 6th.

(c) In nocturnal maps ♂, ♀ and ☽ angular in opposition to ♄ in ♉, ♌, ♐, or ♓.

(d) ♄ in ♓, ☍ ♂ or ☉ or ☽.

(e) ♄ in ♍, ♐ or ♑ in 6th or 12th, □ or ☍ ♂, ☉, or ☽.

5. FEMALE AILMENTS. (a) ☽ in conjunction with or in good aspect to ♀ causes regular catamenia, but if afflicting each other they will be profuse and weakening especially if at the same time ♂ afflicts ♀.

(b) ♄ afflicting ♀ causes catamenia to be irregular painful, or suppressed.

(c) ♄ and ♀ in ♑, afflicted by ☽ in ♎ indicates danger of the catamenia never occurring, and consequent barrenness.

6. CONVULSIONS are caused by afflictions from fixed signs, ☿ being at the same time afflicted by ♂ or ♅.

HEALTH AND ACCIDENTS.

7. STONE. In a diurnal map ♄ and ♂ in 7th or 8th, or ♂ in 6th in ♎ or ♏, afflicting ☽, or ☽ in ♎ or ♏ afflicted by ♄.

8. TUMOURS AND ABSCESSES are caused by the planets or luminaries afflicted in ♋ or ♑. If the afflicting planet be in ♍ or ♓ it often produces an abscess on or near the liver.

ACCIDENTS.

Accidents are caused by serious afflictions from ♂, ♄, or ♅, especially when these planets are rising or afflicting a rising planet. The signs most conducive to accidents are the "violent" signs ♈, ♎, ♏, ♑ and ♒, and to these may be added ♊ also. It is found that the latter half of ♎ is frequently productive of accidents when containing the malefics or afflicted luminaries. The cardinal signs and angles are of chief importance and the position of the ☉ or ☽ afflicted in houses 4, 5, 6, 10, 11, 12, is also conducive to accidents.

1. Afflictions from ♂ cause accidents through fire, burns, cuts, scalds (especially if ☿ be in a watery sign), wounds and bullets (when ♂ is in one of the the "human" signs ♊, ♐, or ♒), and bites (especially when ♂ is in ♏ or ♓). ♂ in the 12th in ♊, ♌, or ♎ gives danger from horses or large animals. The nature of the sign, whether watery, fiery, etc., or human or animal, together with the house, will show the source of danger and the nature of the accident.

2. Afflictions from ♄ cause falls, (especially in airy signs) blows, bruises, sprains, dislocations, and accidents from falling bodies. If in ♐ there are falls from horses, and in ♒ from steps or downstairs. When ♄ is elevated in the 10th

and afflicting the luminaries there will be violent falls especially if ♄ rules the 1st or 8th. ♂ ♂ ♄ gives liability to accidents under directions even when these planets do not afflict the luminaries, and if the conjunction takes place in ♉ in the 4th there is danger from the fall of ruined buildings.

3. Afflictions from ♅ cause sudden and unexpected accidents from machinery, electricity, lightning, and explosions.

The part of the body affected is in all cases shown by the sign containing the malefic or the afflicted luminary. In general there is frequently a mark, scar, or mole on the part of the body ruled by the signs containing malefics, and often on the face if the malefics be rising.

The severity of the accidents must be judged from the strength of the afflicting planets and the amount of help received. Good aspects from ♃ and ♀ when themselves strong will avert serious danger and give "miraculous escapes".

CHAMPTER VI

FINANCE.

The 2nd house rules money and property ; the 5th speculation ; the 8th loss but also legacies, inheritance, and the money of the wife, partner, and general public, and the 11th, income from business. Planets in these houses or their lords will indicate gain or loss through these matters.

1. Note the planets in the 2nd, its ruler, and their signs, and also planets aspecting them with their house and sign positions. Favourable aspects will bring gain by means of the matters, people, and occupations ruled by the aspecting planet and its sign and house, and bad aspects will similarly indicate the sources of loss. Any planet in the 2nd will bring gain if well aspected but if it is a malefic and weak by sign the gain may not prove durable. The same method of judgment is to be applied to planets in, or the rulers of the 5th, for speculation, the 8th, for legacies, and so on.

2. Particular attention should be paid to the ☉, ☽, ♃, and ♀, as they are natural significators of money. The ☉ is more important in a woman's map, and the ☽ in a man's. If these bodies are afflicted the fortunes are poor, but favourable aspects denote gain. A good aspect between ☉ and ☽ is very beneficial and if these

bodies afflict one another the fortunes are uncertain or fluctuating.

3. Examine the position and aspects of the Part of Fortune in a similar way.

4. Judge wealth or poverty by the greater number of indications and the relative strength of the planets. Cardinal signs and angles give increased fortune or misfortune, while mutable signs and cadent houses tend to obscurity and little success.

The following are the influences of the signs and planets on finance, and certain specific effects of some of the planets in the signs. It should be remembered that the position of a planet in a sign merely indicates connection with the matters mentioned and the question of loss or gain depends upon the nature of the aspects it receives.

ARIES. Gain by own endeavours and shrewdness. ♄ here, acquisitive, gain or loss through deaths of uncles or aunts, competence at end of life if well aspected by ♃. ♃, voyages shipping or foreign investments. ♂, private sources, loss through marriage. ♀ gain through deaths of inferiors, secret affairs, and mother's relatives.

TAURUS. Economical, fond of investment, cautious and careful, gain by marriage. ♄, industry and investment ; fortunes improve later. ♃, investment and speculation, money from women. ♂, acquisitive, and persevering. ♀, profession. ☽, inheritance from parents, money from companies or wholesale trading. ♅, from partnership

GEMINI. Fluctuating, double sources of gain, do not save until latter half of life. ♄, questionable means. ♂, by wits, ♀, by relatives, speculation, friends' advice, and secret methods.

FINANCE

CANCER. Acquisitive and careful. Gain through water or voyages. ♄, occultism. ♃, property, intellect. ♂, servants, agencies, travel, public affairs. ♀, meeting public needs. ☽, property and shipping.

LEO. Speculation or public work. Often gives wealth. ♄ domestic or foreign affairs. ♃, marriage, mining. ♂, government or public work, music, success at end of life. ♀, inheritance. ☉, rarely in want.

VIRGO. Foreign affairs, shipping, health, service. ♄, religious people and things. ♃, investment, literature, secondhand dealing. Richer than parents. ♂, speculation, investment. ♀, speculation, help of partner. ♅, state or public work. ☉, wealth in middle age.

LIBRA. Business and association with others. ♄, labour and employment. ♃, institutions, partner or wife, inferiors, commerce, science, or employment of agents. ♂, loss through inferiors. ♀, loss through marriage.

SCORPIO. Gain by others' death or losses and by marriage. ♄, public companies, popular enterprises, life policies. ♃, arbitration, mining, unsound speculation. ♂, marriage. ♀, union or secret alliances.

SAGITTARIUS. Legacies and speculation. ♄, investment. ♃, marriage, sick relatives, speculation. ♂, or ♀, marriage, speculation. ☽, inferiors.

CAPRICORN. Foreign affairs or abroad, investment. Acquisitive. ♄, speculation and investment. ♃, commerce, relatives' deaths. ♂, travel. ♀, diplomatic alliances. ♅, catering on large scale.

AQUARIUS. Corporations and associations. ♄, quiet effort. ♃, associations, inheritance. ♂, parents or relatives. ♀, inheritance or public affairs.

PISCES. Gain from friends. ♄, disregards money. ♃, associations and companies, mining ♅, charity.

Cardinal signs give good earning powers but free expenditure and bring success from enterprise and public recognition. Fixed signs tend to hoard up money but give sudden losses. They favour government work. Mutable signs bring gain through service and in the employment of others.

The influence of planets on money is as follows :—

SUN. Money from father, superiors, business. Gives much money but also free expenditure.

MOON. Money from the mother, females, public service, if elevated and strong from factories. Causes thrift but fortunes are changeful. Afflicted by ♃, improvident, indiscreet, and too generous ; by ♄, financial failure and if ♂ ♄ in an angle causes poverty. Ruling 2nd, in reception with ruler, and placed in Asc. well aspected gives great wealth.

MERCURY. Gain by commerce, writing, agencies, travel, skilled work ; danger of loss by theft. Aspected by ♀, refined occupations ; ♂, industry and skill ; ♃, judgment ; ♄, diplomacy ; ♅, inventiveness or speculation.

VENUS. Friends, pleasures, women. Free expenditure on pleasure or finery. Aspected by ♄ investment or banking ; ☽ public ; ♃, friends and foreign affairs ; ♅, acquaintances, peculiar methods. Afflicted by ♂, waste and extravagance; ♄, fear of poverty, unavoidable loss; ♅, sudden losses. Afflicted in 2nd, loss by females or wife.

FINANCE

MARS. Strength and energy, legacy, marriage. Earns easily but spends freely. Afflicted by ♃ extravagance; ♄, poverty. If in 2nd afflicting ☽ loss by war, fire, or theft.

JUPITER. Religious affairs, shipping. Gives wealth. In good aspect to ♄ or ♅ (especially from 8th or 4th or these planets rule those houses) legacies and inheritance. Afflicted by ♄ or ♅ loss by law or trustees, often poverty. In 8th gain by marriage. If strong in 2nd. in good aspect to ☽ or lord of Asc. in an angle gives ample fortune.

SATURN. Thrifty. Labour, investment. In good aspect to ♀ or ♃, investment and companies. In 7th bad for trade.

URANUS. Out of the way sources, sudden windfalls, government, fluctuating fortunes, danger of smashes. In 7th harassed by creditors, loss after marriage.

NEPTUNE. Institutions, hospitals. Danger of fraud or bubble schemes. Sometimes gain by fraud or blackmail.

The position of the lord of the 2nd is of importance and its influence in each house is as follows :— 1st. By energies, or else well off. 2nd. Riches, especially when well aspected by lord of Asc. 3rd. Loss from relatives, gain by journeys. 4th. Inheritance. 5th. Speculation, children. 6th. Loss by servants, health, animals. 7th Loss by marriage, partners, theft and wars. If afflicted in ♈, ♏, ♐, or ♒, loss by enemies and robbed by wife, unless lord of Asc. is in good aspect with lord of 7th. 8th. Legacies, marriage. 9th. Voyages, shipping, or abroad. 10th. Profession, eminent people. 11th. Friends, societies, companies. 12th. Gain from enemies, servants, .

and animals, loss by theft and imprisonment. As before the aspects received will indicate whether gain or loss is to be expected.

The following are the aphorisms dealing with finance :—

General. 1. Many planets in 2nd bring money in various ways according to the nature of the planets but indicate poverty if afflicted.

2. Lord of 8th in 2nd and well aspected brings gain by legacy and marriage, but if afflicted causes poverty or ruin.

3. Benefics promising money and not afflicted by malefics denote lawful gain, but malefics promising, and afflicted, retrograde, combust or in a bad sign, denote unlawful gain. A benefic in the house or exaltation of a malefic, or a malefic in the house or exaltation of a benefic, denotes both lawful and unlawful gain. Retrogradation and combustion increase the likelihood of unlawful gain in both cases.

4. If the significators of wealth are in houses 12, 11 or 10, money will be obtained in youth ; if in 9, 8, or 7, between the ages of 25 and 35 or 40 ; if in 6, 5, or 4, between 40 and 50 ; and if in 3, 2 or 1 late in life. If the significators rise before the ☉ money will come earlier but if they rise after the ☉, nearer old age. Retrogradation delays the time but swiftness of motion hastens it.

Gain. 1. ♃ strong in Asc. and ☽ well aspected in 2nd gives wealth.

2. ⊕ strong, and its dispositor in 8th in good aspect to lord of Asc., brings legacies.

3. ☊ with ☽, ♃, or ♀, in 2nd denotes durable fortune. The same is denoted if ♃ or ♀ are in good aspect to the cusp of the 2nd.

4. ♄ disposing of ⊕ and in good aspect to ♃ indicates inheritances. If the aspect is in angles or ♃ is in ♊, ♐, or ♓, and in the 7th in good aspect to the ☽ the native is often an adopted child and inherits the wealth of its adopted parents.

5. ☽ in ♉ in 2nd separating from □ or ☍ ♃ and applying to △ ☉ denotes considerable riches.

6. ♀ and ♃ in 7th with ☋, or ☋ with ☿, brings riches through the wife.

Loss. 1. ☋ in 2nd causes want, poverty and, loss by theft.

2. Lord of 2nd combust, ⊕ unfortunate and, 2nd afflicted causes confiscation of estate and bankruptcy.

3. Lord of 2nd ☌, □, or ☍ ♄ or ♂, and both retrograde, cadent, and weak by sign indicates perpetual poverty.

4. The 8th or its lord afflicted may cause loss of estate by the wife's death.

5. ☽ in 8th and lord of Asc. in 2nd or 12th, retrograde, denotes loss by gambling or speculation.

6. ♂ and ♄ in 4th, or cardinal signs on angles and containing ♂ and ♄ gives poverty and misfortune throughout life unless very well aspected by ♃.

7. ♃ in 6th, retrograde, and lord of 2nd in an unfavourable sign or afflicted denotes poverty.

8. The majority of planets retrograde or below the horizon indicates failing fortune.

CHAPTER VII

OCCUPATION AND POSITION.

The 10th house rules occupation, employers, fame, honour, and power; and the 6th, service, inferiors, employees, occupations followed through necessity rather than choice, and ones which give little honour or renown. The following are to be noted in judging the nature of the occupation :—

1. The signs and planets in, or rulers of, the 10th and 6th.

2. The Sun's house and sign position and aspects, and the planet nearest the Sun, especially if rising before it.

3. The ruler's position and the planet in strongest aspect to it.

4. The planet in strongest aspect to the Moon.

5. The dominant planets in the map.

The particular nature of the occupation is very difficult to judge as the field of choice is so large, and many people follow more than one pursuit, especially if the mutable signs are strongly tenanted and the significators receive many aspects. As a rule the exact work is denoted by several positions rather than by one only and follows the general type of map, but the most important factors in addition to the 10th and 6th

116

houses are the strongest planet in the map and the ☉, ☽, ☿, Asc. and its ruler [1]).

The stronger the positions and aspects of any planet the more connection will it have with the profession, and the nature of the aspect does not greatly influence the matter except that good aspects denote the better and more refined occupations of the planets, while the bad aspects denote the more laborious and obscure. The success in any work, however, depends upon the aspects and dignities of the planets concerned, and any occupation denoted by a badly placed or aspected planet will never prove successful. The cause of the lack of success is shown by the position of the afflicting planet and its nature, thus ♄ may cause laziness or neglect ; ♂ pride, obstinacy, carelessness or debt ; ♀, trouble through pleasures or women ; and so on. In *choosing* a profession look to the most favourably placed planets.

The nature of the chief significator and the sign containing it should be combined when judging the nature of the occupation. Thus ♄ denotes work in connection with dark objects, lead, etc., and ♊ has to do with writings and books, so that ♄ in ♊ might denote a compositor

---

[1]) According to Ptolemy the chief significators of the occupation are the planet rising just before the ☉, and the planet in the M. C. If the former is in the M. C. or aspecting it or receiving the application of the ☽ it must be chosen. If it is not in the M. C. and another is, the stronger must be chosen, while if there is no planet rising near the ☉ nor in the M. C., the ruler of the M. C. must be chosen if it is ☽, ☿, ♀, or ♂. These rules are somewhat doubtful. however, and those given above should be followed.

provided the rest of the map were in agreement. Note also that the houses correspond to the signs and rule the same matters, so that a planet in, say, the 6th house has a similar effect to one in ♍.

The matters ruled by the signs, and the effect of certain sign positions of the planets, are as follows :—

ARIES. Pioneer, soldier, short story writer, cattle dealer, groom, coachbuilder, veterinary surgeon, ♄ here, ambition, difficulties in early life. ♃, government work, military success. ♂, work in connection with home. ☽, work involving secrecy, or plebeian.

TAURUS. Dealer in real estate, house agent, broker, dealer in woollen goods, singer, gardener, soap boiler. ♃ religious, philanthropic or philosophical worker. ♂, both gain and pleasure from work. ☽, succeeds to father's business, work remunerative, but secret or plebeian.

GEMINI. Writer, journalist, editor, teacher, schoolmaster, surveyor, astronomer, astrologer, aviator, musician, conductor, or composer, clerk. Often double occupation, ♄ common and public work, science, typing, shorthand, book-keeping, cashier. ♃, obscure, unprofitable, or unpopular work. ♂, better servant than master, gain by wits, cross examiner, detective. ☉, ballooning, mountaineering, unprofitable scientific work.

CANCER. Occupations in which liquid enters, sailor, publican, wine and spirit merchant, barmaid, caterer, washerwoman, occupations connected with the public. ♃, exalted position. ♂, medicine and surgery. ☉, admiral, ship's carpenter.

LEO. Actor, artist, jockey, schoolmaster, manager, coachman, butler. ♄, secret or government work, obstacles from superiors, ♃, government or church dignities, secret service, diplomacy, crime detection. ♂, works to end of life, government work, music, high army position. ♀, help from women of position. ☿, author, if ♂ ☉ jeweller.

VIRGO. Secretary, accountant, stationer, printer, schoolmaster, astrologer, chemist, confectioner, clothes dealer. If rising and ☿ strong good physician but poor salary or bad debts. Bad for legal work. ♄, difficulties in early life, literary critic, proof reader, journalist, chemist. ♃, love of service, magistrate, tutor, guardian, secondhand dealer. ♂, work abroad, ☉, success in police force.

LIBRA. Valuer, assayer, bank clerk, designer, money changer, pawnbroker, linen draper. ♄, career affected by marriage, favours from superiors, trouble every 7 or 9 years. ♂, refined occupations, trouble from competitors, warlike. ☿, subordinate position in law. ☽, work in partnership with someone older or younger, work affected by marriage, success in law.

SCORPIO. Naval man, soldier, chemist, oil and colour merchant, photographer, surgeon, brazier, founder, brewer, maltster. If rising denies success in the Roman Catholic church. ♃, government or chemical work, entrusted with secrets. ♂, peculiar or secret government work, sea voyages connected with work.

SAGITTARIUS. Explorer, lawyer, clergyman, physician, dealer in cattle or horses. Inclines to double occupation. ♄, public service and welfare worker, independent worker. ♃, gain in common work but loss where social interests are involved. ♂, inactive in early life, occult work, unprofitable or risky occupation. ☽, help from women.

CAPRICORN. Political agent, diplomat, government official, dealer in wool or lead, farmer, farrier, chandler, victualler. ♅, distributive work on large scale. ♃, joy in duty, despot, delights in ruling inferiors. ☽ drawback or difficulty in work.

AQUARIUS. Electrician, aviator, scientist, company promoter, painter, poet, ship's carpenter. ♃, work in public institutions, gain in work dealing with liquids or air. ♂, good director, humanitarian interests. ☉, politician, architect, painter, sculptor.

PISCES. Imaginative writer, fishmonger, warder or attendant in prison or hospital, brewer. Tends to double occupations. ♄, trouble with superiors. ♃, public companies or philanthropy. ♂, mental occupation or one requiring uniform. ♀, hospital work. ☽, poet, sailor.

The nature of the signs containing the majority of planets is also important and the following are the group influences of the triplicities and quadruplicities:— *Fire*. Work in fire or metals. Soldier, surgeon, mechanic. *Earth*. Manual labour, agriculture, mining, farmer, corn dealer. *Air*. Intellectual work, literature, artist, lawyer, mathematician, draughtsman, designer. *Water*. Work with fluids, textiles, fabrics, painter, sailor, chemist, brewer, wine and spirit merchant, washer-woman, emotional actor.

Cardinal. Pioneering work, diplomat, manager, director, retailer. *Fixed*. Plodding work, government or old established concerns, naval man, producer, manufacturer. *Mutable*. Better servant than master, agent, traveller, writer, clerk, speaker, importer. Work in public institutions, sometimes needing uniform.

The influence of the planets upon the occupation together with certain of their positions and aspects are as follows :—

SUN. King, nobleman, courtier, manager, government worker, goldsmith, jeweller, gilder. In 10th, occupation of power and trust, honour and success in middle age, help from superiors. Afflicting ☽, changes trouble with superiors and in finding work.

MOON. Sailor, traveller, fisherman, barmaid, servant, nurse, advertiser, caterer, washer-woman midwife, work to do with water or the public. In 10th, fluctuations and changes, and if afflicted by ♂, scandal ; if in good aspect to ♃ or ♀ and they in good aspect to the lord of Asc. or significator of profession gives great success. In ♈, ♌ or ♎, fanatics, false religionists, enthusiastic preachers. In ♒, or ♓ disfavour of superiors. Afflicted by ♅ sudden changes. With ♂, butcher.

MERCURY. Writer, editor, accountant, teacher, schoolmaster, interpreter, secretary, clerk, postman, carrier, bookseller. In Asc. afflicted by ♂ or ♄ and in no good aspect to ♃ or ♀, thief, or forger. In 4th afflicted, shoemaker. With ♅, musician. With ♄, geologist, mining engineer, bookbinder, printer, dyer, antiquarian. Afflicted by ♄, potter, turner, thief. With ♃, painter, barrister, parish clerk ; if in ♂, ambassador, merchant. With ♂, sculptor, carver, quarryman, wrestler, strong man, footballer, etc., chef, steward, dairyman, scavenger, lavatory attendant. ♀ above the earth inclines to oratory, but below, to science or art.

VENUS. Painter, poet, artist, maker of toilet accessories, dealer in scents and flowers, embroiderer, confectioner, milliner, dealer in women's goods or luxury trades. In 9th, poet, especially if in ♂ or aspect to ♄, ☿, and ☽. With ♃, haberdasher. With ♂, dyer, perfumer, barber, metal worker. With ☿ ℞, singer, music master. With ☽ seamstress, engraver, upholsterer, glover. Afflicted by ♄ and both weak, harlot.

MARS. Soldier, surgeon, dentist, chemist, iron and steel worker, barber, cook, agitator. In 2nd, unfortunate with merchandise. In 10th, energy but no success except in martial work, slander. With ♄, miner, plasterer, bath or exhibition attendant; if in bad aspect, sweep, bailiff, labourer. With ♃, soldier, tobacconist, mechanic, tax collector, innkeeper. With ⊙, in nocturnal map, soldier. Separating from ⊙, shipwright, stonemason, carpenter, labourer.

JUPITER. Judge, councillor, clergyman, lawyer, doctor, banker, trustee, clothier, grocer. If in ♍, with ☽ in ♓, poet. With ♀ and ♂, prison keeper, in charge of women.

SATURN. Dealer in land and property, miner, coal merchant, plumber, architect, undertaker, jailer, grave digger, beggar, monk, antiquarian, labourer, worker in dark or heavy materials. In 7th loss through public affairs. In 10th, rises high by industry but falls. With ♀ or ♂ curate, undertaker, work connected with religious ceremonies. Afflicting ☿ and ♂, thief, and swindler, especially if ☽ also afflicts ☿; if ♄ is in 7th may be hung, if in 12th trasported or imprisoned; if ♂ also afflicts ☽, robber and assassin.

URANUS. Government official, aviator, traveller, engineer, inventor, electrician, antiquarian astrologer, hypnotist, engaged in uncommon work. In 7th, loss through public affairs. In 10th, chequered career.

NEPTUNE. Sailor, medium, dealer in cotton, tobacco, drugs, tea, coffee. Occupations connected with psychic or spiritual matters or in which water enters. In 10th, scandal and treachery, sometimes adopts assumed name.

The position of the ruler of the 10th is important and its influence in each house is as follows:— In 1st, authority over public. 2nd, wealth. 3rd journeys in connection with work. 4th, land property, mines, success at end of life. 5th, help through or work in connection with children. 6th, poverty or service. 7th, help through marriage. 8th, by deaths. 9th, church, law, voyages, shipping, abroad. 10th, honour and success, favours from superiors. 11th friends or companies. 12th loss, treachery, imprisonment

RANK AND POSITION.

The rank and position depend upon the strength of the planets in the map, their house and sign positions, the condition of the 10th house, and the number of planets attending the luminaries.

Planets above the earth or in the eastern half of the map (i.e. in houses 10, 11, 12, 1, 2 and 3) give ambition, and denote that the native will rise to a good position ; while if below the earth they tend to obscurity, and if in the western half of the map (i.e. in houses 4, 5, 6, 7, 8 and 9) they give a more altruistic nature, a greater dependence upon others, and a more fated life. It is frequently stated that if the majority of planets are below the earth there is no likelihood

of fame, but this is entirely erroneous unless
they are also weak in other ways.

If the majority of planets are in cardinal
signs or angles the native works his way into
prominence usually early in life ; if in fixed signs
and succeedent houses progress in slower but
more stable ; and if in mutable signs or cadent
houses the life is obscure, or passed in the service
of others, and the native is frequently unstable
or too versatile. Dignified planets increase the
reputation or fame, but debilitated or retrograde
ones cause obscurity and hindrances. Strong
aspects, especially in cardinal signs and angles
cause fame or notoriety but if the aspects are
unfavourable there is at the same time much
criticism and an unfavourable ending.

♃, ♀, or the ☉, if well aspected, in the 10th
raise the native above his birth position, and
♄ and ♅ have the same effect but in their case
there is usually a corresponding fall or crash
afterwards. The continuance of honour and
rank depend upon the strength and positions
of the planets promising them. The house
positions of these planets moreover, indicate the
approximate age at which fame or notoriety may
be expected, as already explained in connection
with the significators of wealth, and the rank
or position will be obtained through the people
and things ruled by the planets promising them.
Planets in the 10th indicate the position attained
in middle life, and those in the 4th that at the
end of life. The condition at these periods may
be judged by the nature and aspects of the planets
concerned or of the rulers of these houses. The
☉, ♃, or ♀ in the 4th promise success at the
end of life, but ♂ causes trouble and quarrels,

OCCUPATION AND POSITION

♄ loneliness and isolation, and ♅ confinement in some institution.

Furthermore the 4th denotes the result of business activities and if afflicted indicates changes and unsatisfactory endings to all occupations.

A satellitium or group of planets in any house or sign tends to bestow fame or notoriety the nature of which will depend upon the dispositor of the planets or the house in which the satellitium occurs. If ♄, it will come from elderly people or Saturnian things or occupation; if ♃, from professional people, etc.; if ♂, through war or murder; if ♀, through women; and if ☿, through intellect, writing or speaking.

The following are the aphorisms relating to rank or position :—

1. ♈, ♌, or ♐ rising, and lord of Asc. in 10th causes the native to aim at things above his present station.

2. Fortunate planets in 9th make famous clergy or lawyers. The same is caused by benefics in trine to the lord of the 9th.

3. ♀ and ☿ in 10th, in the houses of either ♂ or ☿ give eminence in arts and sciences.

4. ♂ ruling Asc. and posited in 10th gives dignity and power accompanied by injury and cruelty.

5. ⊙ and ♃ in 10th give great honour and position, but they are lost if ♄ or ♂ are in □ or ☍. In general ♄ or ♂ afflicting the 10th or its lord cause the native to be unexpectedly cast down.

6. ♀ in 11th, ☿ in 12th ⊙ in Asc., ♃ in 2nd, ♄ in 6th, and ☽ in 9th cause so many and great accidents that the life may be justly esteemed prodigious.

7. ☽ in 10th in ♑, ☍ ♄ or ♂ in ♋ in 4th make the native incapable of honour.

8. ☽ in ♏, in 10th ☍ ♂ in ♉ causes an unfortunate life.

9. Lord of Asc. between 15° ♎ and 15° ♏ cause trouble in business.

10 Lord of 10th or ☉ afflicted by ☽ or ♄ causes misfortune.

11. ♄ on cusp of 4th, and lord of 10th ☌ ♂ in a fiery sign causes a catastrophe.

12. The following positions are all indicative of honour and preferment;— (*a*) ☉ in ☌ with ♀ in ♌, or with ♃ in ♐, or with ♂ in ♈, (*b*) ☉, ♃, and ♂ in trine to each other in fiery signs. (*c*) ☉, ☽, and lord of 10th all in trine. (*d*) ☉ in ♋ in trine to ♃ in ♓ and ☽ in ♏. (*e*) ☽ in 28° ♌, ♃ in 10th △ ♂, and ☉ ☌ ☊. (*f*) ☽ ☌ ♃ in ♋ in 10th. (*g*) Lord of Asc. rising in its own sign. (*h*) ☽ exactly rising in ♉, or ☉ exactly rising in ♌, and unafflicted. (*i*) ☉ in 0° ♈ on M.C. (*j*) ☉ ☌ ☽ in 10th. (*k*) ☽ in good aspect to lords of M.C. and Asc.

CHARTER VIII

PARENTS, RELATIVES AND HOME.

Parents. The 10th and 4th houses rule the parents, but it is not quite certain by which house a particular parent is ruled (see p. 30) The general significators are the ☉ and ♄ for the father, and the ☽ and ♀ for the mother (according to some authors the ☉ and ♀ by day, and the ☽ and ♄ by night), and it is usually advisable to base conclusions on the conditions of these planets. If well aspected or accompanied (within 30°) by benefics a long and fortunate life is indicated, but afflictions to these significators or to planets in, or the rulers of, the 10th and 4th denote trouble or death. If the significators are afflicted, debilitated, and not assisted by 24 or ♀ the parents will be unfortunate, obscure, or humble. If ♄ afflicts the ☉ and both are weak and cadent, or ♂ is elevated above and rising before them the father is full of infirmities, and if the aspect falls in other houses and especially in angles he may die. ♂ elevated above the ☉ causes sudden death or injuries in the face and eyes, but if above ♄, bodily pains. The significators of the parents afflicting each other and afflicted by malefics often denotes trouble between the parents themselves or their separation. If ♀ is in conjunction with ♄ and either rules the 7th in a child's map, there is some likelihood of its being illegitimate, especially if ♅ is also afflicting. Illegitimate children are said often to have the Asc. in aspect with the ☽ and not the significator of the father, further indications being the absence of aspect between the lords of the 4th and 2nd and the ☽; ♀ joined with ♂ or ☿; and ☽ ☌ ☋ as a slight indication. The fortunes and length of life of the parents must be carefully estimated by balancing the indications.

Brothers and Sisters. The 3rd house rules brothers, sisters, and contemporary relatives in general, and the brother or sister next younger than the native in particular. That one next older than the native is ruled by the 11th, the next above that by the 9th, and so on, while the next but one below the native is ruled by the 5th, the next below again by the 7th, and so on. Planets in these houses or their rulers indicate the circumstances of the particular brother or sister. According to Ptolemy the M.C. 11th, ☽, and ♀ must be considered for general indications of brethren, and their sex, conditions, and fortune judged by the planets aspecting the significators and the amount of affliction received. If the ☉ is surrounded by strong malefics there will be few brethren, and if it is afflicted by ♄ from the Asc. it is said to cause the death of the eldest brother from a lingering disease, but if the affliction is from ♂ all the brethren will die. If ♄ and ♂ are in the 1st 1st or 7th houses few brethren are likely.

Other Relatives. The houses ruling other relatives may be estimated by their relationship to the 10th and 4th. Thus the 6th and 12th houses rule uncles and aunts, as they are the third from the 4th and 10th respectively, one being on the father's side and one being on the mother's. Similarly the 7th house rules grandparents, the 9th grandchildren, and so on. In the case of the planets ☿, ♀, and ♂ rule contemporary male and female relatives, ♃ rules uncles and aunts, and ♅ grandparents.

Home. The 4th house rules the domestic life and the residence. Afflictions to planets here or the ruler show unhappiness and changes, while good aspects indicate the reverse. In choosing a residence it is necessary to consider the rising sign and that on the cusp of the 4th. The house should face towards that point of the compass ruled by the sign on the 4th (see Chap. xii). Cardinal signs on the angles denote corner houses and prominent or elevated positions or on a cross road ; fixed signs denote houses in the middle of streets and low lying positions ; and mutable signs houses near the end of streets and flat and inconspicuous positions. The number of the house should harmonise with the planet in or ruling the 4th, the planetary numbers being as follows :— ☉, 1 and 4 ; ☽, 7 and 2 ; ☿, 5 and 9 ; ♀, 6 and 3 ; ♂, 9 and 5 ; ♃, 3 and 6 ; ♄, 8 and 4 ; ♅ 13 ; and ♆ 16. Where two numbers are given the first is positive and the second negative. Any number of several digits must be reduced to unit value by adding the digits together, thus $127 = 1 + 2 + 7 = 10 = 1$, i.e. positive ☉.

The effect of the signs and planets upon domestic matters is as follows :—

ARIES. ♄, early troubles, death of uncles and aunts, ♂, trouble through parents. ♀, feelings affected by father and his affairs. ☽, mother plays an important and often unfortunate part in life.

TAURUS. ♄, loss of brethren, peculiar domestic experiences, death of father if in 8th or 12th. ♃, sorrow through relatives. ☉, fortunate for father. ♀, strong domestic ties. ☽, friendly with relatives, more sisters than brothers, often supports mother.

GEMINI. ♃, eldest or foremost in family. ♂, domestic sorrows. ☉, cleverest or foremost in family, several brothers and sisters, help from relatives. ♀, many relatives through marriage. ☽, frequent changes of residence, numerous brethren, often has step (or adopted) mother or relatives, resembles mother physically or mentally.

CANCER. Attached to home and mother. ♅, close association with mother. ♇, estrangement at home. ♄, domestic trouble, sometimes early loss of parents. ♂, domestic struggles and trouble, danger to mother. ☉, attached to home and mother. ♀, fond of home. ☽, fond of home, often lives near water.

LEO. ♅, loss or trouble through father. ♃, domestic success. ☉, fortunate for father. ♀, mysterious domestic arrangements at end of life. ☽, unfavourable for father.

VIRGO. ♂, many poor relations. ☉, unfortunate for father. ♀, anxiety over relatives. ☽, unfavourable for mother.

LIBRA. ♄, serious domestic troubles late in life. ♃, fortunate domestic conditions at end of life. ♂, many deaths at home. ☉, strong affection for brethren. ☽, fortunate for mother.

SCORPIO. Often indicates a death in the family shortly before or after the native's birth. ♄, inferior, poor, and jealous relatives. ☉, death of or separation from the father. ☽, unfavourable for mother and her relatives.

SAGITTARIUS. If rising, early death of or separation from the father. ♄, trouble through father. ♀, fond of service at home. ☽, frequent changes of residence, may have step or adopted parent.

CAPRICORN. ♃, trouble through family or father. ♅, early family discord, loss of or separation from father. ♂, early death of brethren, survives relatives but does not gain from them. ♀, little or no domestic happiness. ☽, death of or separation from parent, may be illegitimate or badly brought up.

AQUARIUS. ♂, early death of brethren. ☉, unfavourable for father. ☽, unfavourable for mother.

PISCES. ♄, trouble through or danger to father. ♃, help from relatives, ♂, danger to female relatives, harm from family. ☉ unfavourable for father, native foremost in family. ♀, honour amongst relatives. ☽, numerous brethren, native's birth may bring trouble to the mother.

SUN. In 4th good heredity.

MOON. In 4th, many changes of residence, especially late in life; often indicates adoption or early separation from home. If afflicted especially in 4th or 8th, mother makes a bad recovery from childbirth.

MERCURY. In 4th many changes of residence, worry over domestic matters.

VENUS. In 4th, fortunate and happy home life. In 3rd, help from relatives.

MARS. In 4th, domestic quarrels, especially late in life, trouble with parents, danger of fires at home. If angular or succeedent and afflicting ☽ or ♀, accidents and disease to mother. If afflicting oriental ☽, danger of injuries to or sudden death of mother, if ☽ is occidental she may die of miscarriage, childbirth, inflammation, or wounds. If afflicting ♀, death of mother from fever or sudden illness.

JUPITER. In 4th, happy homelife.

SATURN. In 4th, unsatisfactory environment, if afflicted poverty. In 3rd, sorrow through relatives, few brethren. Afflicting oriental ☽, death of mother from disease, cold and fevers, if ☽ is occidental, womb affections or consumption. If slow, retrograde and cadent, and afflicting ☽, accidents and disease to mother, but if both be swift and angular she will have a short and afflicted life.

URANUS. In 4th, domestic trouble, estrangement or death of parent, peculiar disharmony. In 3rd, peculiar relatives.

NEPTUNE. In 4th, peculiar domestic conditions, residence in unfavourable psychic conditions, domestic secrets. In 10th, danger to parents. In 3rd, peculiar relatives.

CHAPTER IX

FRIENDS AND ENEMIES.

Friends and acquaintances are ruled primarily by the 11th house, but the 7th is concerned with open friends, partners, and associates, and the 3rd with secret friends. Enemies, if open ones, are also ruled by the 7th, but if secret by the 12th.

1. For the general testimonies of friendship or enmity and the type of people concerned note the condition of the above houses and their rulers. Planets in the 11th denote the type of friends ; in the 4th home associates ; in the 7th business associates, acquaintances, and open enemies ; in the 12th secret enemies, and so on. The planet and sign in the house, or its ruler, will represent the appearance, character, and occupation of the friend or enemy.

2. Any well aspected planet denotes a friend or friends among people represented by that planet and its sign and house position. Similarly an afflicted planet denotes enemies, and this is particularly true of planets afflicting the ruler of the Asc. and the luminaries. A native with a badly afflicted ♂ will not be on good terms with natives of ♈ or ♏ even if these signs are not occupied in his map. Should they contain benefics, however, the experiences will be mixed and there would be a tendency for friends to fall away or become enemies since ♂ would dispose

of the benefics and therefore to some extent rule the end of the matter.

3. Much detail may be learnt about friends or enemies by calling the sign and house containing the significator that person's first house, the next to it his second, and so on. Afflictions and good aspects to the significator should then be judged according to their house positions in relation to it. If the significator is in, say, the 2nd house and is afflicted by ♄ in the 7th (which is the 6th from the significator) he will probably be an invalid, and so on. The actual house containing the significator denotes the conditions under which the person will be met, or the nature of the link between him and the native.

4. The strength of the significators of enemies in relation to that of the ruler of the Asc. indicates whether enemies will be successful in harming the native or not. The stronger and more elevated the ruler the less the native has to fear.

5. A satellitium in any sign or house brings many acquaintances among people represented by the sign or house, but usually few friends.

The following are the influences of the signs when rising or signifying friends or enemies, together with certain effects due to the planets when posited therein.—

ARIES. Never sees faults in friends. Intellectual friends. ♄, ♃ or ♀, friends among relatives. ♃, acquaintances through travel, gain from enemies. ☿, quarrelsome or assertive friends. ☽, romance or adventures with friends.

TAURUS. Loyal but dominating friends, bitter and unrelenting enemies. Planets here denote friends in the domestic circle. ♄, liable to treachery, trouble from women, a few faithful friends. ♃, spiritually minded friends, often ungrateful. ♂, famous or notorious friends, powerful opponents. ☿, friends among women dogmatic and faithful.

GEMINI. May take advantage of friends. If rising gives enemies. Friends often clever, may be deceitful. ♄, deceitful friends, treachery at home, jealous enemies. ♃, noble friends, religious enemies. ♂, influenced by pleasure lovers. ♀, clerical or legal friends. ☽, dual friendships.

CANCER. Jealous and fickle, imperious, very devoted. If rising difficulty in making friends, especially when ☽ is weak and afflicted by ♃. Planets here give friends among inferiors. ♄, sickness of friends, enemies affect honour. ♃, powerful but inconstant friends. ♂, wounds from secret enemies. ☽, friends in the home, strange experiences.

LEO. Warm hearted, generous, loyal, never see faults in friends. ♄, secret enmity from inferiors, treachery of servants, a few faithful friends among equals or superiors, friends become enemies. ♃, enemies become friends. ♂, trouble through inferiors, powerful enemies. ☿, noble friends. ☽, poetical and artistic friends.

VIRGO. Discriminating in friendship, difficult to know, seek to know rich or distinguished people. Planets here often give sorrow through death of friends. ♄ or ♃, occult or mystical friends; ☿, learned. ☽, peculiar friendships, attached to inferiors.

LIBRA. Popular, very just, fond of society, seek admiration. Artistic, scientific, or philosophical friends, sometimes made abroad. ♄, sorrow through death of secret friend, strange experiences, open female enmity at 21, 35 and 42. ♀, sorrow through death of friends, danger from women but help from society ladies. ☽, vindictive female enemies.

SCORPIO. Magnetic, dominating, champion oppressed, strong likes and dislikes, reverence for well known people. Treacherous friends. ♄, elderly, ambitious or secret friends, honour through them. ♃, intrigues with superiors, treacherous friends, powerful and jealous enemies. ♀, mystical or doubtful friends who attack reputation, secret enemies among servants or near relations. ☽, secret attachments and tragedies. ♂, dangerous enemies, but often overcomes them.

SAGITTARIUS. Friendly and genial, very attractive. If rising gives enemies. ♄, public friends, mental opponents. ♂, refined intuitive friends, danger of secret and often undeserved scandal. ☉, in nocturnal map, danger from secret enemies. ♀, powerful friends, strange enemies, enmity through women, ☿, friends showy and clever but shallow and ungrateful. ☽, loyal friends.

CAPRICORN. Good friends, bitter enemies. ♄, treacherous friends or sorrow through them, influenced by inferiors. ♃, treacherous friends, involved in sorrows of friends which have caused their confinement ♂, difficulties through friends, dangerous secret enemies who affect honour. ♀, strange or doubtful friends, treachery. ☿, crafty friends. ☽, deceived.

AQUARIUS. Courteous, very attractive and magnetic, faithful. Faithful friends, often old, learned, or scientific. If rising gives enemies. ♄, faithful friends easily made, suffers passively

from others. ♂, social friends, meets violent
people. ♀, friends made easily often inferiors ;
indirect gain through enemies. ☉, enemies
among nobles.

PISCES. Attractive, changeable, crave sympathy. ♄, unfavourable ties, loss through
friends, many enemies, danger from secret ones.
♃, generous to enemies ; enemies in high position who will not be harmful. ♀, friends among
weak or afflicted people, gain from friends,
enemies through marriage or rivals. ☿, many
chance acquaintances, talkative and inquisitive
friends. ☽, mediumistic friends.

The general influences of the planets over
friendship and enmity are as follows :—

SUN. Friends among superiors. Some osten-
tation. In 7th, powerful enemies.

MOON. Large number of acquaintances, often
among women, inferiors, or the public. Afflicted
by ♄, false friends. In ♒ or ♓, trouble from
powerful or noble people, especially if afflicted
by ♃ or ♄, but if in good aspect to these denotes
pretended friendship from such people.

MERCURY. Mental friends, young people, often
deceitful. In 7th commercial rivals, slanderous.

VENUS. Friends among women and gain from
them. Aspecting ☽, love of pleasure and popularity.

MARS. Few real friends unless well aspected.
Dominated by friends, and lose through their
advice. If in a watery or airy sign friends
become enemies. In 7th violent enemies. Afflicted by ♅, trouble through peculiar people,
dipsomaniacs, or by plots; by ♇ tragic friendships, legal troubles; by ♄, violence, deceit,
injury ; by ♃, lawsuits and loss ; by ☿, scandal.

JUPITER. Fortunate, friendships. Aspecting ♅, mystical friends; ♄, lasting attachments.

SATURN. A few elderly faithful friends, but ruin if afflicted. In 7th persistent enemies, deceitful opponents.

URANUS. Peculiar sudden friendships and estrangements. Afflicting ♄, powerful enemies. In 7th public rivals.

NEPTUNE. Peculiar and unfavourable friendships, highly romantic or unique. In 7th, plotting and scheming enemies.

The following are the aphorisms dealing with friendship and enmity :—

Friends. 1. Ruler of Asc. in 12th causes solitary life.

2. Ruler of Asc. in 11th or aspecting its lord gives many friends.

3. Planets in 11th in good aspect to Asc., its ruler, ☉ or ☽ give faithful friends.

4. ♃, ♀, or ☿ dignified in 11th gives constant eminent friends, but if debilitated, poor or unfortunate friends.

5. ☉, ☽, ☿, and ⊕ in 11th denote many faithful friends, but if afflicted few false and treacherous ones.

6. Lord of 11th separating from lord of Asc. denotes few friends and disagreements with them.

7. Cardinal signs on 11th or its lord in a cardinal sign denote ambitious friends who may prove treacherous ; fixed signs, faithful friends; and mutable signs fickle and inconstant friends.

8. Lord of Asc. in any sign in good aspect to lord of 11th in fixed sign gives faithful friends. The same occurs when ☽ is in good aspect to lord of 11th; if ☽ or lord of 11th is in a mutable

sign friends do not often fail the native, if in cardinal sign they promise more than they perform, but if badly aspected friends are few.

9. Lord of 10th separating by retrogradation from lord of Asc. or 11th, friends, if any, will be poor, and rich people will dislike the native.

10. If the same sign occupies the cusps of the 11th and 12th there will be a tendency for friends to become enemies, and vice-versa. (This rule is a general one and applies to all cases. When such occurs the two houses blend and the matters ruled by them alternate or are associated.)

Enemies. 1. Lord of Asc. in 12th, or planets afflicted there, gives many secret enemies.

2. Lord of 2nd a malefic and in 12th afflicting lord of Asc. the native will be his own enemy, and will also be cheated in business.

3. Significators of enemies afflicting the luminaries denote treacherous and secret enemies. If the significators be strong in an angle the enemies will be powerful; if in a succeedent house not so powerful; and if cadent poor people.

4. Lord of 12th and 7th in conjunction in 7th the wife or husband will be the chief enemy.

5. Lord of 12th combust, cadent, weak by sign, or afflicted by ♄, ♂, or ☋, the enemies will be few and unfortunate.

6. Lord of Asc. in no aspect to lord of 12th denotes few enemies.

7. The following positions indicate that the native is able to overcome his enemies : (*a*) Luminaries or lord of Asc. in reception with ♂ in his houses or exaltation; (*b*) Lord of 12th in 10th weak, or lord of 10th in 12th; (*c*) ♂ and ♀ in 7th or 4th ; (*d*) lord of Asc. aspecting lord of 12th and disposing of it. (*e*) lord of 12th afflicted by

malefics, especially in 6th, and ♃ or ♀ in 12th.

COMPARISON OF HOROSCOPES.

The likelihood of friendship or enmity between particular individuals is best judged by comparing their horoscopes and noting the aspects formed between planets in the one and those in the other.

Draw two columns side by side on a sheet of paper and head them with the names of the natives. Take the ☉ in one map and observe if it forms any conjunctions, parallels or aspects to the planets and angles in the other map. Write down the Sun's symbol in the column of the native whose ☉ it is, and the aspect and aspected planet in the other column. Having completed the aspects formed by the ☉ do the same with the ☽, then ☿, then ♀, and so on, finishing up with the Asc. and M.C. This gives in a convenient form all the aspects between the maps, and the amount of attraction and repulsion is to be judged by the nature and strength of these aspects and of the planets involved.

The strongest sign of affinity is when the luminaries in the two maps are in conjunction or good aspect, as this indicates radical harmony. In cases of marriage the best possible link is when the ☉ in the woman's horoscope is in conjunction with or in good aspect to the ☽ in the man's. If a malefic in one map falls on or afflicts one of the luminaries in the other there will be enmity, and the native whose luminary is so afflicted will be the one to suffer most. A benefic falling on a luminary is correspondingly favourable, and the owner of the luminary will be the one to receive most benefit. The relationship existing between the respective Ascendants is also important and a favourable aspect disposes to friendship. The greater the number of links that exist the stronger will be the tie for good or evil.

In maps of opposite sexes the opposition aspect is frequently more complementary than evil, though something depends upon the planets concerned. ♀ in opposition to ♂ creates a strong sex attraction and is not necessarily unfavourable, but ♂ in one map afflicting ♄ in the other by any aspect is extremely evil, and while often leading to warm attraction at first, if the sexes are opposite, gradually cools the ardour and culminates in coldness, hatred, or even violence. The same applies to ♂ afflicting ♅ except that the effects are more sudden.

The general effect of aspects from planets in one map to those in another is as follows:—
♃ causes attraction through mysticism, music, psychism, or peculiar immorality, and gives an intense and subtle fascination ; ♅, romantic friendships, and those arising through occultism, antiquarianism, etc., if afflicting ♀ it may cause seduction ; ♄ aspecting ♃ causes a link through inheritance, business, or agriculture ; ♄ and ♂, quarrels, fraud, murder ; ♄ and ♀, kindred, cool steady affection that will not last if aspect is unfavourable; ♄ and ☿, partnership ; ♃ and ♂, politics, ♃ and ♀, women or clerical and legal matters ; ♃ and ☿ literature and science ; ♂ and ♀ sex, danger of seduction; ♂ and ☿ fraud, rivalry in trade ; ♀ and ☿, correspondence, may be schoolfellows.

To a much less extent the *mundane* positions in the respective horoscopes are important.

Thus if the ☉ is on the Asc. in one map, and the ☽ on the Asc. in the other there will be an attraction even if no aspect occurs between them, as they hold equivalent mundane positions. The houses in a map in which the other person's planets fall also produce some effect, and the benefics of one falling in the 11th of the other will produce friendship, in the 10th, help in business, and so on.

So far we have treated of the radical maps, but the same remarks apply to progressed positions. Thus, ♀ in one map progressing to a luminary in the other sets up a strong temporary attraction that will persist if the radical maps harmonise, but die if they are not in accord. The progressed ☽ brings acquaintances in this way and causes temporary association. The course of a friendship can easily be foretold by observing the aspects formed by the progressed planets across the maps, and it should be noted that parallels are of great importance. In cases of marriage it is often easier to determine the actual date of the event in this way than by directions in one horoscope alone, as it is usually marked by strong aspects between the maps.

CHAPTER X

LOVE AND MARRIAGE.

The 7th house rules marriage (or union whether legal or otherwise), and the wife or husband; and the 5th love affairs apart from marriage. Planets in, or the rulers of, these houses denote the success or otherwise of love and marriage and describe the appearance and characteristics of the marriage partner or people to whom the native becomes attached. In addition to these the significators of love and marriage in a male horoscope are the ☽ and ♀, and in a female one the ☉, ♀, and ♂.

Love affairs apart from marriage are to be judged chiefly from the 5th and 11th houses, their rulers, and aspects to the above significators. The rising sign and the sign and house position of the planets concerned will indicate the native's attitude towards love affairs, their success, and the type of people to whom he is attracted.

Marriage or the likelihood of union must be judged by the sign positions of the significators. (a) *Male*. In male horoscopes marriage is indicated if ☽ and ♀ are strong, especially in the "fruitful" signs ♋, ♏, or ♓; if ♂ aspects ♀; if ♀ and the ☽ are not afflicted by ♄; and if fruitful signs are on the 1st or 7th or the lords of these houses are in good aspect. The indications preventing or delaying marriage are ☽ and ♀ weak, afflicting each other, and afflicted by a strong ♄, especially when they are in the "barren" signs ♈, ♊, ♌, ♍, or ♑; ☽ ☌ ☉ in ♑ or ♒ and afflicted by ♄; and ☽ in ♏ afflicted by ♄. (*b*) *Female*. This is judged similarly from the positions of ☉, ♂, and ♀. If these are strong, in fruitful signs, not afflicted by ♄ or ♅, and the ☉ is in aspect to ♂, marriage may be expected. The indications denying or delaying it are ♂ weak and in no aspect to ☉; and ☉, ♂, or ♀ afflicted by ♄, ♅, and sometimes ♆, and weak or in barren signs.

Time of Marriage. (*a*) *Male*. The general strength and positions of the significators must be carefully considered and the probable time of marriage estimated by balancing the indications. An early marriage is indicated if the ☽ is unafflicted in a fruitful sign; ☽ or several planets between 1st and 10th or 7th and 4th; ☽, increasing in light; or ☽ and ♀ unaspected by ♄. These indications may sometimes also denote marriage to a very young partner. Delay is shown (or alternatively marriage to an older or elderly partner) when ☽ or ♂ are afflicted by ♄; ☉ and ☽ afflict each other; significators in barren signs; ☽ between 10th and 7th or 1st and 4th, or decreasing in light. (*b*) *Female*. Consider the sign positions and aspects of the ☉ and ♂. If strong, unafflicted, and in fruitful signs, and also if the ☉ is strong and between 1st and 10th or 7th and 4th an early marriage may be expected; but if in barren signs, or afflicted by ♄ or ♅, or if ♂ does not aspect ☉, or if ☉ is between 10th and 7th or 1st and 4th, marriage is delayed, or in some cases the partner is elderly.

LOVE AND MARRIAGE

Several marriages are denoted by the ☽ (or ☉)
in fruitful signs, or in ♊ or ♐ aspecting many
planets; ♊, ♐, or ♓ on 7th or containing
several planets ; or lord of Asc. in 7th aspecting
lord of 7th in ♊, ♐, or ♓. In such cases there
is often a malefic in the 7th or one afflicting the
marriage significator denoting the death of the
first partner.

The partner is described by the planets to
which the ☽ (or ☉) next applies by strong aspect
after birth, together with planets in the 7th or
its lord ; but any planet in strong aspect to
the ☉ or ☽ has some significance in the matter.
It is generally considered that application should
be as shown in the ephemeris and not as in
directions, namely both bodies should be considered as moving instead of one being fixed.
The successive applications of the luminary concerned denote the various attachments formed,
marriage occurring with that person whose significator is strongest. Application to retrograde
planets usually denotes broken attachments, but
sometimes separation from, or the death of, the
partner, especially if the planet rules the 7th.
The appearance and character of the partner are
denoted by the sign containing the significator
and the aspects to that planet, and the circumstances or place of meeting by the house containing it. By calling the significator's house
that person's first house and renumbering the
houses accordingly a great amount of detail may
be obtained. The happiness or otherwise of
marriage must be judged from the nature of the
significator and its aspects, and also in all cases
by a comparison of the horoscopes of husband
and wife.

The fortunes after marriage are best determined by erecting a horoscope for the moment of marriage and treating it as a radical map, the first house representing the husband and the 7th the wife. Directions formed in this horoscope (calculated exactly as in the case of a nativity by the rules given later) affect the married life and denote happenings that influence the union, while directions between this map and those of the husband and wife are also indicative of the course of domestic events.

The following are the effects of the signs and of planets contained therein :—

ARIES. Intense love nature ; too impulsive ; often unhappy marriage. ♄, jealous or older partner, poverty through marriage. ♃, ambitious partner. ♂, financial loss, difficulty in consummating union. ♀, idealistic, changeable, demonstrative, secret or mental attachments, early marriage but may not marry, often unhappy if a woman. ☉, gain through husband if a woman. ☽, mysterious affairs, wounds from women.

TAURUS. Extreme love nature ; lustful ; often marries money ; often two marriages, the first early and hasty, and the second happy. ♄, love troubles, death of partner or financial trouble. ♃, chaste and mystical partner, happy marriage. ♂, early love affairs, tragic or unfortunate marriage, ruled by partner, harm to or from women. ♀, strong feelings, voluptuous, physical attractions. ☿, trouble through women. ☽, intrigues.

GEMINI. Fickle; nonmoral; sex complications and dual love affairs ; fairly late marriage. ♄, marriage to foreigner or abroad. ♃, marries relative. ♂, several love affairs often at once, partner religious or a relative. ♀, dual love affairs or marriage, peculiar, intrigues necessitated by home life. ☽, peculiar marital relations.

CANCER. Very sentimental ; rather fickle, but exact faithfulness from others ; rarely happy in marriage. ♄, grief through love, partner rises by industry. ♃, social success by marriage. ♂ scandal by marriage, discontented partner. ♀, fickle, secret love affairs, marriage abroad or to a foreigner, or union while travelling, danger of separation or divorce. ☉, unfavourable for marriage if a woman.

LEO. Intense love nature ; very rarely happy marriage ; often marry for children. ♄, disregards pleasure, marries friend, sometimes two marriages. ♃, marries influential or rich friend. ♂, secret alliances, ardent affections returned by partner. ☉, often unhappy marriage, ♀, ardent, jealous, marries friend, sometimes believes in free love.

VIRGO. Inclined to be sentimental and romantic ; critical ; very- self-controlled ; undemonstrative ; dutiful ; usually chaste. ♄, romantic courtship, trouble from or disinclined to marriage, happier if partner is older, sometimes two marriages. ♃, secret love affairs, peculiar marriage, sometimes to inferior. ♂, peculiar ties, secret love affairs with inferiors, led astray, unhappy ; may marry soldier if a woman. ♀, intrigues with inferiors, illicit love, tragedy, secret and obscure marriage; if afflicted by ♄, immorality. ☽, secret sorrows in marriage.

LIBRA. Fond of pleasure ; always desire admiration and attention ; often selfish and shallow; often unhappy marriage. ♄, separation, especially if ♀ is afflicted. ♃, happy marriage, ♂, responsibility by marriage. ☉, danger of separation. ♀, pure, fiery passions, love affairs with relatives, responsibility and financial sacrifice through marriage. ☽, secret love affairs.

SCORPIO. Intense sex nature; seek admiration; critical and nagging; jealous; often marry money; secret love affairs; often two marriages. ♄, passionate, secret and sad love affairs. ♃, injury in love, jealousy, gain by marriage but often unhappy. ♂, struggles, gain by marriage, unhappy partner; if in 6th, 8th or 12th violence to or from women unless the benefics prevent. ♀, jealous, marries widow or widower, risky love affairs, may be frail or betrayed if a woman. ☉, danger of separation.

SAGITTARIUS. Impulsive; affectionate; often unhappy but usually conceal it; often two marriages, ♄, danger of separation. ♃, two love affairs or marriages, one to a relative. ♂ mental improvement and gain by marriage. ♀, mental improvement, marries relative, more than one marriage and early widowhood. ☽, happy marriage.

CAPRICORN. Deep love nature; undemonstrative; often lustful. ♄, entanglement with inferiors, opposed to marriage or unhappy. ♃, parents concerned in marriage, unsatisfactory. ♂, early entanglement with inferior, social gain and changes by marriage. ♀, ambitious, intrigues with inferiors, disappointments, marriage of convenience, cold partner, adultery. ☽, inconstant and unfortunate marriage. ☉, bad for marriage and husband's health if a woman.

AQUARIUS. Very idealistic; easily led; usually faithful but may be the reverse. ♄, faithful, romantic and lasting tie, good marriage. ♃, love marriage, partner older than native. ♂, good and faithful marriage. ♀, chaste, often long .courtship and late love marriage.

PISCES. Affectionate ; fickle ; inclined to be wanton. ♄, unfavourable ties, beginning romantically and ending tragically, ailing partner, unhappy marriage, trouble through servants after marriage. ♃, marries inferior, often two marriages, danger of scandal. ♂, passionate, unhappy, two attachments, disappointing love affairs, delay in marriage, separation. ☉, rich but unhappy marriage. ♀, discriminating in love affairs, early marriage ; if ♂ ☽ afflicted by ♄, fickle, separation or divorce. ☽, adultery.

The following are the influences of the planets :-

SUN. Proud and honourable or vain and domineering partner ; marries in middle life. In good aspect to ☽, happy. If afflicting ☽, unhappiness.

MOON. Fickle love affairs ; intrigues ; early marriage ; partner fond of change and travel. If afflicted unfortunate in choice. In 4th wife dies first. In 7th marries between 24 and 28 ; if afflicted tragedy. In 12th indiscreet in love affairs. Afflicted by ♅, cruelty to or from women; by ♄, slovenly wife ; by ♀, untidy wife, If ☍ ♃ or ♀, bereavement. If separating from ♂ and applying to ♀ in western half of the map, several wives. If ♂ ♀ and ♄ in 12th, death of wife and difficulty in obtaining one.

MERCURY. Clever and quick witted or busybody and malicious partner ; wrangling if afflicted ; anxiety over love affairs ; marriage through correspondence or journeys ; partner younger or a cousin. If afflicted, especially in 5th,

149

scandal. In 7th afflicted by ♂ or ♅ denotes partner with nerve disorders or unsound mind. If with ♀ in 4th afflicted by ♂ denotes evil conduct.

VENUS. Attractive, pleasant and affable or bold, arrogant, and wasteful partner; happy love affairs. Afflicted by ♅, very romantic attachments or sudden separations; by ♄, sorrow in love; by ♂, impulsive and extravagant love affairs. If in Asc. with ♄ in signs ruled by either planet, dishonourable or aged wife. In 2nd, marries for money. In 4th, afflicting ☽ in ♒, inconstant wife. In 6th, marries servant. In 7th unafflicted, good house wife; and if in good aspect to ♄, ♃, or ☿, provident, attached to home, late marriage, fond of harlots. If ♂ ☉ in 7th, wife is a stranger. Ruling 9th and placed in 1st or 10th, foreign wife. In 12th secret or obscure love affairs, early marriage but separation later, especially if afflicted by ♄ or ♅; particularly bad if ♀ is in ♈, ♋, ♏, or ♑. If oriental, dignified, and aspecting Jupiter, wife will rule. If ♂ ♄ and afflicted by ♂, much jealousy and strife. If afflicted in ♌, womanhater.

MARS. Cordial, honest, and forceful or combative, vicious and violent partner. Quarrels or violence if afflicted. Afflicted by ♅, foolish infatuation; by ♃, unrestrained feelings. In 5th delays marriage if a woman. In 7th or 8th afflicted by ♃, ruin through extravagant wife. If in ♋, ♏, or ♓ afflicting ☽ (or ☉), the wife (or husband) may drink.

JUPITER. Successful love affairs; honest, faithful, religious partner, often older than native. If in 5th or 7th in a woman's map often

150

denotes attachment to a widower. If afflicted in ♓ on cusp of 7th or just below and receiving the application of the ☉, denotes an adulterous husband in a woman's map.

SATURN. Elderly, discreet, prudent, persevering and industrious or lazy and envious partner; delay and disappointment; steady and enduring love. In 7th in good aspect to ☽ (or ☉), marries widow (or widower) who will have a family if ♂ aspects ♄, and will be wealthy if ♄ is dignified and in good aspect to ♃. In 12th afflicting luminaries, sorrow through death of loved ones. Afflicting ♂ or ♀ in 5th, danger of unnatural affections. With or afflicting ♀ in his own dignities, vicious and sordid partner.

URANUS. Romantic attachments; hasty engagement and marriage; danger of separation, particularly if afflicted in 7th. Afflicted by ♂ violence. Afflicting ♀, intrigues with girls; sometimes homo-sexual or other positive sex perversions, especially if in or from ♈ or ♐, ☿ being also afflicted. Afflicting ☽, intrigues with married women; afflictions from ♂ or ☿ cause scandal, but ♃ or ♄ keep the matter secret. Afflicting ☉ in a woman's map, elopement or seduction, especially if ♂ also afflicts ☽ or ♀; often denies marriage entirely.

NEPTUNE. Peculiar union, platonic or reverse; seduction; crippled, drug taking, or musical partner. If afflicting ☽ or ♀, especially if in or from negative signs, causes negative sex perversions. In 7th gives intense desire for marriage but may prevent it or make it unsatisfactory.

The following are the aphorisms dealing with love and marriage:—

Love Affairs. 1. Significators of marriage or

♀ in cardinal signs, especially if ♀ or ☽ are in ♋ or ♑ cause inconstancy in love and marriage.

2. ♀ badly placed and afflicted by ♂ causes much trouble in love especially if a woman.

3. ☽ in a nocturnal map separating from ♂ and applying to ♄ denotes many troubles from women.

4. ♀ in Asc. afflicted by ♂ or ♄ or both gives sensuality, dissipation, scandal and ill-fame, especially if the malefics occupy the 10th.

5. ♉, ♎, or ♏ rising, and ♂ afflicting, causes the native to do harm to women.

6. ♂ or ♀ in an angle in ♋ or ♑ and afflicting the ☽ gives vicious inclinations.

7. ♄ elevated above and in square to ♀ makes the native shameless and a woman hater, but if ♀ be elevated above ♄ he is a great friend to women.

8. ☽ in ♏ □ ♄ in ♌, or ☍ ♄ in ♉ rarely gives either wife or children. If ♄ be in ♒ the native will be a woman hater.

9. ♉, ♎, or ♑ ascending with ♂ therein in a woman's map leads to immodesty.

10. ♂ ☌ ☉ in a woman's map causes intrigues with inferiors, but if ♀ be well aspected, with equals or superiors.

11. Malefics aspecting each other and afflicting ♀ and ♃ caused secret indecency in men, but if ♂ and ♀ alone they will be licentious.

12. ♂ separating from ♀ and ♄, and in good aspect to ♃ causes men to be decorous in sex matters, but if ♂ aspects ♄ alone they will be dull and careless.

13. ☽ ☌ ♄ or afflicted by it causes men to be of solitary habits and to lead single lives. A combust planet or the ☉ in ♉ greatly afflicted has the same effect on women.

14. Lord of 5th afflicted in 12th causes secret love affairs or self-abuse.

15. ♀ with ♄ and aspecting lord of Asc. causes the native to be attracted to old, ugly or dirty women, or to be sexually perverted.

Marriage. I. ♄ ☍ ♂ from 1st and 7th, or ♄ alone near 7th, or ♀ in ♌ or ♏ unaspected by ♂, or ♂ in ♉, ♍, or ♑ in 7th whether aspecting ♀ or not, give great difficulty in obtaining a partner, and finally a hasty marriage, though the native is often lascivious.

2. ♄ lord of 7th often delays marriage to middle life. Barren signs on cusps of 1st and 5th delay marriage and deny children. If, however, ♀ or ♃ be in Asc. in good aspect to ☽, an early marriage is likely.

Type of Partner. I. ♃ in good aspect to ☽ and in reception denotes a wealthy and well born wife, especially if ♃ be in 7th or 8th.

2. Lord of 7th in 8th if a benefic denotes a rich marriage partner or one born to ample inheritance.

3. ♀ afflicted in 6th denotes a poor wife unless ☽ be well aspected by ♃, or ♃ be unafflicted in 7th.

4. Lord of 7th in 12th afflicted by ♄ denotes an immodest partner.

5. ♂ ☍ ♀ from 6th and 12th denotes an inconstant and vicious partner especially if one of these planets is the ruler of 7th.

6. Part of Marriage afflicted by malefics or ☋ denotes a partner of evil life or diseased. (The Part of Marriage for both sexes is found by adding the longitude of the Asc. to the longitude of the 7th cusp and from the sum subtracting the longitude of ♀).

7. ♀ ☌ ☿ in 4th, or in ♊ or ♍, and ♄ in 10th denotes a low wife, and if also aspecting ♂ she will be evil. If in ♋ or ♑, a harlot.

8. ☽ decreasing in light and ☌ ♂ in cardinal signs indicates that the wife loves another man.

9. ☽ in man's map or ☉ in woman's afflicted by ♂ denotes a headstrong and wilful partner.

10. ♂ ruling Asc. in woman's map with ♀ in it, or ♀ ruling Asc. with ♂ in it or ♂ ruling Asc. and in M.C. causes her to be unfaithful in marriage.

11. ♂ in mutual reception with ♀, ♄ and ☿ indicates marriage between persons of same age ; if in 1st or 10th with an older relative.

Agreement. 1. ♂ and ☿ afflicting lord of 7th and elevated above it causes the native to kill his wife, partner or enemy, especially if either has power in the Asc.

2. ♃ in 7th no matter how strong, afflicted by malefics denotes strife in marriage.

3. In a man's map ♀ afflicting ☽ denotes trouble in marriage. If ♀ be in 12th ☌ ♂ he will be cruel to his wife.

4. If in a man's map the Part of Marriage falls in the obedient signs ♎ to ♓, and in a woman's in the commanding signs ♈ to ♍, the woman will rule the man.

5. In a woman's map lord of 7th in Asc. indicates that she will domineer over her husband.

Death of Partner. 1. ♀ rising after ☉, weak and afflicted, indicates a short lived wife.

2. ☽ in a man's map or ☉ in woman's applying first to ♃ and then to ♅ denotes death of marriage partner, especially if ♅ or ♄ occupy 7th.

CHAPTER XI

CHILDREN.

The 5th house rules the children of the native and the 11th those of the marriage partner since it is the fifth house from the 7th. According to Ptolemy if these houses are unoccupied and unaspected the 10th and 4th are to be considered, but this rule is usually ignored. The ☽ and planets in these houses or their rulers and the signs concerned indicate whether the native is prolific or the reverse, the sex of the children, and their disposition and fate.

The nature of the signs is as follows: —♋, ♏ and ♓, are very fruitful signs and give a large family; ♊ and ♐ are often fruitful also and disposed to the birth of twins; ♉, ♍, ♎, and ♒, are only moderately fruitful and give few children; ♈, ♌, and ♑ are barren or give only a very small family. The nature of the signs on the Ascendant and 5th or containing planets there, and those occupied by the ruler of the 5th and the ☽ indicate whether a large or small family is likely. Afflictions to these planets from the malefics limit the family and denote death of children in infancy, especially if the malefics occupy the 5th or 11th or rule those houses. If the malefics occupy fruitful signs in the 5th or 11th children will be born but will die early, but if well aspected by ♃ or ♀ the children will

be reared after much difficulty. The strength
of the afflictions and the nature of the signs
will determine whether children are denied
or whether they will merely be very sickly. It
is necessary also to balance the testimonies of
of the 5th and 11th houses, as if they contradict
some of the children will die in infancy.

The sex of the children is to be judged by the
signs and planets signifying them. The even
signs and houses are female, and the odd signs
and houses male, while ☽, ♀, and ♅ are female
and ☉, ♂, ♃, ♄ and ♇ are male, ☿ being indifferent and taking the nature of that planet in
strongest aspect to it. The predominance of
male or female indications will determine the
sex. According to some writers the 5th house
in a male horoscope rules the first child, the 7th
rules the second, the 9th the third and so on, while
in a female map the first child is ruled by the
4th, the second by the 6th, the third by the 8th,
and so on. The condition of the house concerned
will denote the sex, disposition and fate of the
child it represents. In all cases it is necessary
to examine the horoscopes of both husband and
wife and balance the indications so obtained as
one map may contradict the other.

Twins. If the planets denoting children in a
fruitful map are placed in the double signs ♊,
♐, and ♓ or are in a fruitful sign and strongly
aspected from double signs there is likelihood
of twin or multiple births. The same may also
occur if the map is very strongly fruitful and all
the significators are in fruitful signs. According
to Ptolemy sex is chiefly to be judged from the
signs containing the Asc. the luminaries and
their dispositors. When the majority of these

are in double signs twins will be born, and when all are so placed and most of the other planets similarly situated the birth will be triple, or even more in extreme cases and when the significators are in angles especially in the M.C. ♄, ♃, and ♂ in masculine and double signs and aspecting the Asc., luminaries, or their dispositors in fruitful signs are said to cause the birth of three males ; ♀, ☽, and ☿ so placed and in feminine signs, three females ; ♄, ♃ and ♀, two males and one female ; and ♀, ☽ and ♂, two females and one male. In most cases, however, the children are born with some defect or deformity.

The influence of planets in the various signs is as follows :—

ARIES. ♃ gain through children ☉ slightly favourable for birth of sons.

TAURUS. ♄, anxiety through children. ♃ position obtained through care of children. ♂, strange experiences through them. ☉, children gain through parents.

GEMINI. ♄, no children or few and sickly in infancy, sorrow through them. ☉, favours birth of twins, children gain through parents. ♀, likelihood of twins in female map.

CANCER. ♄, sorrow through children. ♂, unfortunate children. ☉, children sickly or do not prosper if afflicted. ♀ or ☽, large family.

LEO. Passionately fond of children. ☉, favours birth of son but danger of trouble to him if afflicted.

VIRGO. Not fond of children but very dutiful to them. ♃, fine children.

LIBRA. ♃, good children, ♂, many and intelligent.

SCORPIO. ♃, notoriety through children, premature loss of first child. ⊙, death of son. ♀, death of or trouble through children. ☽, many children but death or sorrow through one ; danger of sterility, miscarriage, or death in childbirth, especially if afflicted and in a diurnal map.

SAGITTARIUS. ♄, fortunate children. ⊙, premature loss of children. ♀, affectionate children who gain social success. ☽, many children.

CAPRICORN. ♄, suffer through selfish children. ♃, troubles in birth or rearing of children. ♂, sickly children. ⊙, illhealth or death of son. ♀, danger of sterility in female map.

AQUARIUS. ⊙, favours birth of sons but causes trouble with one. ♀, premature loss of children.

PISCUS. ♄, separation from children or sickly ones. ♂, denies children or gives early death of one. ⊙, death of eldest child or unfortunate children. ♀, healthy and fine children.

The influence of the planets is as follows: —

SUN. In 5th denies children or gives trouble at their birth. If well aspected gain through them.

MOON. In 5th famous or notorious children, life bound up with children ; if afflicted from 8th or 12th death of children. With ♀ in fruitful signs in 5th, many healthy children. In ♈, ♌ or ♐ afflicted by ⊙ or malefics, barrenness.

MERCURY. In 5th fatalistic affair with, or worry over children. In Asc. ☍ ♄ in 7th causes children to live with native only a short time. If occidental and well aspected by benefics gives many children, but if oriental and afflicted by malefics causes barrenness.

VENUS. In 5th artistic or musical children.

CHILDREN

In Asc. and ♃ in 7th gives fortunate children. In 1st or 7th afflicted by ♄ causes barrenness in both sexes, miscarriage, or death of children at birth.

MARS. In 5th denies children or causes trouble at their birth, often kills one of them, gives bold and refractory children. If ☍ ♃ or ♀ destroys the children.

JUPITER. In 5th, good and dutiful children. Ruling 5th and ☍ ♄ kills most of the children.

SATURN. In 5th, stubborn children and trouble through them. Afflicted by ♂ or ♀, lack of sympathy. If ☍ ♃ or ♀, destroys some of the children or denies issue.

URANUS. In 5th, eccentric children, separation from children, and anxiety and scandal. Miscarriage.

NEPTUNE. In 5th, great desire for children but often sterile. Peculiar or afflicted, or adopted or illegitimate children.

The influence of the house positions of the ruler of the 5th is as follows:— In 1st, many good children. 2nd, dutiful ones. 3rd, children gain from friends. 4th, children obtain inheritances, but if afflicted will suffer and some will die in prison. 5th, prosperous and honoured children. 6th, children will have few serious illnesses and will assist their father, or he will gain through them. 7th, children side with marriage partner against native and cause injury. 8th, children obtain money through deaths; if afflicted few children or they die before the native, especially if the lords of 5th and 8th afflict each other. 9th, religious and pleasure loving children. 10th, sickly but may be eminent. 11th, trouble to children through enemies and quarrels. 12th, few, troublesome, or hateful children.

The following are the aphorisms dealing with children:—

Fruitfulness. 1. ☽ and ☿ in 5th and their dispositors unafflicted give many children.

2. ♃, ♀, or ☽ in 5th in fruitful signs give many children. If ☽ is in good aspect to ♃ or ♀ the number is increased.

3. ♃, ♀, or ☊ in 5th indicates happiness and fortune through children who will gain honour and dignity.

4. ♃ △ ☽ in human or watery signs, or ☽ and ♀ with ♃ in an angle denote many children who become prosperous.

Barrenness. 1. ♄ in 5th and ☉ □ ♃ denies issue.

2. ☉, ♄, or ♂ ruling 1st, 5th, and 11th, without good aspects from benefics, or if posited in 5th, deny issue.

3. ☉ with ♄ and ☿ in 5th or 11th aspecting ☽ denies issue or causes children to die soon after birth.

4. The greatest testimony of barrenness is when lords of 5th and 1st are combust or retrograde especially if malefics, and ☽ is weak and afflicted also.

Sickness or Death. 1. ♄ ♂ ♀ and afflicting ☽ in 5th denotes little comfort from children, and much sickness amongst them.

2. ☽ in 5th gives children, but ill-conditioned ones if ♄, ♂, or ☋ are there.

3. Lord of 5th afflicted by malefics or by lord of 12th (eight from fifth) indicates that the children live but a short time.

4. ☉, ♄, and ☿ in conjunction in M.C. afflicting ☽ causes death of children.

CHILDREN

5. ♄ and ♂ in 5th or 11th or in opposition from those houses causes death of children, and if ☉ rules, or is exalted in, 5th and is afflicted by ♄ or ♂ no children are left alive.

CHAPTER XII

TRAVEL

The 3rd house rule short journeys such as can be completed in a day, and the 9th long journeys and voyages. Planets in, or the rulers of, these houses denote the probability and success of journeys and the countries to visit or avoid. In addition, attention should be paid to the ⊙, ☽, ☿ and ♂ which are general significators of travel.

If the significators or majority of planets are in cardinal or mutable signs, or angular or cadent houses, many journeys will be made, but if in fixed signs or succeedent houses the native will tend to remain in one place, especially if ♄ is strong. Watery signs, or ♅ or ♃ strong, indicate voyages especially if the 9th house is prominent. The house positions of the significators denote the cause or reason of travel and their aspects indicate gain or loss. Afflictions to the significators of travel denote the nature of any dangers encountered. Afflictions from fiery signs indicate accidents, burns, fevers, etc.; earthy signs, famine, falls, foundering, grounding; airy signs, falls and tempests; and watery signs, floods, wrecks, drowning, or being left in desolate places. Cardinal signs indicate privation or sickness; fixed signs, falls or tempests; and mu-

table signs, attacks from pirates or savages or if
♐, from wild beasts.

If the 3rd and 4th houses, or their rulers,
are stronger and more favourable than the 9th
and 10th it is inadvisable to reside abroad and
the native should remain in his birthplace, but
if the 4th is unfavourable it is better to remove.
In the selection of a place choose those countries
ruled by the signs containing the benefics if
they are favourable, but if not then choose those
of the best aspected planets especially if in good
aspect to the luminaries. The countries and
points of the compass ruled by the signs are
given below. In the case of short journeys the
direction in which to travel is often better indicated by the house, and the points of the compass ruled by the houses are as follows:— 1. E.
2. ENE. 3. NNE. 4. N. 5. NNW. 6. WNW.
7. W. 8. WSW. 9. SSW. 10. S. 11. SSE. 12. ESE.
The nearer the house is to the 4th the nearer is
the place to be chosen, the 3rd and 5th showing
places quite near and the 10th the antipodes.

Some authors recommend altering the radical
(and progressed) map to the longitude of the
place of residence when abroad. This is done by
taking the G.M.T. of birth as fixed and erecting
the map for the corresponding L.M.T. of the place
of residence. The new house positions of the
planets indicate the prospect of success in that
place. A further key to the chances of success
in any place lies in a comparison between the
native's map and one for the place. The town
map should be erected for the foundation of
the town or for the date on which a charter was
given, the time being rectified by events or taken
roughly for noon.

The points of the compass and countries ruled by the signs, and the effects of planets in signs are as follows :—

ARIES. E. England, Germany (parts), Denmark, Palestine, Syria, Burgundy, Lesser Poland. ♄, few and dangerous journeys. ♃, gain by voyages. ☉, fond of travel and exploration, voyages on missions with or for influential people. ♀, pleasure from travel. ☿, danger of exile.

TAURUS. S by E. Ireland, Persia, Poland, Grecian Archipelago, Asia Minor, Caucasus, Cyprus, White Russia, Georgia, ♃, voyages affect health. ☉, fond of travel. ♀, sickness in travel.

GEMINI. W by S. Belgium, Flanders, Wales, West of England, Lombardy, Brabant, Sardinia, Armenia, Tripoli, Lower Egypt, N. E. Africa, United States of America. ♂, unfortunate journeys. ☉, fond of short journeys. ♀, travel for pleasure. ☿, fond of travel. ☽, many short journeys.

CANCER. N. Scotland, Holland, Germany (parts), Prussia, Mauritius, N and W. Africa, Paraguay, China (parts), Zealand, ♄, troubles in travel and residence. ♃, safe voyages. ♂, journeys on business. ☉, much travel but danger by water. ☿, much travel by water. ☽, unprofitable voyages.

LEO. E by N. France, Italy, Alps, N. Roumania, Apulia, Bohemia, Sicily, Chaldea to Bassorah, ancient Phoenicia near Tyre and Sidon, Australia (parts). ♂, danger of exile.

VIRGO. S by W. Turkey, Switzerland, Assyria, Mesopotamia, Crotia, Silesia, Crete, Babylonia, Morea, Thessaly, Greece (parts), Kurdestan, W.

Indies, Lavadia, Virginia, Brazil. ♃, foreign travel on business. ♂, business abroad. ♀, foreign travel on business or to safeguard reputation. ☽, many short journeys often for peculiar reasons.

LIBRA. W. Austria, Japan, N and Indo-China, Tibet, Caspian, Savoy, Upper Egypt, Livonia, Argentina, Burma. ♃, lasting friendships abroad. ☉, short journeys by land, fond of travel and of the country. ☽, journeys to avoid legal proceedings.

SCORPIO. N by E, Algeria, Barbary, Judea, Cappadocia, Morocco, N. Syria, Catalonia, Bavaria, Jutland, Norway, Transvaal, Queensland ♄, unpleasant voyages, residence abroad. ♃, long voyages and strange adventures. ♂, unfortunate journeys. ☉ or ☽, danger in travel. ♀, romance on voyages. ☿, danger of exile.

SAGITTARIUS. E by S. Spain, parts of France near C. Finisterre, Provence, Tuscany, Madagascar, Hungary, Istria, Moravia, Sclavonia, Dalmatia, Arabia, Australia (parts). ♂, fond of travel. ☉, travels and voyages. ♀, marriage union while travelling. ☽, travel, changes and voyages.

CAPRICORN. S. India, Punjaub, Afghanistan, parts of Persia near Korassan, Circan, and Maraccan, Greece, Thrace, Macedonia, Morea, Illyria, Balkan States, Hesse, S. W. Saxony, Styria, Romandiola, Mecklenburg, Lithuania, Mexico, Orkneys. ♀, gain or allowances from abroad.

AQUARIUS. W by N. Arabia, Abyssinia, Circassia, Tartary, Lithuania, Westphalia, Wallachia, Piedmont, Prussia (parts), Poland (parts), Red Russia, Sweden. ♂, danger on voyages.

PISCES. N by W. Portugal, Galicia, Calabria, Normandy, Nubia, Sahara. ♀, travel for business. ☽, travel by water.

The influence of the planets is as follows :—

SUN. If in 9th influential position abroad.

MOON. In 9th fond of travel. Aspecting ♅ and either in angles or 3rd and 9th, sudden changes and removals. Rising or in M.C. in ♊ or ♐, fond of travel and long voyages. In ♊, ♐, or ♓, frequent and usually sudden changes, if in ♓, advantageous. In 5th in good aspect to ♃ or ♂, either ruling 9th, pleasure in travel.

MERCURY. Many short journeys often on business, mental benefit through travel. If ♂ ☽, in reception, or both in 1st, 3rd or 9th, many long journeys. If afflicting significators, danger of piracy, imprisonment or poison.

VENUS. In 9th, travel for pleasure, fond of yachting and boating. If afflicted unpleasant journeys.

MARS. Impulsive and dangerous journeys. If aspecting luminaries often gives changes. If descending, especially in 9th and afflicting luminaries causes tramping or itinerating.

JUPITER. Travel and residence abroad, financial success. Afflicted by ♂ danger of accidents or shipwreck.

SATURN. Unfavourable for travel and often gives love of home.

URANUS. Sudden and unexpected journeys.

NEPTUNE. Long voyages, and journeys by water.

The following are the aphorisms dealing with travel :—

1. ♂, ♀, and ☽ just setting in a watery sign cause voyages or long residence near water.

TRAVEL

2. ☉ or ☽ setting in 7th denote journeys for gaining employment or evading enemies.

3. Lord of Asc. in 9th, or lord of 9th in Asc. indicates fondness for travel.

4. Significators of travel with lord of 10th or ♄ elevated, native will be sent on a mission by an influential person, but if significators are in Asc. or in good aspect to it he will travel by his own wish.

5. ♃ ruling Asc. and posited in 9th and afflicted by malefics causes forced journeys on account of religion or law.

6. ♀, ruling 7th, in 9th afflicted by malefics denotes travel on account of love affairs.

7. ⊕ cadent is some indication of numerous journeys.

CHAPTER XIII

DEATH.

The 8th house rules death, and the 4th the end of life. It is usually said that the 4th denotes only the old age conditions, but this is incorrect as it also indicates the state at the end of life, at whatever age that may be, and sometimes affords clearer indications of death than does the 8th. Planets in the 4th, or its ruler, considered in connection with their sign and aspects will show the circumstances under which the end of life is passed.

In the case of death note the hyleg, the planets afflicting the luminaries, and those in the 8th and 4th or the rulers of these houses. If the significators are free from serious affliction judge that natural death will occur and do not anticipate a violent one unless the afflictions are severe and unmistakable. Good aspects from ♃ or ♀ interposing among afflictions will often change the death from tragedy to natural suddenness. The character of a natural death may be judged from the planets in the 8th and 4th and the afflictions to the significators, together with the signs concerned. Death will be due to the illnesses ruled by these factors as given in chap. V.

Violent Deaths. These occur when there are severe afflictions from the malefics to both ☉

DEATH

and ☽, and usually to the Asc. also, especially from ♈, ♉, ♌, ♏, ♐, or ♑; when no help is given by the benefics; when the malefics are elevated or angular; and when there are afflictions to the 4th and 8th, or their rulers. Afflictions are increased when coming from cardinal signs, angles or the 8th house.

The time of death can be known only from directions, and even then precise determination is difficult and should never be attempted as even a small benefic aspect will frequently preserve life. Death is denoted by a long train of evil directions of which the first shows the time of death and the others its nature.

☿ and ♅ rarely, if ever, kill alone and only influence the type of death. The influence of the signs and planets is as follows:—

ARIES. Indirectly causes own death. ♄, suicidal tendencies if ☿ also afflicted. ♃, honour at end of life, heroic death. ☽, danger of drowning

TAURUS. Sometimes death by surgical operations. ♂, death by beheading or cutting throat.

GEMINI. ♄, strange death, liable to violence through jealousy, end hastened by relatives. ♂, unfavourable end amongst hostile relatives.

CANCER. ♄, difficulties at end of life, death abroad or by drowning. ♃, notable end, peaceful death abroad with honour.

LEO. ♄, danger of death from overwork or heart disease. ♃, honourable death. ♂, death in office or labour to end of life, danger of violent death abroad or in exile. ♀, possibility of death to save honour.

VIRGO. ♄, drowning or suffocation if afflicting ☽. ♂, quiet end affected by relatives.

LIBRA. ♄, trouble at end of life, danger of

tragic and notorious death. ♃, peaceful end amongst family.

SCORPIO. ♅, liable to sudden end. ♄, liable to sudden death, solitary and mysterious end, death through secret enemies, animals, or drowning. ♃, liable to tragic death through society or politics. ♂, indirectly causes own death, sudden or violent end often through secret enemies, murder, especially if ☽ is afflicted by ♄, ☉, danger of early or sudden end. ♀, danger of death by poison, suicide through love affairs, or death at the hand of a woman. ☿, danger of death from poison, bites, or enemies. ☽, danger of early death by violence, drowning, epidemics, or childbirth.

SAGITTARIUS. ♄, death amid good surroundings and with religious thoughts. ♂, danger of murder especially if afflicting ☽ from angles, ♀, peaceful end.

CAPRICORN. ♄, danger of death through chronic and tragic mental ailments. ♂, death by drowning.

AQUARIUS. ♄, end of life better than beginning. ♃, sudden end. ♂, death in strange land or among strangers. ♀, tragedy or shock at end of life.

PISCES. ♄, retired or secluded and tragic end, sometimes suicide, grief, or drowning. ♃, quiet and religious end. ♂, death through pleasure or abroad. ☉, danger of violent death from secret enemies.

SUN. In 8th, death through hereditary weakness, heart trouble, or heroic end; honour after death. If afflicted sudden or violent death in middle life.

MOON. In 8th, public death, death in presence of strangers or in hospital, drowning.

MERCURY. In 8th, liable to death through

brain or nerve disorders, melancholia, etc. Fully conscious at death.

VENUS. In 8th, peaceful death ; if afflicted death through pleasure, poison, wasting diseases, diabetes, kidney or venereal diseases.

MARS. In 8th, sudden or violent death, suicide, accident, fever, or operation. In ♊, ♍, ♒, or first half of ♐, death by human hands or in war ; if ♀ is also involved, through women ; and if ☿ also, through burglars or robbers. In ♉ or ♏ afflicting hyleg, death by operation, burning, or smallpox. If setting in opposition to the luminaries, death by fire.

JUPITER. In 8th, peaceful end. If afflicted death through heart, liver, blood, tumours, cancer, or consumption.

SATURN. In 8th, slow lingering death, suffocation, falls, consumption ; if in watery sign, drowning ; if well aspected, death in old age; if in fixed sign, suffocation, strangling or hanging. If afflicted by ♃ death by judicial sentence. If in ♈, ♉, ♌, ♐, or ♑, death by bites of animals. If in opposition to luminaries rising, death in prison. If in M.C. and afflicting ☉ and ♂, falls from heights especially if in an airy sign. If conjunction ♀ and ☿ and afflicting hyleg, death by poison or female treachery.

URANUS. In 8th, sudden or uncommon death, suicide, epilepsy, paralysis or death from electrocution, explosions, or machinery.

NEPTUNE. In 8th, strange and mysterious death, disappearance, death in trance, through drugs, in hospital or asylum ; danger of being buried alive.

The following are the more important aphorisms dealing with death ;

1. A planet exactly on the 7th cusp in its own sign will partly indicate the nature of the death.

2. Malefics afflicting from angles denote a public death.

3. ♄ in 12th and ♀ in 8th indicate early death or suicide.

4. One malefic in 12th, another in 6th, and lord of Asc. in 8th, afflicted by either, indicates death by plots of secret enemies.

5. ☿ afflicted in 6th is some indication of death in prison.

6. Significators in earthy signs indicate death in prison or by starvation or poison.

7. Lord of 8th weak and afflicted by ♄ or ♂ in watery signs denotes death by poison or venomous stings.

Animals. The following positions indicate death from the kick or bite of an animal.

1. ♄ in Asc. ☽ in 7th, □ ♂ in 4th in one of the "bestial" signs ♈, ♉, ♌, ♐, or ♑.

2. ☽ with ♄ and ♂ in M.C. in a bestial sign.

3. ♂, ruling 8th, with ☽ in bestial sign.

4. ☽ in an angle and ♃ weak in a bestial sign, especially ♌.

Mutilation. The following positions indicate mutilation :—

1. ☉ with Caput Algol (in ♉ 25 or its line of R.A. in ♉ 15) in no aspect to benefics, no benefic in 8th, and the ☉ by day or the ☽ by night afflicted by ♂, the native will be beheaded ; if the luminary culminate he will be wounded, maimed, or torn to pieces alive ; and if ♂ be in ♊ or ♓ his hands or feet will be cut off.

2. ♂ with Caput Algol and afflicting ☉ in ♌ or ♏ indicates beheading.

DEATH

Drowning is indicated by the following positions:—

1. Significators afflicted in watery signs.

2. ♄ in ♋ in 4th rising after ☉ and afflicting ☉, ♂, or ☽.

3. Lord of 4th in 7th in a watery sign and a watery sign on 4th cusp.

Burning is indicated by the following positions:—

1. Significators afflicted in fiery signs.

2. ♂ afflicting luminaries from ♏ indicates accidental burning; from ♈ or ♌ sentenced to be shot; from ♐, sentenced to be burnt.

3. ☽ ☌ ♂ in fiery sign in 8th.

4. ☽ ruling 7th, and ♂ and ☉ in affliction from 7th and 10th in fiery signs.

5. ☉ in conjunction with lord of Asc. in ♌, no benefic in 8th, and ♂ neither ruling nor exalted in Asc.

Hanging or Falls are indicated as follows:—

1. Significators afflicted in airy signs.

2. ♄ ruling 8th and ♃ with ♂ in 7th not aspecting 4th cusp.

3. ♄ or ♂ with ☋ in 7th.

4. ♂ with Pleiades (♉ 29), ♄ with Regulus (♌ 29) or Antares (♐ 9), and ☉ with Caput Algol, indicate hanging or beheading.

CHAPTER XIV

ESOTERIC ASTROLOGY.

Esoteric Astrology or Astrotheosophy is that branch of astrology which deals with the natal horoscope from a theosophical point of view and seeks to discover the operations of evolution and the unfoldment of the Ego behind the map. According to its teachings the horoscope is the result of a series of past lives in which the present environment and character have been built up, and by a study of the map the trend of former lives may be discovered, and the line of development most fitted for the native may be picked out. The general argument is that an affliction in a horoscope indicates some disharmony, abuse, or lack of development in matters represented by the planets concerned, and that one of the aims of the present life is to correct this failing and to fight against it in order that the proper quality may be evolved and the disharmony be removed. Thus a badly afflicted Mars indicates misapplied energy, cruelty, or passion, in a past life, and it is therefore necessary to combat the passionate tendencies indicated in the present map as a result of the past life, and to utilise the stronger and better qualities in the horoscope in order to rise above it. This may be done by the help of favourable aspects. If in the example Mars has a favourable aspect to one of the other planets the qualities ruled by that planet should be developed as they may be applied to check the martial disharmony through the channel of the good aspect. Failing a good aspect the sign ruled by a planet, if favourably occupied, may be used for the same purpose.

The law of cause and effect, or Karma, by which thought in a past life becomes character in the next, desire becomes opportunity, and action decides environment, gives us a clue to the type of life of which the present is the outcome. Symbolically the planets are the qualities, the signs character, and the houses environment, so that in general a planet in a favourable sign but unfavourable house indicates a fairly well developed character functioning in an unfavourable environment, as would be the case if a man had performed a bad action from which good results had proceeded, and the same would hold true of the converse position. It is necessary, however, to distinguish between bad character and bad Karma. The most highly developed people have frequently the most strongly afflicted horoscopes, the bad aspects working out in physical trials and struggles and producing a series of disaster in order that the Ego may be freed from past unfavourable links. *Only intuition can decide whether the native is of high or low development, and our present knowledge is unsufficient to read this from the map.*

The greater part of an esoteric judgment must be based upon symbolism, and it is found that the planetary symbols employed are all made up of three separate characters, namely, the circle, symbolising spirit, the cross matter, and the semi-circle or crescent, soul, or the emotional and desire nature. The aspects and signs are arranged according to the symbols of the triangle and cross or square, of which the triangle represents the three aspects of the Deity and spirit, and the cross or square matter. All aspects formed by dividing the circle into three parts, or equal divisions of these, such as the trine, sextile, and semisextile, are favourable, while those formed on the cross, such as the square and semi-square are unfavourable. Similarly signs of the same triplicity are harmonious as they form a triangle, whilst those of the same quadruplicity are inharmonious being formed on a cross.

The signs and houses correspond to the three divine attributes of Will, Wisdom, and Activity, and also rule the planes and human principles.

Cardinal signs and angular houses correspond to Activity and the physical world.

Fixed signs and succeedent houses correspondto Will and the desire world.

Mutable signs and cadent houses correspond to Wisdom and the mental world.

Cardinal and fiery signs are in affinity as are fixed and earthy, and mutable and airy and watery. The triangles of the fiery and airy signs represent the inner nature or Individuality, and those of the watery and earthy the outer nature or Personality, planets in these triangles indicating the development and nature of each. Furthermore:—

Airy signs correspond to the Higher Mental plane and Causal body.

Fiery signs correspond primarily to the Spirit, but also on a lower level to the Lower Mental plane and Mental body.

Watery signs correspond to the Astral plane and Astral body.

Earthy signs correspond to the Physical plane and Phsysical body, and the condition of these signs indicates the condition of the corresponding principle in the native.

The following are some esoteric notes on the signs and planets :—

ARIES. The symbol denotes the uprushing fountain of life become individualised and entering this plane to gain development. It is the sign of the separate self and rules the personal vitality.

TAURUS. The symbol represents a coiled serpent. It is the hidden impulse to action, blind desire, inertia, and the creative instinct, and forms the centre to which the physical activities of Capricorn converge through the agency of Virgo.

GEMINI. The sign of mental relationship. It acts as a channel along which the mental activities of Libra converge into Aquarius, or through which the will of Aquarius re-acts upon Libra.

CANCER. The symbol represents the life springing from the cell. It is the activity of the senses and the outgoing emotions, which come from or go to the fixed centre Scorpio.

LEO. The symbol is a partly uncoiled serpent. It is the heart of the Individuality and the fixed centre of the fiery triangle.

VIRGO. The sign of service and discrimination, and the medium through which the physical energies and activities are transmitted.

LIBRA. The balance or turning point between the first or outgoing half of the Zodiac, and the last or absorbing half. It is the point at which a new departure is made when the previous experiences are balanced up and the Ego definitely turns inwards.

SCORPIO. The symbol is a moving serpent denoting the waking of the fixed centres which began in Taurus and culminates in Aquarius. It is the sign of generation and re-generation in which the creative forces may be turned outwards or inwards.

SAGITTARIUS. The symbol is an arrow shot into the unknown. It is the sign of initiation and rebirth, and the beginning of a new and higher life.

CAPRICORN. The symbol is usually said to be a goat ascending a mountain typifying the evolution of the personality through work and service, but the real ancient symbol as depicted on the old star maps is a creature half goat and half fish denoting the physical energies and service evolving through sensation and desire, and the transmutation of the latter into the former.

AQUARIUS. The symbol is a white serpent gliding over water and its dark reflection, or a man pouring water out of a vessel. It denotes the free gift of the spirit and the ceasing of rebirth, when the spiritual forces flow through the native for the good of humanity and are not absorbed for himself. There is a light and a dark side to the sign, and the spiritual forces are frequently distorted through the "water" of the astral plane.

PISCES. The sign of universal solution and of self-undoing. It is the passage from this plane to another and to freedom from bondage, or the universal love and sympathy into which all things are to be resolved.

It will be seen from the above that the triplicities form groups that react from one to the other. The cardinal sign of any triplicity denotes its activities, the mutable sign the channel along which they pass, and the fixed sign their centre. In the lower stages the fixed centre attracts for itself, but in the higher stages it acts as a part of the Divine Will which moves outwards through the other signs. The positions of the planets in these signs indicate the type of activity of each sign of the triplicity, and the help or hindrance to the moving forces.

The esoteric nature of the planets is as follows:

SUN. The symbol is the point within the circle denoting the manifesting spirit. It represents the spark of Deity in all, and rules the Individuality or permanent part of man.

MOON. The symbol is the semi-circle, or the soul of man and the desire or emotional nature. It represents the Personality, and its rapid motion indicates the many and fluctuating changes that take place in the outer nature.

MERCURY. The symbol is the semi-circle over circle over cross, or the predominance of soul and spirit over matter and the blending of all three. The central position of the spirit denotes the. alternation of emotion and matter through which the spirit is reached and to which it forms a point of balance. It rules the Buddhic or Intuitional consciousness, and the Second Ray.

VENUS. The symbol is the circle over the cross indicating the predominance of spirit over matter. It is said to rule the Higher Mind and the Third Ray but this has been disputed.

MARS. The symbol is the cross over the circle denoting the predominance of matter over spirit.

It rules the astral plane and the desire nature.

JUPITER. The symbol is the semi-circle over the cross denoting the predominance of emotion over matter. It rules the human bodies and the physical body in particular.

SATURN. The symbol is the cross over the semi-circle denoting the predominance of matter over emotion. It is the planet of limitation and fate or Karma, and marks the dividing or limiting line between the Personality and Individuality which has to be passed or overcome before true progress can be made.

URANUS. The symbol represents the life emerging from the spirit, passing through matter, and converging into onepointedness. It is the planet of individualisation, and represents the will or spirit that is ever pressing forward through changing matter.

NEPTUNE. The symbol represents the life emerging from the spirit, passing through matter, and diverging into unity with the Divine along the three lines of Will, Wisdom and Activity. It is the Christ planet denoting the suppression of self and universal love and charity, and is probably the real ruler of the Second Ray.

The practical application of these esoteric principles is largely a matter of intuition and cannot be laid down in a series of hard and fast rules. The general nature of the map will indicate the part of the character that is functioning to the greatest extent, afflictions will denote the sources of disharmony and the hindrances to development, and good aspects the powers that may be utilised for development. The nature of the afflictions roughly indicates their cause in past lives. Thus the position of Saturns in a sign or house indicates a check on the activities ruled by them, and therefore denotes something damped out probably because of past excesses. Thus Saturn in Leo might well represent past abuse of power, and the same might also be shown by a map in which the majority of planets were in powerful and ruling signs with a weak and serving ascendant. It is said also that rising planets and those in the succeedent houses, especially the 5th and 2nd, denote past Karma, while the 9th indicates the line upon which the future is being built.

In general the following are the afflictions in a map that are said to result from various abuses in past lives of the nature of those indicated :—

♅ afflicting ♂. Deceit, unnatural practices, black magic.

♯ „ ♂. Anarchy, suicide, murder, destruction.

♄ „ ♃. Hypocrisy, religious injustice, imposition.

♄ „ ♂. Cruelty, violence, hatred, selfishness.

♄ „ ☿. Dishonesty, treachery, cowardice.

♃ „ ♂. Waste, conceit, extravagance.

♂ „ ☿ Lying, slander, malice.

♂ „ ♀. Sensuality, abuse of emotion and affection.

In all cases the path of development lies in checking the existing tendencies to these vices and developing the opposite virtue by the aid of the strong and favourable positions in the map.

CHAPTER XV

AN EXAMPLE NATIVITY.

As an example of the foregoing rules and methods of procedure the following nativity may be considered. It is not proposed to give a detailed delineation as the student should work this out for himself, and therefore only the facts and a few explanatory notes are set down.

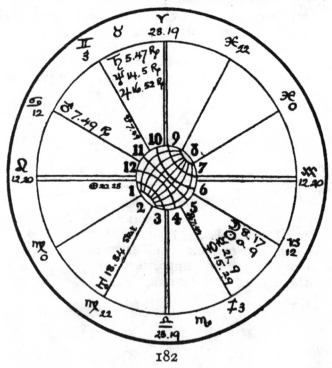

Planets	Lat.	Decl.	ASPECTS ☉	☽	☿	♀	♂	♃	♄	♅	♆
Sun		23 S 27	☉	☌	∥		☍	⟎	△		⟎
Moon		20 S 29		☽				☍	△		△
Mercury		23 S 44			☿		☌		⟎	□	
Venus		22 S 9				♀		⊼		□⟎	⊼
Mars		26 N 37					♂		✶	△	✶ ☌
Jupiter		15 N 51						♃		⟎	
Saturn		11 N 4							♄		△
Uranus		5 N 15								♅	
Neptune		14 N 21									♆
Ascdt.			ASC.								
M.C.			M.C.								

Length of life. The Asc. is hyleg and is badly afflicted by the squares of ♄, ♅, and ♃ from the 10th, but is △ ♀ from the 5th. A strong sign is rising but ☉ and ☽ are weak and badly afflicted, though △ ♄ ruler of 6th. The afflictions from ♂ give vitality but do not promise length of life. The testimonies are more unfavourable than favourable and a comparatively short life is all that could be expected. Native died at 37 years of age.

Appearance. The personal appearance is fairly well described by ♌. The native was tall with a large frame and big bones, walked erectly, had sherry coloured and rather catty eyes, but was very dark owing to the strong Saturnian influence (♄ □ Asc., ☉ ☌ ☽ in ♐). He was thin and unhealthy looking, largely owing to ☉ ☌ ☽ in ♐. Sight and hearing were good, but the native stammered at times through nervousness (☿ □ ♅, ∥ ☉ in ♐, ⟎ ♄ in ♉). Teeth were good and there was no apparent deformity.

Character and Mind. The ♌ characteristics were marked and the influence of ♑ was also pronounced. The strong fixed and earthy signs gave a dogmatic nature, materialism, ambition, great conscientiousness and plodding power in work, and a good deal of despondency. There was much love of statistics, and also of philosophy and peotry (☿ ♂ ♀ in ♐) and the mind was very idealistic, always evolving utopian schemes (☿ ☐ ♅), strongly pacific (☿ ♂ ♀), and yet at the same time Bolshevistic (afflictions from ♅ and ♆). The native always wanted to do good but only succeeded in offending everybody (☉ ♂ ☽ in ♑, ♅ ☐ ☿ ♀, and the cramping influence of ♄ and the earthy signs). The mental balance was not good and there were serious nervous breakdowns and some insanity (☽ ♂ ☉ in ♑, ☽ and ☿ in no aspect, ☿ in ♐ afflicted by ♅ on cusp of 3rd, ☿ afflicted by ♄ in night map. etc.)

Health. The health was fairly good owing to the strong sign rising but ☽ on cusp of 6th ♂ ☉ gave weakness and digestive trouble (♋), ☉ afflicted in 5th with ♌ rising and fixed positions heart trouble, and the afflictions from ♂ on the 12th cusp together with the afflicted ☿, insomnia. Much of the ill-health came from overwork (♄ ruling 6th in 10th) and domestic worries (afflictions from ♂, part ruler of 4th.)

Finance. All the native's money came by his own endeavours and by hard work (strong ♄ and fixed signs). He was careful over money matters (♄ and ♑), but at the same time impulsively generous to women and friends (☿ ruling 2nd and 11th ♂ ♀ ☐ ♅, ♌ rising, ♃ in ♉ ☐ ☉).

Occupation and Position. The native held a

position under a large body (♄ and ♐). He was at one time engaged in work connected with the land (♉ ♐) in Ireland (♉), but met with much opposition. Later he was engaged on work connected with land and sea (♆). His final position was a good one (☉ ☽) in a cardinal sign, three planets in 10th including ♄ and ♃), but the responsibility hastened his death owing to overwork and apprehension lest he should be unable to carry on (♐ afflictions, ♄ in ♉).

Parents and Relatives. The father was an invalid and confined to his bed for many years. (♄ and ♆ in 10th, ☉ afflicted in ♐). The cause of his death was heart trouble (♉ operating through ♌ by transverse polarity). The mother died of cancer (♂ ruling 4th afflicting ☽ from ♋). There was one brother and one sister. Domestic affairs were extremely unhappy (♂ ruling 4th in 12th in ♋ afflicting luminaries).

Friends. The native had few friends but a large number of acquaintances mostly among young people, clerks, or writers (☿ ruling ♊ on 11th).

Love and marriage. The views on love affairs and marriage were peculiar (☿ ☌ ♀ in 5th □ ♅), and the passions were strong. Marriage was unhappy (♌ rising, ☽ ☍ ♂, etc.) and there was temporary separation (♀ □ ♅). The wife was described by ♂ in ♋ and ♄ in ♉. There were two children, the first being a girl who died in infancy, and the second a boy, born with ♌ rising.

Death. A violent death is clearly shown. The native committed suicide by drowning after having unsuccessfully attempted to poison himself (watery signs on 4th and 8th, ♂ in ♋ in 12th ☍ ☉ ☽) and elevated, ♃ ruling 8th, ♂ ♆ afflicting ☉, etc.).

SECTION III

DIRECTIONS AND RECTIFICATION

CHAPTER I

SECONDARY DIRECTIONS.

Directions or the calculating of future events are divided into two main headings, Primary and Secondary. The processes are based on the fact that after birth the planets and houses "progress", or pass on to form different positions and aspects amongst themselves and to their birth positions, and therefore denote changing influences that enter into the life after birth. The secondary system, which is that commonly in use and which may conveniently be treated first, is concerned with the passage of the planets in their orbits on successive days after birth. *It is found that one day after birth is equivalent to one year of life, and that if we wish to know the influences in force during say the 20th year of life we must examine the planetary positions on the 20th day after birth, so that all the directions acting in a life of 90 years are actually formed in the heavens within three months after birth.*

The horoscope of birth is thus not only significant of the whole of life but also relates in a more particular manner to the period from age 0 years to age 1 year, or from the actual birthday to its first anniversary. The most simple method of obtaining the "progressed horoscope" is to count as many days after birth as the native is years old and erect a map for the same time as at birth but on the day thus found. Suppose a person were born at 6.49 p.m. on 3rd April, 1864, and wished for a progressed horoscope for 1879. The age on the birthday in 1879 would be 15 years, and therefore the map must be cast for 6.49 p.m. on the 15th day from birth. The day after birth is called 1, and the 15th would therefore be 18th April, 1864, so that a map for 6.49 p.m. on 18th April, 1864, would show the course of events taking place between 3rd April, 1879 and 2nd April, 1880, or to put the matter rather more accurately aspects formed during the 24 hours from 18th April to 19th April would operate between 3rd April, 1879 and 2nd April, 1880.

The movement of most of the planets is so slight that few aspects are formed in any given day, but in the case of the Moon a large number may be formed and it is necessary to sub-divide the period in order to obtain the exact months of their operation. Therefore, since the whole day is equivalent to one year, it is necessary to divide the daily motion of the Moon by 12 in order to find its progressed motion per month.

There are three main methods of obtaining the progressed horoscope, each of which gives the same result but begins the progressed year at a different point. Method A should be thoroughly grasped as it gives a clear idea of the principles involved, but in practice method B is the most speedy and convenient.

A. BIRTHDAY METHOD. This is the most simple to understand and is the one already outlined above. It gives the progressed positions as on the birthday, so that the year counts from one birthday to the next. The following are the rules for erecting the map:—

SECONDARY DIRECTIONS

1. Add one day for each year to the date of birth in order to obtain the progressed date for which the positions must be calculated.

2. Compute the cusps for the actual birth time but use the Sidereal Time of the progressed date. The local Mean Time of birth should be used as in erecting an ordinary horoscope.

3. Compute the planets' positions for the time of birth on the progressed date using Greenwich Mean Time. The whole process consists in imagining the native to be born again at the same time of day on the progressed date, and the map is cast in the ordinary way. The result is the progressed positions of the planets as on the birthday anniversary.

4. Calculate the Moon's position for the same time on the next day and so find the number of degrees and minutes it moves in the 24 hours (or one year).

5. Divide this quantity by 12 to obtain its monthly progress (which will be more or less than 1°.)

6. Add this quantity successively to the position originally found and the result will be the Moon's progressed longitude on the birth date in each month.

7. Follow rules 4 to 6 using the Moon's declination instead of its longitude.

EXAMPLE. *Native born 2 May, 1922, 6 a.m., G.M.T., London.*

Required progressed map for age 10 to 11 (May, 1932 to May, 1933).

10 years after birth is equivalent to 10 days and therefore the progressed map showing the progressed positions as at 2 May, 1932, should be cast for 6 a.m. on 12 May, 1922. Then :—

Sid. Time at noon 11 May, 1922	3	13	57
Add local time elapsed	18	0	0
Add correction		2	57
Sid. Time at 6 a.m. 12 May, 1922	21	16	54

With this Sidereal Time turn to the proper Tables of Houses and write down the cusps. Next find the planetary positions for this time and insert them in the map.

The Moon's position for the required time will be found to be 3° ♐ 44', which is therefore its progressed place as on the birthday anniversary of 2 May, 1932. To find its place on 2 May, 1933 calculate its position at 6 a.m. on 13 May, 1922. The result will be found to be 17° ♐ 27'. Therefore it follows that the Moon moves from 3° ♐ 44' to 17° ♐ 27' in the year from 2 May, 1932 to 2 May, 1933. The annual progressed motion is therefore obtained by subtracting the former from the latter and is found to be 14° 43'. To obtain its mothly motion divide this by 12, the result being 1° 13'$\frac{7}{12}$. We may now erect a table of the Moon's monthly position as follows:—

Moon's prog. place on 2 May, 1932	3°	♐	44'
Add monthly motion	1		13$\frac{7}{12}$
Moon's place on 2 June, 1932	4		57$\frac{7}{12}$
Add monthly motion	1		13$\frac{7}{12}$
Moon's place on 2 July, 1932	6		11$\frac{1}{6}$

and so on

Write these in a column and then repeat the whole process to find the monthly value of the Moon's declination.

SECONDARY DIRECTIONS

The process of calculating directions will be explained after the other methods of computing the positions have been described.

B. NOON DATE METHOD. This is the method most commonly employed in practice as it does away with the necessity of calculating the planets' places.

It is clear that if one day after birth is equivalent to one year the following proportion holds good:—

$$24 \text{ hours} = 12 \text{ months}$$
$$2 \text{ hours} = 1 \text{ month}$$
$$1 \text{ hour} = 15 \text{ days}$$
$$4 \text{ mins.} = 1 \text{ day}$$

In the above example we found that 6 a.m. on 12th May was equivalent to 2 May, 1932, and 6 a.m. on 13th May to 2 May, 1933. Therefore *noon* on 12th May must correspond to some date in between 2 May, 1932 and 2 May, 1933, and if we find this date we can simply copy the noon positions from the Ephemeris on the 12th May as they will be the correct progressed positions for this intermediate date which is known as the "Noon Date".

The following is the easiest method of finding the Noon Date :—

1. Find the time elapsing from birth to the *nearest* noon. The Greenwich Mean Time of birth is to be used for this purpose.

2. Convert the hours and minutes thus found into months and days by means of the proportions given above.

3. (*a*) If the birth is a.m. add the months and days so found to the date of birth.

(*b*) If the birth is p.m. subtract them.

The result is the noon date for any year. [1]) Thus in our previous example 6 a.m. is 6 hours before noon. 6 hours are equivalent to 3 months and as the birth is a.m. 3 months must be added to the birth date to give the noon date which will, therefore, be 2nd. August. Then the noon positions each day after birth in the Ephemeris will be equivalent to their progressed positions as at 2nd August of each year, the noon positions on the day of birth itself (2 May, 1922) being equivalent to 2 August, 1922.

The rules for erecting the map are as follows:—

I. Calculate the cusps for the time of birth on the progressed date as in method A[2]).

[1]) The above method treats all the months as consisting of 30 days, and a more accurate method is as follows :—

1. *For an a.m. birth.* Subtract the Sidereal Time at birth from the Sidereal Time at noon on the day of birth and to the result add the Sidereal Time at noon on the day of birth. The Noon Date will be the day whose noon Sidereal Time is the same as that found in the above result.

2. *For a p.m. birth.* Subtract the Sidereal Time at noon on the day of birth from the Sidereal Time at birth. Subtract the result from the Sidereal Time at noon on the day of birth. The result is the Sidereal Time at noon on the Noon Date as before.

If the birthplace is not London it will be necessary to find Sidereal Time at Greenwich for the moment of birth. This may be done by supposing the native to be born at London and using the Greenwich Time of birth instead of the Local Time in finding the Sidereal Time at birth.

[2]) The slight discrepancy between the cuspal and planetary dates is immaterial as a whole year alters the M. C. by only 1°, but if absolute accuracy is desired proceed as follows:—

1. Find the Sidereal Time at the time of birth on the progressed date as before.

2. Find the time elapsing in hours and minutes between the Greenwich time of birth and the nearest and noon.

3. Find the correction for this from the Table on p. 243 of the Appendix.

4. If the birth is a.m. add the correction to the Sidereal Time found is 1, and if p.m. subtract it. The result is the Sidereal Time corresponding to the Noon Date.

2. Insert the *noon* positions of the planets in the map, making a note as to the date to which they measure.

3. Find the Moon's motion in longitude and declination from that noon to the next and divide by 12 to obtain its monthly position as before.

Example. As before. The noon date is 2 August so that the planets at noon on 12 May, 1922 are their progressed positions as at 2 August, 1932. Calculate the cusps as before and make a note "cusps as at 2 May, 1932" (unless the cusps are also adjusted to the noon date, in which case the Sidereal Time will be 21^h 17^m 53^s instead of 21^h 16^m 54^s as already determined).

Insert in this map the positions of the planets at noon on 12 May, 1922. The Moon's longitude on this date is 7° ♐ 13', and on the next noon it is 20 ♐ 52. Therefore it moves 13° 39' in the year, or 1° 8'¼ a month. Then:—

Moon's position as at 2 Aug. 1932   7° ♐ 13'
      Add monthly motion   1°   8¼

Moon's position as at 2 Sept., 1932   8°   21¼
      and so on

It will be noticed that the positions in this Table and those in the last show a discrepancy of 2 or 3 minutes. These are due to the method of obtaining the noon date and may be eliminated by employing the Sidereal Time method.

C. First of January method. It is sometimes convenient to calculate the planetary positions for the 1st January of each year and for the 1st of each succeeding month instead of for intermediate dates. The method of doing this is as follows:—

1. Subtract the month and day of birth from

the 1st January next following so as to obtain the native's age on the 1st January in months and days.

2. Convert the months and days thus obtained into hours and minutes at the rate of 1 month = 2 hours, and 1 day = 4 minutes.

3. Find the time elapsing from birth to the nearest noon and add it to the above result if the birth was p.m. or subtract it if a.m. The result will be the time counted from noon on the birthday that measures to the 1st January of the following year

The above method can be modified so as to find the time for which calculation must be made to obtain the progressed positions on the first of any month. All that is necessary is to find the age on the 1st of the required month next following as in rule 1 above, and then to proceed exactly as there shown.

Example. As before. Required the directions for 1932.

	Year	Month	Day
1st Jan. 1923 =	1923	1	0
2nd May 1922 =	1922	5	2
Age	0	7	29

0^y 7^m 29^d	= 0^d 15^h 56^m
Subtract time of birth from nearest noon	6 0
Time from noon on day on birth	9 56

= 9.56 p.m.

Therefore the planets positions for 9.56 p.m. on the day of birth measure to 1st Jan. 1923, and by adding the required number of days we find that their positions at 9.56 p.m. on 11th May, 1922 measure to 1st. Jan. 1932.

The cusps are computed in the usual way and the planets positions for 9.56 p.m. are inserted in the map.[1])

The Moon's monthly motion is obtained in the usual way. Thus the Moon's place at 9.56 p.m. on 11 May, 1922 is 29° ♏ 1', and on 12 May, 1922, 12° ♐ 52'. Its annual motion is therefore 13° 51', and its monthly progress 1° 9'¼. Then:—

Moon's position as at 1 Jan. 1932   29° ♏ 1'
    Add monthly motion   1   9¼

Moon's position as at 1 Febr. 1932   0 ♐ 10¼
    and so on.

Having now described all the methods of calculating the progressed map we may proceed to the further task of finding the directions in force. The following rules will make this clear:—

1. Take the progressed position of the Sun and notice whether it forms any aspects to any of the planets in the birth horoscope (which is usually called the "radical" map, as it is the radix or root from which changes proceed). Parallels are also to be included. If any aspects are formed during the year under consideration note the approximate month in which they become exact. The Sun moves about 1° or 60' per annum by progression, and its monthly movement will therefore be about 5'.

2. Next note whether the progressed Sun forms any aspects or parallels to the progressed

---

[1]) If desired the cusps can also be corrected to 1st Jan. by adding to the Sidereal Time at the time of birth on the progressed date the correction for the age expressed in hours and minutes on the 1st. Jan., following as in method B.

planets with the exception of the progressed Moon. Note these and their months of operation also.

These two classes form the *Solar Directions*.

3. Take the progressed ☿ and note any aspects and parallels it may form to radical positions and then to progressed positions. Note the months in which such aspects are formed by estimating the monthly movement of ☿.

4. Do the same with ♀, ♂, ♃, ♄, ♅, and ♆ respectively. When looking for aspects to progressed planets omit the progressed Moon in all cases.

These form the *Mutual Directions*.

5. Tabulate the Moon's monthly progressed positions and then write down against the months in which they are formed any aspects or parallels made by the progressed Moon to the radical and progressed places of the Sun and planets. These form the *Lunar Directions*.

6. If the birth time is reliable the aspects formed by the progressed M.C. and Asc., may be tabulated also, but if there is any doubt as to the accuracy of the time they should be omitted. The directions are now complete.

When writing down directions it is customary always to write the moving body first, and to mark the radical and progressed positions by the letters "r" and "p" respectively. Thus, ☉ p ⚹ ☽ r means that the Sun has progressed to form the sextile of the Moon's place at birth, whereas in the case of ☽ p ⚹ ☉ r it is the Moon that moves to the sextile of the Sun's radical position. An aspect formed between 2 progressed bodies may be written either in the form ☉ p ⚹ ☽ p or simply ☉ ⚹ ☽. When a letter is omitted after the planet's symbol it is to be understood that the body is a progressed one and that it is "p" that is omitted. These distinctions are important and should always be observed.

The final step in the process is to obtain an Ephemeris for the actual year for which the directions are required, or if this is unobtainable a set of Transit Tables should be obtained. A shilling publication by Raphael entitled "The Geocentric Longitudes of the Major Planets from 1900 to 2001" will serve the purpose admirably.

A *transit* is the passage of a planet in the heavens on any day over a radical or progressed position. The theory is that a radical planet retains its birth position and influence throughout life and that its progressed position is also a sensitive point. Both these points may be stimulated at any time by the passage of a planet over them and it is this that constitutes a transit. It is customary to ignore the transits of ♀, ☿, and the ☽ when dealing with major influences, as the transits of these bodies are of minor importance and are chiefly of use in marking favourable and unfavourable days. A strong transit will hasten or retard the operation of a direction as will be explained later and a note should be made of the dates of all the major transits over both the radical and progressed positions of all the planets. The directions are now ready to be interpreted.

CHAPTER II

INTERPRETATION OF DIRECTIONS.

The progressed horoscope cannot be read in quite the same way as a radical map. The birth horoscope is fixed and rules the whole of the life as it represents the character, environment, and type of life into which the native is born or with which he is furnished. By the gradual progression of the planets away from their birth positions, however, a certain amount of freedom arises and the native is able to expand or to change along the lines indicated by the progression. The progressed horoscope changes only very slightly from year to year and therefore if read as a birth map it would hold good for many years. But all changes in the progressed horoscope must be interpreted in terms of the birth map, as that is the radical or root map of the life and therefore has the major significance and power, so that the most important point is not so much where the planets are in the progress as in what relations they stand to their birth positions.

The following are the rules for judging a progressed horoscope and for estimating the happenings at any time in the life:—

1. The Solar and Mutual directions are the most important as they are the slowest in for-

mation and may be in force for many years. Tabulate the aspects made by the progressed Sun and keep them together, and do the same with the other directions, keeping each set of aspects to a particular planet in a class by itself. Suppose the Sun is in trine to Jupiter at 19 years of age, and next forms a square to Saturn at 27. The mid-point between these aspects occurs at 23, and the influence of the trine to Jupiter will extend to that age when it will be gradually replaced by the influence of the square to Saturn which will reach a maximum at 27 and then gradually decline in power until it is superseded by the next aspect formed by the Sun. At any time in the life of an aspect it may be stimulated by lunar directions and transits, and so a direction such as ☉ △ ♃ will operate in various ways and at different times during several years, the nature of the effect being modified by the kind of stimulation it receives. When two successive aspects of an opposite nature are formed, as in the above example, the mid-point is critical and secondary effects, such as lunar aspects, will operate freely, but when the major aspects are similar in nature the mid-point is a very strong one. During the time in which a major aspect is in force, secondary aspects will act strongly if of the same nature as the major one but will be repressed if of an opposite nature. Thus under ☉ △ ♃ a lunar aspect such as ☽ □ ♄ would not be strongly felt, but if the same aspect fell under ☉ □ ♄ it would mark the climax of the major influence and would operate with great power. A major aspect need not operate exactly to date as it is usually dependent upon minor causes and operates many times, or overshadows and characterises a long period of time.

2. As already stated each class of direction should be kept separate from the others. The successive aspects of the progressed Sun form an ordered series, and the same is true of the successive aspects of the other planets with the exception of the Moon. These separate series interpenetrate but do not cancel each other, so that a bad aspect in the Saturn series may coincide with a good one in the Jupiter series, the total effect probably being sorrow through a death but at the same time benefit by a legacy. The worst and most dangerous periods of the life are indicated by a train or series of bad aspects.

3. In interpreting a direction consider the planets involved and the signs and houses occupied and ruled by them. For this purpose the direction of a progressed planet to a radical one is to be interpreted in terms of the radical map and consideration given to the radical houses involved ; but a direction falling between two progressed planets must be referred to the progressed map.

4. The strength of a direction depends upon the strength and nature of the radical planet. If Jupiter in the horoscope of birth is badly afflicted a good direction to it in after life does not produce as good results as when it is free from affliction, and similarly a bad direction to a malefic well aspected at birth is not so serious as if it had been afflicted. Remember that the radical map symbolises the whole life and that directions must conform to it. Therefore unless the horoscope shows a violent death do not

judge it from a severe and violent direction, and if the radical map shows a life of poverty no good direction will produce riches.

5. The function of the lunar aspects is to indicate the monthly course of events through the aspects formed by the Moon and its stimulation of major influences. The sign and house of the radical map through which the Moon is passing will always be prominent in directions, and the exact effect will be denoted by these, combined with the house and sign occupied by the aspected planet, together with the houses ruled by it either in the radix or progress according to whether it is a radical or progressed planet. Thus suppose the Moon is passing through the radical second house in the sign Leo and meets the opposition of the radical Mars, which rules the 5th and 10th houses in the horoscope of birth. If the major influences are not antagonistic there will be heavy expense (☽ ☍ ♂) connected with business and speculation (10th and 5th houses) and probably over children (5th) or a death (8th). These indications may be narrowed down by a study of the transits in force. It should be noted that when the Moon passes from an aspect of a radical body in one month to an aspect of that same body's progressed position a month or two later, a period is formed that is under the continuous influence of that planet.

INFLUENCE OF PLANETS IN DIRECTION. The general influence of the planets in direction is as follows :—

The Sun. Directions involving the Sun affect the father, husband, male relatives, profession, fame, health, life, and constitution. Bad directions will cause trouble in these affairs of the nature indicated by the aspecting planet and the houses and signs concerned, while good aspects will produce good results.

The Moon. The mother, wife, female relatives, health, functional changes, residence, and journeys. Aspects between the Sun and Moon are always critical, especially to women, as they denote changes in the constitution.

Mercury. Commerce, business, journeys, writings, papers, documents, mental affairs, nerves, critiscism, aunts, and young men.

Venus. Pleasures, love affairs, money, ornaments, sisters, and young women. Afflictions to Venus frequently produce bereavement.

Mars. Accidents, fevers, wounds, (especially if in human or airy signs), loss of blood, passionate, impulses, slander, and brothers.

Jupiter. Prosperity, religion, legal and professional matters, legacies, and uncles. Good aspects bring great prosperity and give optimism, and joviality, but afflictions tend to blood disorders through intemperance or excess.

Saturn. Diseases, falls, hurts, deaths, colds, rheumatism and slow lingering ailments, teeth trouble, contact with aged people or old associations, death of elderly people, investments and business. Good aspects cause steadiness, contemplation, and sometimes bring legacies ; bad ones cause melancholy and suspicion.

Uranus. Association with large firms, the Government, corporations, and very aged people, such as grandparents. Electrical, occult, or antiquarian matters excite interest. Unexpected changes occur and there may be some very romantic episodes. If afflicted there are sudden and unexpected crashes. The influence of Uranus is always sudden and peculiar. Under affliction it frequently brings most promising looking opportunities which if taken lead to sudden disaster.

Neptune. Psychic and spiritual interests or experiences. A sea trip or journey to the seaside. Interest in music or speculation, association with hospitals and places of confinement, peculiar and irrational fears or desires. If well aspected it brings idyllic or highly spiritual experiences, but if afflicted leads to drug taking, excessive smoking, or peculiar excesses, and gives great danger of fraud and trickery.

Midheaven. Aspects to the midheaven are similar in nature to those to the Sun and affect profession, honour, business, and the parents.

Ascendant. Aspects to the Ascendant are similar to those to the Moon, affecting the health and causing changes and journeys.

Any of the above matters may be stimulated by direction, the effect being favourable or the reverse, according to the nature of the aspect, the conjunction being good or evil according to the bodies concerned. The particular influence can only be judged by a consideration of the signs and houses involved, and it is therefore of little use to give details of the effect of each planet upon the others. In Mutual Directions the matters pertaining to each planet are affected, but in lunar aspects the chief effect comes from the planet aspected by the Moon and the houses and signs containing it and ruled by it, as the Moon is this case acts in a negative manner and excites the influence of the other body. It should be remembered that directions not only produce events but also bring into the life people of the types ruled by the bodies forming the aspects, and who answer in personal appearance or character to the planets, signs and aspects that are being stimulated. The conjunction and parallel in particular always introduce the native to new people or surroundings.

TRANSITS. A transit over a point affected by direction will precipitate the effect, but to be strongly operative the transit must be of the same nature as the direction, and if it is of an opposite nature its power will be held in check. Transits are subsidiary to directions except in the case of a transiting planet that is stationary upon a radical or progressed body, as this has the power of a direction. A strong conjunction or opposition of two transiting bodies on a sensitive part of the map is always important. The power of transits should not be over-exaggerated and their effect should always be interpreted in the light of the directions in force, but they are of extreme use in marking the exact date when a given direction is most likely to operate.

NEW MOONS. Particular notice should be taken of New Moons, especially when no lunar aspects are in force. The house and sign of the radical map in which a New Moon falls will always be affected, and the nature of the effects may be judged by the aspects made by the New Moon to the radical planets and also by the aspects in the New Moon map considered by itself and in relation to the radical map. The relation to the progressed map is also of some importance but its influence is not so marked as a rule unless there are few aspects to radical planets and a great number to progressed ones. The effects of a New Moon are in force for one month, but are modified by the quarters and full Moon which have a secondary influence.

ECLIPSES. An eclipse falling on any planet in the map is of great importance and is usually adverse, as it cuts off the things signified by that body in the radical map. Unlike an ordinary new or full Moon an eclipse lasts much longer than a month and its influence is often not felt for a long time. The effects of an eclipse of the Sun are said to last for as many years as the eclipse is hours in duration, and those of the Moon for as many months as the lunar eclipse is hours in duration. During these periods the eclipse effects will be felt whenever stimulated by directions or transits, and the most marked effect will always occur when a planet is in transit over the eclipse point, the nature of the effect being shown by the nature of the transiting body, Mars causing cuts and burns, Saturn falls and deaths, and so on. The affairs of the house in which the eclipse falls in the radical map will also be disturbed. Although usually adverse an eclipse may sometimes produce ultimate good, and in the case of an eclipse falling on Jupiter, and to a lesser extent when on Venus the immediate result is unpleasant but the final result is advantageous. Eclipses are of extreme importance and should always be most carefully studied. The most dangerous are those that fall upon the Sun, Moon or Ascendant, as they usually disturb the health and frequently denote death when the directions are sufficiently severe

CHAPTER III

PRIMARY DIRECTIONS.

Primary directions are formed by the rotation of the earth alone, and ignore the progression of the planets in their orbits. By the earth's rotation a planet is carried up to an angle or to the place or aspect of another planet which is supposed to remain fixed and the time at which an event so symbolised will happen is represented by the "arc of direction" or the number of degrees of right or oblique ascension through which the moving body has to pass.

Primary directions are either *mundane* or *zodiacal*. The former are computed with reference to the mundane positions of the planets in the houses, and the latter are concerned with the zodiacal degrees occupied by the planets irrespective of their house positions. In the mundane system a direction is termed *direct* if the motion of the moving body is clockwise, and *converse* if it is anti-clockwise, while in the zodiacal system a direct direction is formed by motion in the order of the signs (i.e. anticlockwise) and a converse one by motion against the order of the signs (i.e. clockwise). As before it is usual to write the moving body first and to state after the aspect whether it is mundane or zodiacal and direct or converse.

It is not possible within the limits of a general

text book to treat the subject of primary direct-ions so fully as could be desired, but their great importance renders their inclusion neces-sarry to any complete outline of astrological practice, and it will therefore be possible only to give the full rules, lengthy examples being necessarily omitted.

The object of primary directing is to obtain the arc of direction which is finally converted into time by a simple proportion. It should, however, be understood at the outset that the system requires that the time of birth be known to great accuracy, for an error of 4 minutes in the birth time throws a direction one year wrong in its date of operation, and therefore unless the birth time is exactly known, or can be found by rectification, it is useless to compute primary directions.

The Sun, Moon, Ascendant, Midheaven, and Fortuna are the bodies to which direction is made and are termed Significators, the other planets being called Promittors. It is usual to direct promittors to significators and vice-versa, but it is not generally held to be legitimate to direct the promittors among themselves, or in other words directions corresponding to the Mutual Directions of the Secondary system are not usually computed as it is considered that all events are indicated by directions between promittors and significators.

In order to facilitate calculation it is neces-sary first of all to prepare a "Speculum" or table showing the Right Ascension, Meridian Distance, Semi-arc, and Cuspal Distance of each of the planets. It is necessary also that the latitudes of the planets should be known and these may be obtained direct from the Ephemeris. The following are the elements included in the speculum:—

Right Ascension. (R. A.) is the distance of the planet or point from ♈ 0° measured along the equator. *Meridian Distance* (M. D.) is the distance of the planet in degrees of R. A. from the M.C. or I.C. and is called upper and lower M. D. respectively. The *Semi-arc* (S.A.) is half the time the planet remains above or below the horizon expressed in degrees and minutes of space, the former being called the diurnal S.A. and the latter the nocturnal S. A. One third of its S. A. is the extent of a house for the planet concerned. The *Horizontal Distance* (H.D.) is the distance of the planet from the eastern or western horizon, and the *Cuspal Distance* (C.D.) is the distance of the planet from the cusp of a house measured in accordance with its S.A.

For the purposes of calculation it is customary to use Ternary Proportional Logarithms, a table of which will be found on pp. 398—413 of Chambers' Mathematical Tables. This table should be altered so that the words "1 degree or hour" and "2 degrees or hours" at the head of the tables read 60° and 120° respectively; the minutes heading each column should be changed to degrees, and the seconds on the left should be changed to minutes.

The following formulae are necessary :—

1. *To convert the longitude of the Sun or of a zodiacal degree into R. A.*

Log. cos. obliquity of ecliptic (23° 27′) + log. tan. long. from ♈ or ♎ (or log. cotan long. from ♋ or ♑) = log. tan. R. A. from ♈ or ♎ (or log. cotan R. A. from ♋ or ♑.). If in ♈, ♉, or ♊ the answer is the required R. A. ; if in ♋, ♌, ♍ add 90°; if in ♎, ♏, ♐ add 180°; and if in ♑, ♒, ♓ add 270°.

2. *To convert the long. of the Moon and planets into R. A.*

Log. cos. declination (*arithm. comp.*) + log. cos. latitude of planet + log. cos. long. from ♈ or ♎ (or log. sine long. from ♋ or ♑) = log. cos. R.A. from ♈ or ♎ (or log. sine R.A. from ♋ or ♑).

3. *Given long., to find the declination of the Sun or of a zodiacal degree.*

Log. sine obliquity of ecliptic (23° 27′) + log. sine long. from ♈ or ♎ (or log. cos. long. from ♋ or ♑) = log. sine declination.

4. *Given declination, to find the long. of the Sun or of a zodiacal degree.*

Log. sine declination — log. sine obliquity of ecliptic = log. sine long. from ♈ or ♎ (or log. cos. long. from ♋ or ♑).

5. *To find Meridian Distance* subtract the R.A. of the planet from the R. A. of the M. C. or I. C. whichever may be nearer, if it is west of the M. C. or east of the I. C. If it is east of the M. C. or west of the I. C. subtract the R. A. of the nearer Meridian from the R.A. of the planet.

6. *To find Ascensional Difference* (A. D.) Log. tan. declination + log. tan. latitude of birthplace = log. sine A. D.

7. *To find Oblique Ascension.* (O. A.) With north declination, R. A. — A. D. = O. A. With south declination, R. A + A D. = O. A. (For places in south latitudes reverse these rules).

8. *To find Semi-arc.*

For diurnal S. A. with N. declination, 90 + A.D.

,, ,, ,, ,, ,, S. ,, 90 — ,, ,,

,, nocturnal ,, ,, N. ,, 90 — ,, ,,

,, ,, ,, ,, ,, S. ,, 90 + ,, ,,

(Reverse the rules for southern latitudes).

9. *To find Horizontal Distance.* Subtract the M.D. of the planet from its S. A.

10. *To find Cuspal Distance.* In the following rules use lower M. D. and nocturnal S. A. for a planet in houses 1 to 6 inclusive, and upper M. D. and diurnal S. A. for one in houses 7 to 12 inclusive.

If in houses 1 or 7	S.A.—M.D.	is the distance	below 1 or above 7
„ „ „ „ „	M.D.—⅔S.A.	„ „ „	above 2 „ below 8
„ „ „ 2 „ 8	⅔S.A.—M.D.	„ „ „	below 2 „ above 8
„ „ „ „ „	M.D.—⅓S.A.	„ „ „	above 3 „ below 9
„ „ „ 3 „ 9	⅓S.A.—M.D.	„ „ „	below 3 „ above 9
„ „· „ „ „	M.D.	„ „ „	E. of 4 „ W. of 10
„ „ „ 4 „ 10	M.D.	„ „ „	W. of 4 „ E. of 10
„ „ „ „ „	⅓S.A.—M.D.	„ „ „	below 5 „ above 11
„ „ „ 5 „ 11	M.D.—⅓S.A.	„ „ „	above 5 „ below 11
„ „ „ „ „	⅔S.A.—M.D.	„ „ „	below 6 „ above 12
„ „ „ 6 „ 12	M.D.—⅔S.A.	„ „ „	above 6 „ below 12
„ „ „ „ „	S.A.—M.D.	„ „ „	below 7 „ above 1

The preliminary step is to compute the speculum and for practical work it will be found convenient to include the following columns. 1. Lat. 2 Dec. 3 R.A. 4. M.D. and its ternary prop. log. 5. H.D. and its log 6. both S.A.'s and their logs. 7. one third of both S.A.'s. 8. both C.D.'s and their logs. 9. Constant log. The constant log. is found by adding the arithmetical complement of the ternary prop. log. of the S.A. to the ternary prop. log. of the nearest C.D. The S.A. used should be diurnal if the planet is above the horizon and nocturnal if it is below. The arithmetical complement of a log. is of frequent use and is found by subtracting the log. from 10.00000. The quickest way to do this is to write down the numbers necessary to make each figure of the log. add up to 9 working

from left to right, and making the last right
hand figure up to 10. Thus the arithm. comp.
of 0.32568 would be 9.67432.

When it is desired to calculate the mundane
directions of Fortuna that point must be computed in a special way, and it is not possible to
use its position in the zodiac as usually determined. According to the method of Negusantius
the *mundane* position of ⊕ is to be found as
follows :— Add the R.A. of the ☽ to the O.A.
of the Asc., and from the sum subtract the O.A.
of the ☉, adding or subtracting 360° if the
subtraction requires this or the sum exceeds
that amount. The result is the R.A. of ⊕. Its
declination is the same as that of the ☽ and its
S.A. is also the same as that of the ☽ if they
are both on the same side of the horizon, but if
one be above and the other below it is found
by subtracting the S.A. of the ☽ from 180°.

A. Mundane Directions to Angles. A
planet on the cusp of the Asc. is in mundane
square to the M.C., one on the cusp of the
12th is in mundane sextile to the M.C. and
semi-sextile to the Asc. and so on.

(*a*) *Direct Directions*. The C. D. of a planet
measured from the cusp to which it will next
come if moving in a clockwise direction gives the
first arc of direction. Thus a planet 9° 30'
above the 8th cusp will be ⚹ M.C. and ⚻ Asc.
after moving 9° 30', and this is therefore the arc
of direction. To this keep adding one third of
the planet's S.A. to bring it to the cusp of
successive houses, noting the arc of direction
in each case. The ∠ and ⚼ are formed in the
middle of houses and one sixth the S.A. must be
added to obtain these. While the planet is above

the horizon the diurnal S.A. must be used and while below the nocturnal S.A. If it passes across the horizon the S.A. must be changed.

(b) *Converse Directions*. The method of procedure is identical with the exception that the first arc of direction is the distance of the planet from the cusp to which it would next come if moving in an anti-clockwise manner. Successive thirds of the appropriate S.A. are then added as before.

B. MUNDANE DIRECTIONS BETWEEN SUN, MOON AND PLANETS. One body is considered to be fixed and the other to be brought up or down to its conjunction or aspect by the rotation of the earth. *Rule:— As the S.A. of the fixed body is to its C.D. so is the S.A. of the moving body to its second distance from that cusp from which the aspect is formed*. The correct S.A. belonging to each body should be used. If the moving body crosses the cusp to form the aspect the sum of its first and second C.D.'s is the arc of direction, but if it remains on the same side of the cusp the difference of the distances is the arc of direction. Further directions are found by adding one third of the S.A. of the moving body (or one sixth for ∠ and ⬓) to the first arc of direction. If the moving body crosses the horizon the above proportion must be calculated again using the opposite S.A. of the moving body. Suppose ♃ is 3° above the cusp of the 2nd and the ☉ is 4° above the cusp of the 6th. The ☉ will form the trine of ♃ when it is about 3° below the cusp of the 6th measured in proportion of its S.A. Then the first arc of direction will be the Sun's distance above the 6th plus its second distance below as it has to cross the

PRIMARY DIRECTIONS

cusp. Adding one third of its nocturnal S.A. brings it to □ ♃, another third gives ⚹ ♃, another sixth gives ∠ ♃, another sixth gives ⊻ ♃, and another third brings it to ☌ ♃. The converse series begins with a proportion to find the Sun's second distance below the 7th. Then a further proportion is necessary using the diurnal S.A. to find its distance below the 8th. In a case like this it is more convenient to use the C.D. of ♃ below the 1st and then to find the proportional distance of the ☉ above the 7th which can then be added direct to the Sun's H.D. to obtain the arc of direction. In working out proportion sums like the above find the arithm. comp. of the log. of the first term and add to it the logs. of the second and third terms. The sum is the log. of the answer.

C. MUNDANE PARALLELS. These are formed when two bodies are at equal distances from the Meridian measured in proportion to their S.A.'s Both bodies may be on the same side of the Meridian or on opposite sides. *Rule:*— As the S.A. of the fixed body is to its M.D. so is the S.A. of the moving body to its second distance from the Meridian on which the parallel is formed. The arc of direction is the difference between the first and second distances if the body remains on the same side of the Meridian, and the sum of these distances if it crosses.

D. RAPT. PARALLELS. In this case both bodies are considered to move until they occupy proportional distances from either the Meridian or horizon. One of the bodies will be approaching the Meridian or horizon and the other receding from it, and it is the applying body that is directed. The S.A.'s employed are those proper

to the bodies when the direction is complete
and the M.D.'s or H.D.'s should both be measured
from the same Meridian or horizon. *Rule:*— As
half the sum of the S.A.'s of the two bodies is
to half the sum of the M.D.'s (or H.D.'s) so is
the S.A. of the body applying to its distance
from that Meridian (or horizon) when the aspect
is complete.

E. ZODIACAL DIRECTIONS TO THE M.C. Zodiacal
directions are concerned only with the zodiacal
degrees occupied by the planets or in which
their aspects fall. In directions to the M.C. calculate
the R.A. of the degree and minute in which the
conjunction or aspect falls and find the difference
between it and the R.A. of the M.C. Suppose
the M.C. is ♊ 5, and the ☉ ♋ 7. When the M.C.
comes to ♊ 7 it will form the direction M.C.
⊻ ☉, zod. dir. To compute this find the R.A.
of ♊ 7 and subtract the R.A. M.C. The answer
will be the arc of direction. The next aspect formed will be M.C. ☌ ☉, to calculate which the
R.A. M.C. must be subtracted from the R.A.
of ♋ 7. In zodiacal directions every aspect needs
a separate calculation and as the directions are
concerned only with the *longitude* of a body the
quantities given in the speculum must not be used

Zodiacal Parallels to the M.C. These are formed
when the M.C. arrives at a degree having the
same declination as one of the planets in the
horoscope. Find the longs. of the zodiacal degrees to which the given planet's declination
corresponds by means of formula 4. Then find
the R.A. of this degree and take the difference
between this and the R.A. M.C. as the arc of
direction.

F. ZODIACAL DIRECTIONS TO THE ASCENDANT.

PRIMARY DIRECTIONS

The Asc. is directed by oblique ascension. The O.A. of the Asc. is found by adding 90° to the R.A. of the M.C. To direct the Asc. find the R.A., Dec., A.D. and finally the O.A. of the degree and minute in which the aspects falls. The difference between this and the O.A. of the Asc. is the arc of direction.

Zodiacal parallels to the Asc. Convert the dec. of the body whose parallel is required into long. Find the O.A. of this long. and take the difference between it and the O.A. of the Asc. as the arc of direction.

G. ZODIACAL DIRECTIONS BETWEEN SUN, MOON, AND PLANETS. These are formed by one body passing up or down to a zodiacal degree to form the aspect or conjunction of another body. Either the moving body or the fixed point will occupy the foremost position in a clockwise direction and whichever is the further advanced in this way is called the *preceding* body or point, the other being the *succeeding* one. The preceding body or point is always further back in the zodiac than the succeeding one, but further advanced if both are thought of as moving in a clockwise direction. The rule for both direct and converse directions is:— As the S.A. of the preceding body or point is to its M.D. so is the S.A. of the succeeding body or point to its second distance from the Meridian. If the succeeding body crosses the Meridian the sum of its first and second distances is the arc of direction, but if it remains on the same side the difference of the distances is the required arc. Use that S.A. and M.D. which belong to the preceding body or point and if they are diurnal then all must be diurnal.

In all cases one of the two factors is a body and the other a point, or in other words a body is always directed to a longitude which may be the actual longitude occupied by a planet or one in exact aspect to it. In computing the direction the S.A. and M.D. of the *point* must be calculated but those of the *body* may be taken from the speculum.

Zodiacal Parallels are to be treated in a similar manner, the longitude corresponding to the planets' declination being computed and used as the point to which direction is made.

This completes all the classes of directions that can be formed. It is a tedious process to compute all the arcs for a life time but it is worth the trouble and it will be found easier to compute a long series than to select only those due to operate in any one year.

Having a list of all the arcs of direction arrange them in numerical order and at the side write the date to which each arc corresponds. For this purpose it is necessary to convert the arc of direction into time, and the most usual and generally satisfactory method is that is Ptolemy namely 1° is equivalent to one year of life and 5' to one month. Thus an arc of direction of 35° 25' will operate at the age of 35 years 5 months.

Certain other measures of time have also been suggested of which the following are the most important :—

Naibod's Method. The Sun's mean daily motion (59' 8") represents one year of life. In other words each degree of R.A. measures 1 year 5 days 8 hours, and each minute 6 days 4 hours.

Simmonite's Method. The Sun's actual daily motion after birth represents one year of life.

PRIMARY DIRECTIONS

In other words the increase in the Sun's R.A. from noon on the day of birth to noon on the next day is the measure for the first year ; that from noon on the first day after birth to noon on the second is the measure for the second year and so on. A variety of this method is to employ the Sun's actual daily motion in R.A. on the day of birth as a constant measure for the whole of life.

Placidus' Method. Add the arc of direction to the Sun's R.A. The direction will operate when the Sun in its daily motion after birth attains this R.A., the time being measured at the rate of 1 day to a year, and 2 hours to a month.

Each of these methods has its advocates, but the simple Ptolemaic measure of $1° = 1$ year is that in greatest favour and the student would do well to follow it.

The interpretation of primary directions is similar to that of secondaries with the exception that lunar aspects are of much longer duration and importance. Note the planets, signs, and aspects involved and interpret accordingly having regard to the houses occupied and ruled and remembering also that the house into which the moving body has passed is likewise of influence.

CHAPTER IV

MINOR METHODS OF DIRECTING

Apart from the two main systems already described there are a number of minor methods of directing, all of which give more or less good results. The multiplicity of systems that have been advocated tends rather to embarrass the student, especially if he begins to apply them all, but it is at least as well for him to know of their existence and something of the principles upon which they rest in order that he may form his own opinion as to their merits.

In general the Primary system is the most reliable, but the complicated and tedious nature of its practice and the necessity for absolutely reliable birth data render it unsuitable in the majority of cases. Next to that in general utility and reliability comes the Secondary system and the greater number of astrologers use no other. Some, however, also employ converse secondary directions and the Solar Revolution, but beyond that the other methods herein explained are practically never used. With this brief apology we may now turn to a rapid survey of the most important minor systems that have been put forward.

1. CONVERSE SECONDARY DIRECTIONS. These are frequently termed "pre-natal" directions since they are all formed in the heavens before birth.

MINOR METHODS OF DIRECTING

The process of calculation is exactly the same as that used in the ordinary secondary system except that the number of days corresponding to the native's age in years is counted *backwards* from birth, 30 days before birth representing the events of the 30th year of life. The horoscope and the Solar and Mutual aspects are calculated as usual and the Moon's daily motion is divided by 12 to obtain its monthly position, the only difference being that everything is passing backwards and the Moon moves about 1° backwards each month instead of forwards. This is probably the most important of the minor methods and forms a useful adjunct to the ordinary Secondary system.

2. Solar Revolution. This is a map erected each year for the moment the Sun returns to the exact degree, minute, and second that it occupied at birth. Unlike the Secondary system the map must be erected for the actual year for which a forecast is required. The horoscope so obtained is judged partly as a separate map but chiefly with reference to the radical horoscope. Thus the ruler of the radical Asc. in the revolutional 6th is an indication of ill-health, and so on. The position of planets in the revolution in aspect to, or on the places of planets at birth is important, and these act almost like directions. The times of happenings denoted in the revolution are indicated by transits over the revolutional positions during the year.

3. Precessional Solar Revolution. It has been suggested that as the whole zodiac is moving backwards owing to the precession of the equinoxes, the ordinary Solar Revolution does not represent the return of the Sun to its real birth

position. The amount of precession is 50".25 per annum, and before erecting the precessional revolution this amount should be added to the radical longitude of the Sun for each year of life, the Solar Revolution being calculated in the ordinary way but using this revised longitude as that which must be occupied by the revolutional Sun.

4. PROGRESSIVE SOLAR REVOLUTION. This is equivalent to counting a year and a day for each year of life. Add to the date of birth as many days as the native is years of age. Use the position of the Sun on that date but erect the rest of the map in the usual way for the current year for which the revolution is required.

5. SYNODICAL LUNATIONS. A Synodical Lunation is the return of the progressed Moon to the same distance from the progressed Sun as the radical Moon was from the radical Sun. Each Synodical Lunation, which occurs once every $29\frac{1}{2}$ days or thereabouts, measures to one year of life, and a map should be erected for the moment when the relationship of the luminaries to each other is exactly the same as at birth. The first return of the luminaries to their birth relationship will take place in the month after birth, and will measure from age 1 to age 2, and so on. Synodical lunations are subsidiary to directions and are to be interpreted in the same way as a Solar Revolution.

6. CURRENT SYNODICAL LUNATIONS. These are maps erected for any given month in the current year when the luminaries are in the same relationship as at birth. Their rule is limited to the space of one month.

7. LUNAR REVOLUTION. This is exactly ana-

logous to the Solar Revolution and is a map erected for each month of the current year and for the moment when the Moon returns to its exact longitude at birth. It rules for one month.

8. DIURNAL HOROSCOPE. This is a map erected for the time of birth on each day in the current year and rules for one day only. Its chief uses are for finding the exact date of operation of an aspect, and for determining good and bad days, those days being bad on which the malefics or their radical places pass across the angles of the diurnal horoscope.

9. PERIODIC DIRECTIONS. These are directions formed by the planets in their motion through the signs in accordance with their Kabalistic periods of revolution. These periods are said to be as follows :— ☉ 19 years, ☽ 4 years, ☿ 10 years, ♀ 8 years, ♂ 15 years, ♃ 12 years, and ♄ 30 years, and to these might, perhaps, be added ♅ 84 years and ♆ 165 years. In this system of directing each planet is said to pass through the 12 signs once in its period, so that ♂, for example, will take 15 years to come back to its birth position, and will, therefore, move at the rate of 24° a year and 2° a month. A table should be formed showing the place of each planet each year, and directions will be formed by the aspects made by the progressed planets to radical bodies and among themselves in their passage through the various houses of the birth map.

10. PROFECTIONAL DIRECTIONS. These are of three kinds, Annual, Monthly, and Diurnal, and are, perhaps, more Kabalistic than purely astrological. In annual profections the Ascendant advances one complete sign in one year, and the

other signs are arranged in their normal order round the cusps of the other houses. Thus if the birth Ascendant is ♊, that for the next year of life will be ♋, and so on, the birth Ascendant returning every 12th year. The planets remain fixed in their birth positions and judgment is drawn from their passage over or aspects to the angles, the exact time of such aspects being easily determined by proportion. A similar process is also to be applied to the M.C., ☉, ☽, and ⊕, each of which advances one sign per year.

Monthly profections are formed in a similar manner one sign being added for each month, and in the case of Diurnal Profections one sign is added for every 2 days 8 hours.

II. ALFRIDARIES. An Alfridary is an arrangement by which the life is divided into periods ruled by the planets in a definite order. A number of alfridaries have been put forward, the most famous being that of Ptolemy, in which the ☽ rules from birth to 4 years of age, ☿ from 4 to 14, ♀ to 22, ☉ to 41, ♂ to 56, ♃ to 68, and finally ♄ to 98. It has been said that ordinary directions to a planet act more powerfully in the period of life ruled by it.

CHAPTER V

RECTIFICATION

It has been shown that if a birth time is accurately known it is possible to arrive at a knowledge of the times and natures of events that happen during the course of the life time, and from this it follows that a converse process is possible, namely to determine the time of birth when the dates of a number of happenings are known. This process is termed "rectification" and it may be employed either to find a quite unknown birthtime, or to correct one that is defined as lying between certain limits. In the latter case absolute accuracy of result is easily obtainable, but when the birthtime is not known to within 24 hours the process is usally exceedingly difficult and requires the most expert manipulation.

The first step in any system of rectification is to determine the rising sign, as once that is obtained it is comparatively easy to find the exact degree required. In some cases this may be done from a photograph, and the detailed descriptions given in the chapters on appearance and character will be found of great assistance. It is often impossible, however, to be certain of a result obtained in this way, and in such cases the first step is rectification by Secondary directions, the rules for which are as follows :—

1. Given the date of an important event, count as many days after birth as the native was years old at the time the event happened.

2. Take the position of the progressed Moon on the day so found and see whether during the 24 hours it formed any strong and appropriate aspect to a radical or progressed planet.

3. If an appropriate aspect is seen to have taken place on the progressed day find by means of proportion the time of day in hours and minutes at which it became exact, and write it down in years, months, days, hours, and minutes.

4. Find the native's age at the date of the event in years, months and days and convert it into days, hours and minutes by calling the years, days and taking 2 hours as equivalent to 1 month, and 4 minutes to 1 day. Write the result below that found in 3.

5. Subtract the result of 4 from that of 3 and the answer will be the date and approximate time of birth.

Thus suppose a person was born on 24 July, 1872, and an important event took place on 9 September, 1894. The age on this date would be 22 years, 1 month, 16 days, which is equivalent to 22 days, 3 hours, 4 minutes. The progressed date would be 22 days later than 24th July which measures to 15 August, 1872. Let us suppose that an appropriate aspect was formed by the Moon to a radical or progressed planet at 4.30 p.m. on that date.

		Yrs.	Mths	Days	Hrs.	Mins.
Then :—	Aspect formed	1872	8	15	4	30
	Subtract age			22	3	4
	Birth	1872	7	24	1	26

Birth is therefore indicated as having taken place at about 1.26 p.m. on 24th July.

The result thus obtained should be checked by applying the same method to other important dates in the life. The final result should be correct within about 2 hours, but greater accuracy cannot be obtained in this way owing to the slowness of the Moon's progressed motion. The method serves, however, to narrow down the field of enquiry and to give a choice of 2 or 3 ascending signs.

The next step in the process is to erect a series of maps, (say one for every 15° on the M.C.) between the limits determined upon. Take the list of events and turn the age at each event into degrees and minutes at the rate of 1 year = 1°, and 1 month = 5', and then convert the arcs so obtained into time at the rate of 15° = 1 hour, 1° = 4 mins., 1' = 4 secs. Find from the correct Tables of Houses the Sidereal Time when one of the given degrees is on the M.C., or in other words the Sidereal Time for which one of the trial maps is erected. Add the arc in time to this Sidereal Time and look up the M.C. and Asc. corresponding to the sum in the Tables of Houses. Do this with each of the maps in turn, and notice what planets are brought to the conjunction or aspect of the progressed angles. If any aspects appropriate to events are formed in any of the maps or would be formed in some map intermediate between two of the trial ones, look up the Sidereal Time which gives the exact aspecting degree on the M.C. or Asc. when the proper arc is added and adjust the map accordingly. Check this map by other aspects to angles in a similar manner. The aspects so far examined are direct, and to obtain the converse ones *subtract* the arc in time from the given Sidereal Time and look up the corresponding M.C. and Asc. If the tentative map is correct there should be converse directions also in force.

Being satisfied of the approximate accuracy of the horoscope so obtained, work it out in full detail, calculate the speculum, and then compute accurate Primary directions to angles. If discrepancies exist between the arcs obtained and the true arc of the event adjust the former to the latter and calculate the exact R. A. M. C. so obtained. Slight differences of a few minutes will probably still exist, and the final R. A. M. C. should be taken from the most accurate arc or from the direction likely to operate most exactly to time. Aspects to ☿, ♂, and ♅ are usually well defined and act promptly, whilst those to ♄ are usually too slow and long drawn out to be of use in estimating the time with great exactness.

The only directions that are of much use in rectification are Primary directions to angles and Rapt Parallels, since these depend entirely upon the accuracy of the map, and a mistake of 4 minutes in the time of birth makes an error of 1 year in the time of their operation. Rapt Parallels are of great assistance in arriving at the correct Asc., but directions to angles are handier to use and should be computed first, the former being used to check the final results.

Primary directions among the Sun, Moon, and planets are not of great use as they are not affected to the same extent by errors in the birth time, but there is a method of employing them that is of service when only the approximate time has been ascertained, as for example by the use of Secondary lunar aspects. This method as given by Oxley and Zadkiel, is as follows :—

1. Reduce the Meridian distance of the ☉ or ☽, whichever is directed, into minutes and call it the *first* position. Add to this Meridian distance one degree, reducing it also to minutes and call it the *second* position. Then opposite the second position place the error of the original arc of direction expressed in minutes, multiply them together and call the amount A. Work the same direction with the altered Meridian distance (taking care to adjust the M.D. of the planet employed also), find the error in this arc of direction and place it opposite the first position. Multiply these together and call the amount B.

2. If *both* errors be *greater* or *less* than the arc for the event, find the *difference* between the errors and call this C. Find also the difference between A and B and call this D. Then D divided by C will give the true Meridian distance of the ☉ or ☽ at the moment of birth, and the R.A. of the M. C. should be adjusted accordingly.

3. If one error be *greater* and the other *less* than the arc for the event call the *sum* of the errors C, and the sum of A and B call D. Then D divided by C will give the true Meridian distance as before.

Having obtained the corrected time by this method proceed as before to adjust the map by means of directions to angles and Rapt Parallels.

The final steps in obtaining the exact degree and minute rising at birth may also be performed by means of a process known as the Pre-natal Epoch but this method cannot be treated here as it is far too vast a subject, and an imperfect outline would be worse than useless.

APPENDIX

PLACE	Fast (+) or Slow (—) of Greenwich	Date of Adoption
	h m s	
Low Archipelago	—10 0 0	Recent
Luxembourg	+ 1 0 0	
Madagascar	+ 3 0 0	Recent
Madeira	— 1 0 0	Recent
Malta	+ 1 0 0	——
Marianne Is. Except Guam	+10 0 0	After 1911
Guam	+ 9 30	
Morocco	G.M.T.	Recent
Marquesas	—10 0 0	Recent
Marshall Is.	+11 0 0	Recent
Martinique	— 4 0 0	Recent
Mauritius	+ 4 0 0	Recent
Mexico L. T. of Mexico City	— 6 36 37	——
Monaco	G.M.T.	
New Caledonia	+11 0 0	Recent
Newfoundland L. T. of St. Johns ..	— 3 30 44	
New Guinea	+10 0 0	After 1911
New Zealand	+11 30 0	
Nigaragua L. T. of Managua	— 5 45 10	
Norway	+ 1 0 0	1 Jan. 1895
Panama L. T. of Colon	— 5 19 39	
Canal Zone	— 5 0 0	After 1911
Persia L.T. of Teheran (Telegraph purposes)	+ 3 25 40	
Peru	— 5 0 0	Recent
Pescadores Is.	+ 8 0 0	1 Jan. 1896
Phillippine Is.	+ 8 0 0	11 May 1899
Poland	+ 2 0 0	16 Sept 1919
Porto Rico	— 4 0 0	——
Portugal	G.M.T.	After 1911
Princes Is.	G.M.T.	Recent
Reunion Is.	+ 4 0 0	Recent
Roumania	+ 2 0 0	Recent
Russia L.T. Petrograd for Telegraph & Railways	+ 2 1 19	
L. T. of place for general purposes		
St. Lucia	— 4 0 0	Recent
St. Pierre	— 4 0 0	Recent
St. Thomas Is.	G.M.T.	Recent

4. THE PRESENT USE OF STANDARD TIME.

PLACE	Fast (+) or Slow (—) of Greenwich	Date of Adoption
	h m s	
Aden	+ 3 0 0	Recent
Africa Somaliland	+ 3 0 0	Recent
British East	+ 2 30 0	Recent
Portuguese East	+ 2 0 0	1 March 1903
Union of South. Natal	+ 2 0 0	1 Sept. 1895
Orange River Colony, Transvaal	+ 2 0 0	1 Oct. 1903
Rhodesia, Cape Colony	+ 2 0 0	1903
French Equatorial, Belgian Congo, Cameroons, Nigeria, Portuguese West Africa, South West Africa	+ 1 0 0	Recent
Gold Coast, Ivory Coast, Gambia, Dahomey	G.M.T.	Recent
Liberia, Senegal, Sierra Leone ..	— 1 0 0	——
Algeria	G.M.T.	11 March 1911
America, United States of		
Maine to S.Carolina (67½° — 82½°)	— 5 0 0	18 Nov. 1883
Dakota and Michigan to Texas and Florida (82½° — 97½°)	— 6 0 0	18 Nov. 1883
Montana to Arizona and New Mexico (97½° — 112½°)	— 7 0 0	18 Nov. 1883
Pacific Coast States and Nevada (112½° — W. coast)	— 8 0 0	18 Nov. 1883
Alaska	— 9 0 0	18 Nov. 1883
Argentine Republic	— 4 0 0	1 May 1920
Austral Archipelago	—10 0 0	
Australia West	+ 8 0 0	1 Feb. 1985
South	+ 9 30 0	1 Feb. 1895
Victoria, New. S. Wales	+10 0 0	1 Feb. 1895
Queensland	+10 0 0	1 June 1895
Austria-Hungary	+ 1 0 0	1 Oct. 1891
Azores	— 2 0 0	Recent
Bahama Is.	— 5 0 0	Recent
Belgium	G.M.T.	May 1892

PLACE	Fast (+) or Slow (—) of Greenwich	Date of Adoption
	h m s	
BISMARCK ARCHIPELAGO	+10 0 0	Recent (1911 or after)
BORNEO	+ 8 0 0	Oct. 1904
BOSNIA	+ 1 0 0	Recent
BRAZIL West	— 5 0 0	———
Central	— 4 0 0	———
East	— 3 0 0	———
BULGARIA	+ 2 0 0	Recent
CALIFORNIA	— 8 0 0	———
CANADA British Columbia	— 8 0 0	18 Nov. 1883
Mountain Zones, Alberta, Assiniboia Athabasca	— 7 0 0	18 Nov. 1883
Central Zones, Keewatin, Manitoba, Ontario (W of 82½°)	— 6 0 0	18 Nov. 1883
Quebec, (W), New Brunswick (W), Ontario (E of 82½°)	— 5 0 0	18 Nov. 1883
New Brunswick (E), Quebec (E), Nova Scotia, Prince Edward Is.	— 4 0 0	18 Nov. 1883
CAPE VERDE IS.	— 2 0 0	Recent
CAROLINE IS. Yap.	+ 9 0 0	Recent
West of 154°	+10 0 0	After 1911
East of 154°	+11 0 0	Recent
CEYLON	+ 5 30 0	Recent
CHAGOS ARCHIPELAGO	+ 5 0 0	Recent
CHILE, Except Valparaiso, L.T. of Santiago	— 4 42 46	———
Valparaiso L. T.	— 4 46 34	———
(Chile is now said to have adopted the Standard of—4ʰ as from 1 Sept. 1918		
CHINA, East Coast, Macao	+ 8 0 0	Jan. 1903
Hong Kong	+ 8 0 0	Oct. 1904
Port Arthur	+ 8 0 0	
French Indo-China	+ 7 0 0	Recent
COLOMBIA, L. T. of Bogotá	— 4 56 54	———
COSTA RICA L. T. of San Jose	— 5 36 17	———
CUBA L. T. of Havana	— 5 29 26	———
CYPRUS	+ 2 0 0	Recent
CZECHO-SLOVAKIA	+ 1 0 0	Recent
DENMARK	+ 1 0 0	1 Jan. 1894

PLACE	Fast (+) or Slow (—) of Greenwich	Date of Adoption
	h m s	
ECUADOR L. T. of Quito	— 5 14 7	———
EGYPT	+ 2 0 0	1 Oct. 1900
ENGLAND	G.M.T.	Legalised 1880
FALKLAND Is. L. T. of Port Stanley ..	— 3 51 26	
FARÖE Is.	G.M.T.	Recent
FEDERATED MALAY STATES	+ 7 0 0	Recent
FERNANDO Is.	— 2 0 0	Recent
FIJI Is.	+12 0 0	Recent
FINLAND	+ 2 0 0	1 May 1921
FORMOSA	+ 8 0 0	1 Jan. 189
FRANCE	G.M.T.	11 Mar. 191
GERMANY	+ 1 0 0	1 Apr. 18
GIBRALTAR	G.M.T.	
GREECE (L.T. Athens, + 1 34 53 adopted) 14[9] 1895 & in use until recently)..	+ 2 0 0	28 July 1
GRENADA	— 4 0 0	Recent
GUADELOUPE	— 4 0 0	Recent
GUIANA, French	— 4 0 0	1 July 1
HOLLAND Railway & Telegraph	G.M.T.	1 May 1
L. T. Amsterdam	+ 0 19 32	
HONDURAS	— 6 0 0	———
ICELAND	— 1 0 0	Rece
INDIA Except Calcutta and Portuguese India	+ 5 30 0	1 Jan.
Calcutta L. T.	+ 5 53 21	
Portuguese India	+ 5 0 0	
Burma	+ 6 30 0	———
IRELAND	G.M.T.	1 Oct.
From 1880 to 1916 L. T. of Dublin —0.25.21		
ITALY	+ 1 0 0	1 No
JAMAICA	— 5 0 0	R
JAPAN	+ 9 0 0	1 Ja
JAVA L. T. of Batavia	+ 7 7 14	
KOREA	+ 9 0 0	1 D
LABUAN	+ 8 0 0	C
LEEWARD Is.	— 4 0 0	-
LIBYA	+ 1 0 0	

APPENDIX

PLACE	Fast (+) or Slow (—) of Greenwich	Date of Adoption
	h m s	
St. Vincent	— 4 0 0	Recent
Salvador L. T. of San Salvador	— 5 56 32	
Samoa	+12 0 0	After 1911
Sandwich Is.	—10 30 0	Recent
Scotland	G.M.T.	Legalised 1880
Serbia	+ 1 0 0	1 Oct. 1891
Seychelles Is.	+ 4 0 0	June 1906
Siam	+ 7 0 0	1 Apr. 1920
Singapore	+ 7 0 0	Recent
Society Is.	—10 0 0	Recent
Spain	G.M.T.	1 Jan. 1901
Straits Settlements	+ 7 0 0	Recent
Sumatra L. T. of Padang	+ 6 41 21	
Sweden	+ 1 0 0	
Switzerland	+ 1 0 0	1 June 1894
Tasmania........................	+10 0 0	
Timor, Portuguese	+ 8 0 0	Recent
Tobago	— 4 0 0	Recent
Trinidad	— 4 0 0	Recent
Trinidad Is. (Brazil)	— 2 0 0	Recent
Tunis	+ 1 0 0	? 1911
Turkey	+ 2 0 0	
Uruguay	— 4 0 0	1 May 1920
Venezuela	— 4 30 0	Recent
Wales	G.M.T.	Legalised 1880
Yukon	— 9 0 0	20 Aug. 1900

NOTE

Early in 1919 the Britsh Admiralty introduced a series of zone or standard times that are now generally adopted. In the above list the word "Recent" implies that the standard there given has been in use only since about 1918 or 1919, while the words "After 1911" indicate that in that year standard time had been proposed, but had not yet been adopted. Prior to the adoption of standard time it was customary for each country to use the local mean time of its capital.

APPENDIX

B. SUMMER TIME

ENGLAND. British Summer Time (abbreviated B.S.T.)

1916	21 May	2 a.m. G.M.T.	to	1 Oct.	3 a.m. B.S.T.
1917	8 April	....	to	17 Sept.	....
1918	24 March	....	to	30 Sept.	....
1919	30 March	....	to	29 Sept.	....
1920	28 March	....	to	25 Oct.	....
1921	3 April	....	to	2 Oct.	....
1922	26 March	....	to	8 Oct.	....

The Summer Time Bill recently passed lays down the following rule for 1923 and subsequent years:—

"The period of Summer Time shall be taken to be the period beginning at two o'clock, Greenwich mean time, in the morning of the day next following the *third Saturday in April*, or, if that day is Easter Day, the day next following the second Saturday in April, and ending at two o'clock, Greenwich mean time, in the morning of the day next following the *third Saturday in September*."

The Bill will not be permanent but will be renewable annually.

FRANCE.

1916	15 June	11 p.m.	to	1 Oct.	1 a.m.
1917	25 March	....	to	7 Oct.	......
1918	9 March	....	to	7 Oct.	......
1919	2 March	....	to	5 Oct.	......
1920	14 Feb.	....	to	23 Oct.	......
1921	14 March	....	to	25 Oct.	12 p.m.
1922	25 March	....	to	7 Oct.	......
1923	26 May				

GERMANY & AUSTRIA-HUNGARY.

1916	1 May		to	30 Sept.	
1917	16 April	2 a.m.	to	17 Sept.	3 a.m.
1918	15 April	....	to	16 Sept.	......

Has not been introduced since.

NORWAY	1916 21 May	11 p.m. to 30 Sept.
SWEDEN	1916 15 May	1 a.m. to 30 Sept.
HOLLAND	1916 1 May	to 30 Sept.
DENMARK	1916 15 May	to 30 Sept.
PORTUGAL	Introduced 17 June, 1916, 11 p.m.
ITALY	1916 4 June to ?
	1917 15 March to 1 Oct. o.o.
GREECE	Introduced 15—28 July, 1916.
RUSSIA	1917 14 July to ?
TANGIER	1918 6 May o.o. to 7 Oct o.o.

APPENDIX

BELGIUM	1920 14—15 March to ?
	1923 21 April to ?
AUSTRALIA	Mainland (including N.S. Wales, Victoria, Queensland, S. & W.
	1917 1 Jan. 2 a.m. to 25 March 2 a.m. Act then repealed.
TASMANIA	1916 1 Oct. 2 a.m. to 1917 25 March 2 a.m.
	1917 28 Oct. . to 1918 3 March .....
	1918 27 Oct. ..... to 1919 2 March ..... Act then repealed.
U.S.A.	Act approved 19 March, 1918.
	1918 31 March 2 a.m. to 27 Oct. 2 a.m.
	1919 30 March ..... to 26 Oct. ...... Act then repealed, but certain towns subsequently used Summer Time.
CANADA	Decided against Summer Time on 27 May, 1919, but certain towns and railways used it.

C. THE CALENDAR
DATES OF ADOPTION OF NEW STYLE

A.D. 1582		Denmark
„	Oct. 15	Italy (parts of), Portugal, Rome, Spain
„	Dec. 20	France, Lorraine
„	Dec. 25	Artois, Brabant, Flanders, Hainault, Holland, Malines
1583—1584		Switzerland (parts of)
1584		Germany (Roman Catholics)
1586		Poland
1587		Hungary
1682	Mar. 1	Strasburg
1699	Nov. 15	Germany (Protestants)
1700	Dec. 12	Friesland, Groningen, Guelderland, Overyssel, Utrecht, Zutphen,
1701	Jan. 12	Basel, Berne, Schaffhausen, Switzerland (Protestants), Zurich
1749 or 1751		Tuscany
1752	Sept. 14	England, all English Colonies, America
1753	Mar. 1	Sweden
1872		Japan
1912		China
1915		Bulgaria
1917		Soviet Russia
1919		Yugo-Slavia and Roumania

APPENDIX

The difference between the Styles is as follows:—

15th Century	9 days		20th Century	13 days	
16th	„	10 „	21st	„	13 „
17th	„	11 „	22nd	„	14 „
18th	„	11 „	23rd	„	15 „
19th	„	12 „	24th	„	16 „

Add   the difference in days to Old Style to obtain New Style
Subtract „   „   „ „ from New Style „ „ Old Style

D. SENSITIVE POINTS

A great deal of interest is now being taken in the so-called "sensitive points", and the student may appreciate a list of them together with the method of computing each. There are two main series but the principles of calculation are similar and the method of calculating one of them (Fortuna) has been described in detail (See p. 33)

SERIES I. THE ARABIC POINTS

1. Part of Fortune, Fortuna or Landmark (⊕) corresponding to ☽
2. Caduceus   or Point of Commerce   „   „ ☿
3. Heart   „   „   „ Love   „   „ ♀
4. Sword   „   „   „ Passion   „   „ ♂
5. Pomegranate   „   „   „ Increase   „   „ ♃
6. Hourglass   „   „   „ Fatality   „   „ ♄
7. Lightning Flash „ „   „ Catastrophe   „   „ ♅
8. Grille or Trident „ „   „ Treachery   „   „ ♇

The position of any of the above points is found by adding the longitude of the planet to which it corresponds to the longitude of the Ascendant, and from the sum subtracting the longitude of the Sun.

It marks the point that would be occupied by the planet if the Sun were exactly rising, and it would probably be more correct to use the longitudes for sunrise.

It has been said that when a planet is retrograde its distance from the Sun should be *subtracted* from the Ascendant instead of being added.

These points respond to aspects and their sign and house positions are of influence. They carry the nature of their corresponding planets and if those are weak the points are also weak.

240

APPENDIX

SERIES II. THE ARABIC PARTS

1. *Part of Life* Asc. + ☽ — New or full moon nearest before birth
2. *Part of Understanding* Asc. + ♂ — ☿
3. *Part of Spirit* Asc. + ☉ — ☽
4. *Part of Fortune* Asc. + ☽ — ☉
5. *Part of Goods* Asc. + cusp of 2nd — lord of 2nd
6. *Part of Brethren* By day :— Asc. + ♃ — ♄
   By night :— Asc. + ♄ — ♃
7. *Part of the Love of Brethren* Asc. + ♄ — ☉
8. *Part of the Father* Asc. + ☉ — ♄
9. *Part of Fortune in Husbandry* Asc. + ♄ — ♀
10. *Part of Inheritances and Possessions* Asc. + ☽ — ♄
11. *Part of Male Children* Asc. + ♃ — ☽
12. *Part of Female Children* Asc. + ♀ — ☽
13. *Part of Plays* Asc. + ♀ — ♂
14. *Part of Sickness* Asc. + ♂ — ♄
15. *Part of Slavery and Bondage* Asc. + ☽ — Dispositor of ☽
16. *Part of Servants* Asc. + ☽ — ☿
17. *Part of Marriage* Asc. + cusp of 7th — ♀
18. *Part of Discord and Controversy* Asc. + ♃ — ♂
19. *Part of Death* Asc. + cusp of 8th — ☽
20. *Part of the Perilous and Most Dangerous Year* Asc. + lord of 8th — ♄
21. *Part of Faith* Asc. + ☿ — ☽
22. *Part of Journeys by Water* Asc. + 15° ♋ — ♄
23. *Part of Travels by Land* Asc. + cusp of 9th — lord of 9th.
24. *Part of the Mother* Asc. + ☽ — ♀ (Not given by ancients)
25. *Part of Honour* (a) Asc. + 19° ♈ — ☉, or according to some
    (b) Asc. + 3° ♉ — ☽
26. *Part of Sudden Advancement* Asc. + ⊕ — ♄ (If ♄ is combust substitute ♃)
27. *Part of Magistery and Possessions* Asc. + ☽ — ♄

APPENDIX

28. *Part. of Merchandise* Asc. + ⊕ — Part of Spirit
29. *Part of Friends* Asc. + ☽ — ♀
30. *Part of Honourable and Illustrious Acquaintance*
    By day :— Asc. + ☉ — ⊕
    By night:— Asc. + ⊕ — ☉
31. *Part of Imprisonment Sorrow, and Captivity* Asc. +
    ⊕ — Part of Spirit
32. *Part of Private Enemies* Asc. + cusp of 12th — lord
    of 12th

These points are to be judged according to their sign
and house positions, and aspects, and their effects in directions should be noted.

Other series of sensitive points may be obtained by taking
the middle distances between any two bodies, and also the
reflection of one body over another, i.e. the distance of
one body from another projected on the other side of the latter.

E. CORRECTION TO BE ADDED TO MEAN TIME TO OBTAIN SIDEREAL TIME.

Hours.	Correction.		Mins.	Cor.	Mins.	Cor.	Secs.	Cor.	Secs.	Cor.
	m	s		s		s		s		s
1	0	9.86	1	0.16	31	5.09	1	0.00	31	0.08
2	0	19.71	2	0.33	32	5.26	2	0.01	32	0.09
3	0	29.57	3	0.49	33	5.42	3	0.01	33	0.09
4	0	39.43	4	0.66	34	5.59	4	0.01	34	0.09
5	0	49.28	5	0.82	35	5.75	5	0.01	35	0.10
6	0	59.14	6	0.99	36	5.92	6	0.02	36	0.10
7	1	9.00	7	1.15	37	6.08	7	0.02	37	0.10
8	1	18.85	8	1.31	38	6.24	8	0.02	38	0.10
9	1	28.71	9	1.48	39	6.41	9	0.03	39	0.11
10	1	38.57	10	1.64	40	6.57	10	0.03	40	0.11
11	1	48.42	11	1.81	41	6.74	11	0.03	41	0.11
12	1	58.28	12	1.97	42	6.90	12	0.03	42	0.12
13	2	8.13	13	2.14	43	7.07	13	0.04	43	0.12
14	2	17.99	14	2.30	44	7.23	14	0.04	44	0.12
15	2	27.85	15	2.46	45	7.39	15	0.04	45	0.12
16	2	37.70	16	2.63	46	7.56	16	0.04	46	0.13
17	2	47.56	17	2.79	47	7.72	17	0.05	47	0.13
18	2	57.42	18	2.96	48	7.89	18	0.05	48	0.13
19	3	7.27	19	3.12	49	8.05	19	0.05	49	0.13
20	3	17.13	20	3.29	50	8.22	20	0.05	50	0.14
21	3	26.99	21	3.45	51	8.38	21	0.06	51	0.14
22	3	36.84	22	3.61	52	8.54	22	0.06	52	0.14
23	3	46.70	23	3.78	53	8.71	23	0.06	53	0.15
24	3	56.56	24	3.94	54	8.87	24	0.07	54	0.15
25	4	6.40	25	4.11	55	9.04	25	0.07	55	0.15
26	4	16.26	26	4.27	56	9.20	26	0.07	56	0.15
27	4	26.13	27	4.44	57	9.37	27	0.07	57	0.16
28	4	36.00	28	4.60	58	9.53	28	0.08	58	0.16
29	4	45.86	29	4.76	59	9.69	29	0.08	59	0.16
30	4	55.71	30	4.93	60	9.86	30	0.08	60	0.16

Index

Index

Index

Index

Index

Index

Index

Index

Index

Geological Curator, Vol. 5, No. 2, 1989 (for 1987), pp. 65-71.
UNCURATED CURATORS. No. 2

Vivian Erwood Robson (1890-1942)
Curator Turned Astrologer
By Hugh S. Torrens

INTRODUCTION

This article was unusually inspired by an article in the daily press, in this case, one in the *Daily Telegraph* for 7 January 1987 entitled 'Towards an Enterprise Culture' by the journalist Paul Johnson. This spoke of the 'spirit of whining mendicancy and parasitism at our British universities', some of which were so bad they should be killed off completely. Johnson felt that the solution for such universities was to expose them to what he called 'the discipline of the market', whereby buyers in that market would now provide the 'educative discipline' and thus decide whether a particular activity or field of research was worthy of that market's support. In short, if people want something researched they will pay for it and if people won't pay for it, directly in the market, then that research should not be supported.

This paper describes the career of a forgotten geological curator, and how his career interacted with the 'discipline of the market' and forced him to abandon the career of geological curator for the new career of journalist, a career shared with Paul Johnson!

ROBSON'S FIRST CAREER AS
A GEOLOGICAL CURATOR

Vivian Erwood Robson was born on 26 May 1890 in Aston, Birmingham, where his father Alfred William Robson was a surgeon, living at 111 Park Road. Aston (C.A. Boardman. pers. comm. 17 July 1981). Some details of medical life in Birming-

253

The Vivian Robson Memorial

ham at the time are provided by one of surgeon Robson's friends, Dr H.W. Pooler (1948), who noted in particular that Robson's family was from Yorkshire (p. 57) and gave other details about Alfred Robson (pp. 54-62).

Robson senior's practice as a surgeon was sufficiently lucrative for Robson junior to be sent to King Edward the Sixth School, Birmingham, in December 1901. His career at the school 'is mainly negative; in that he was not a member of a sports team, not active in the literary society or debating society, and not a prefect' (C.A. Boardman, pers. comm. 17 July 1981). Robson left King Edward's on 2 July 1907.

However, the seeds of his first career as a curator had clearly been sown very early, and at this school. The School Magazine for April 1906 contains a report of its Natural History Society's activities and includes a note that fifteen year old Robson, 'has undertaken the naming and arrangement of the collection of fossils and [that] it is hoped in a short time to have [the School] Museum again in a presentable condition'. Nearly a year later the same source for March 1907 recorded that 'this term V.E. Robson has finished naming the collection of fossils and Mr. Robson has presented the Museum with a handsome catalogue of the fossils of the Museum'. Robson himself later recorded (Bristol City Museum and Art Gallery [BRSMG], Geology File 392) that he was awarded the Walter Myers Prize in Geology and Palaeontology whilst at the school.

After leaving King Edward's, Robson passed to Birmingham University. Unfortunately, no Students Matriculation Registers for this period survive and the University records state only that he took the degree of B.Sc. (unclassified) in June 1913 (B.S. Benedikz, pers. comm. 18 June 1981). But other records (Anon. 1907, p. 27) show that he had arrived at the University in October 1907, when he was recorded as Member 73 of the British Federated Society of Mining Students (Birmingham University Society), living at home at 111 Park Road, Aston.

Charles Lapworth (1842-1920), who was now Robson's Head of Department, later provided further details of Robson's career as a student of geology in a testimonial, written after Robson had graduated (Fig. 1; BRSMG Geology File 392).

At some stage, whilst still an undergraduate, Robson had come into contact with the English ammonite worker Sydney Savory Buckman (1860-1929). This seems to have been after the publication of Part viii of Volume 1 of Buckman's major work, *Yorkshire Type Ammonites*, after 15 June 1912. Buckman's personal copy of this (in the Buckman family's possession) contains his later manuscript annotation that Robson had subsequently reported to Buckman the existence of another copy of the rare work by Martin Simpson *A Monograph of the Ammonites of the Yorkshire Lias* (1843), and which Buckman had in course of revision. This new copy was to be found in the library of the British Museum (Natural history) (Buckman 1909-1930. vol. 1, pt. viii, E).

Other evidence of Robson's involvement with Buckman comes from Vol. 2 of the same work: on p. D of Part xviii (1919) Buckman noted that 'Mr. V.E. Robson has given very considerable assistance in the preparation of the MS and in many other ways'. The Robsons also helped Buckman with material that they had collected, and either Vivian or his father must be the 'Dr Robson of Birmingham' who obtained specimens of the ammonite *Waehneroceras* and associated stratigraphic data, from a quarry at Kayes Cement Works, Long Itchington near Southern in Warwickshire on which Tutcher (1858-1951), the Bristol-based palaeontologist, reported in 1917 (Buckman 1918, pp. 280-281). This was in a paper commenced in the winter of 1914-1915, the data for which must have been gathered earlier.

Fourteen of Robson's letters to Buckman over 1913-1921, and one of Buckman's of 1915 returned to him by Robson, have survived (BGS 1/1151 file M-R). The first is dated 11 March 1913 and shows that the two had already been in contact for some time before this. With this first letter Robson sent Buckman eleven Yorkshire ammonites (perhaps collected on a Robson family holiday in their native county?). The second letter (30 June 1913) was delayed by the intervention of Robson's final examinations at Birmingham. It shows that Robson had unsuccessfully examined for Buckman the Samuel Sharp (1814-1882) collection of Jurassic fossils, which was already in the University Geology Museum at Birmingham (Strachan 1979), in case it contained any type ammonites from Yorkshire needed for Buckman's work. Robson's letter also shows that he had then hoped to spend a month or two after his finals doing private palaeontological research in London. In his third letter (29 July 1913) this had become a reality and he then further offered to carry out additional research for Buckman in London 'for the pleasure and experience it will give' him. August found Robson researching enthusiastically in London, both for Buckman and himself. In the next letter, Robson sent measurements of some Sowerby type ammonites that he had located and studied in London.

In September 1913 Robson applied for his first geological position, as a Demonstrator and Assistant Lecturer in the Department of Geology at University College, Aberystwyth. The Department had been opened only in 1910 under its first Professor, O.T. Jones (1878-1967) (Pugh 1967). Robson's printed testimonials survive (BRSMG Geology File 392) and comprise that from Lapworth (Fig. 1) and one from Buckman which again speaks of his valued assistance in connection with Buckman's *Yorkshire Type Ammonites* revision. Other testimonials were from the London-based dealer in fossils and minerals Francis Henry Butler (1849-1935), who had known Robson 'for many years past', one from the Birmingham-born and based physician and amateur geologist Theodore Stacey-Wilson (1861-1949), one from the then Erdington-based Baptist cleric and fellow amateur geologist Rev. Benjamin Oriel (1865-1936) and a final one from the veteran petrologist and stratigrapher John Wesley Judd (1840-1916). All spoke of Robson's enthusiasm and knowledge of palaeontology (in particular, ammonites). In the event Robson was short-listed but was only placed second (BRSMG Geology File 392; and letter to S.S. Buckman, 30 September 1913) and the post went to Stanley Smith (1883-1955) who had been working on Palaeozoic corals and had graduated from both Armstrong

Curator Turned Astrologer

From Professor C. Lapworth, M.Sc., LL.D. (Aber.), F.R.S., F.G.S.

GEOLOGICAL DEPARTMENT,
UNIVERSITY,
EDMUND STREET,
BIRMINGHAM.

July 29/h, 1913.

Mr. V. E. ROBSON, B.Sc., informs me that he is a Candidate for a post in which a practical knowledge of Geology and Palaeontology is desired, and asks me to write a few words in testimony of his abilities in these subjects. I do so with pleasure.

I have known Mr. Robson since the year 1904, and have throughout observed his interest and indeed enthusiasm in Geology and its various branches. In the years 1904 and 1905 he attended and did well in the Elementary and Local Geology Lecture Courses and Excursions conducted by myself, and in the year 1906 attended the corresponding course in Advanced Geology. In 1907-1908 he joined the Junior Courses in Geology as a University Student, in 1908-1909, the Senior Courses, following up this work in the Session 1910-1911. *1907 — 1911*

The Geological Subjects laid down for the B.Sc. degree, and taken in the various years by Mr. Robson, comprise Petrology, Stratigraphy, Palaeontology, Tectonic Geology, Economic Geology and Geological Surveying. In all his terminal and final examinations in these he did well.

In Palaeontological and Stratigraphical Geology he has always been an enthusiast, and he is a good draughtsman.

His attendance was most regular, his attention and keen interest in the subjects throughout, everything that could be desired.

He is a man of quiet gentlemanly bearing, and his love of Geology and Palaeontology would be certain to infect and stimulate all those whom he might be called upon to instruct.

(Signed) CHARLES LAPWORTH,
Professor of Geology, Birmingham University.

Fig. 1. Testimonial for V. E. Robson written by Professor Charles Lapworth (1842-1920) on 29 July 1913.

The Vivian Robson Memorial

College, Newcastle-upon-Tyne and Cambridge University (Lang 1956).

Robson's letter thanking Buckman for his testimonial for the Aberystwyth job is dated 3 September 1913 and records that he was to return to London for more ammonite research that same month. On his way to London Robson called on Buckman at his home in Thame, Buckinghamshire, bringing with him an ammonite specimen that he had acquired (perhaps during his stay in London) which he thought agreed with the figure published in 1678 by Martin Lister (?1638-1712). This was of a Yorkshire specimen which had since become a type specimen. Buckman too became convinced of the possibility of its being, in fact, the long lost holotype of *Hildoceras bifrons* (Brugière). On Robson's return to London he continued to send Buckman ammonitological data, including the exact text of Lister's original description of the newly discovered possible type specimen. Robson ends his letter 'There is nothing I should like better than specialising in Ammonites'. The Yorkshire ammonite was figured by Buckman in 1918 (Buckman 1909-1930, pl. 114) as a topotype specimen. Buckman's description noted that Robson had 'purchased it in London', probably from what is known of Robson's connections, from some dealer. Buckman recorded how struck he was with the remarkable agreement Robson's specimen showed with Lister's figure and also suggested that it might be Lister's lost type specimen, and thus the long-lost holotype.

To be safe Buckman designated it as the Neotype. A reviewer of Buckman's book (Anon. 1918) sardonically noted of Robson's purchase, 'that London is a big place so that this statement does not throw much light on the previous history of the specimen. Indeed our friend Mr. S. Holmes, Intelligence Department, regards it as a transparent blind'. As we shall see, this was not the only specimen of type status in Robson's personal collection, his acquisition of which was shrouded in much mystery.

The next crucial phase in Robson's career came early in November 1913 when Bristol Museum and Art Gallery finally decided to appoint an Assistant Curator in Geology. The Museum's then Director, Herbert Bolton, (1863-1936), had previously reported (in 1911) on the appalling state of the Bristol Museum's important and historic geology and mineralogy collections (Bolton 1911, pp. 10, 13) and urged that extra funds, which could not come from the Museum's small normal admission-charge income, would be needed to restore them. This, he said, had to come from 'private benevolence', or in a more modern phrase, Paul Johnson's 'educative discipline of the market'. By September 1913 those 'serious hindrances to the development' of the Geological Collections still remained and no satisfactory progress was possible under existing conditions, which Bolton again greatly regretted (Bolton 1913, pp. 12-13).

By November 1913 the financial situation at Bristol had improved somewhat and Bolton was able to write to a number of candidates who had to be graduates, preferably in either zoology or geology, who could be considered for the new geology post at Bristol. Robson was one of those approached, in this case on the recommendation of S.S. Buckman. Robson's handwritten application for the Bristol post survives and is dated 4 November 1913 (BRSMG Geology File 392). It reports that he had studied palaeontology, which was the field in which the assistant was most to work, for nine years, since 1904 when he was, as we have seen, still at school. He had been working privately on ammonites at the British Museum (Natural History) at the same time as he was assisting S.S. Buckman with his work on ammonites (Buckman 1909-1930). Robson knew scientific French and German and some Italian.

Buckman's personal letter of support for the Bristol position also survives (BRSMG Geology File 392). It is dated 9 November 1913 and speaks of Robson as 'a quiet gentlemanly fellow' and that Robson's work for him had shown his 'good sense of systematic methods which is what one often finds lacking in the ordinary school and university students'. Robson's application was accepted on 20 November and he was interviewed successfully on 25 November. His appointment, nominally from

The Vivian Robson Memorial

1 December for a period initially of twelve months at the salary of £120, was soon confirmed, on 21 January 1914. Before the interview he had been to London again for more work on ammonites and to send Buckman final data for the *Yorkshire Type Ammonites* project, work which had to end with his Bristol appointment.

On 25 February 1914 Robson was elected a Fellow (no. 5018) of the Geological Society of London. His sponsors for this included Buckman, Lapworth and Bolton with, in addition, Frank Raw (?1875-1961) who had also taught Robson at Birmingham and S.H. Reynolds (1867-1949), the then professor of geology at Bristol University. In his first year at Bristol, Robson 'devoted himself with considerably enthusiasm and success to the task of arrangement of a palaeontological series of invertebrate fossils' (Bolton 1914, pp. 5-6). He also started a manuscript card index of Type, Figured and Cited specimens in the Bristol Geology collections which survives today. It contains 109 entries, with much useful information and shows how devoted a curator Robson had become in this, his first, curatorial post (BRSMG Geology Manuscript 81). On 18 November 1914 his appointment was confirmed, after the first probationary year. 'The Committee were highly pleased with the character and quality' of his work during the previous first twelve months.

When this appointment was confirmed, it was also agreed that he should receive annual increments to his salary of £10, up to a maximum of £150. So his new salary from December 1914 was to be £130 and, if the agreement was respected, from December 1915 he would have received a salary of £140, and from December 1916 the maximum of £150. However, a document in the Robson file at Bristol City Museum (BRSMG Geology File 392) suggests that he was not actually paid all these agreed increments, presumably because those private benefactors 'who will enable this (Geology] department to rise to the height of its traditions and exhibit its treasures worthily' (Bolton 1916, p. 11) had not come forward in sufficient numbers! So much for the 'discipline' of the market in this period. This document does confirm that Robson was paid the agreed salary (£120) in his first year but that he was only paid £125, instead of £130, in his second year. It further reveals that, from December 1915, Robson was paid not the agreed £140 but only £130. Such financial problems are thought to be the major reason why Robson did not long remain a geological curator, and strongly suggest that Bristol's sponsors of such 'cultural activity' had not lived up to Bolton's expectations.

On 18 November 1916 Robson tendered his resignation from the Museum. He had been offered a position in the Admiralty on War Work and, since he was needed immediately, he asked to be released at once (BRSMG Geology File 392). His Admiralty pay is not known but, apart from any patriotic motives, it is likely to have been much higher and thus a major incentive for Robson's departure from Bristol. He was released from Bristol on 21 November 1916 (Bolton 1917, p. 6) and with this his geological career effectively came to an end.

Details of two of Robson's geological research projects while at Bristol have survived. The first is reported in the *Annual Report*, of the Museum for 1916 (Bolton 1916, p. 16) as follows: 'Mr. V.E. Robson B.Sc., F.G .S., has in hand the preparation of a bibliographic index of Ammonite genera. At the suggestion of Mr. T.W. Stanton [1860-1953], of the American Museum of Natural History, this bibliography is being extended to include all genera of Triassic Ammonites, together with the geological horizon of type species. This has greatly increased the work but satisfactory progress is being made'. This index was later passed, when he abandoned geological work in 1923, to S.S. Buckman. Robson described it, in his letter of 13 August 1923 to Buckman, as being 'complete save for 5 genera he could not trace, up to the middle of 1914'. It may survive in the Buckman papers, either in the British Museum (Natural History) or in the British Geological Survey archives at Keyworth.

The other research project Robson undertook at Bristol concerned further careful curatorial work. Soon after he arrived at Bristol he discovered there most of the type series of ammonites

The Vivian Robson Memorial

which had been described in 1841 (Pratt 1841) from the Oxford Clay exposed in the excavations for the Great Western Railway near Christian Malford in Wiltshire by Samuel Peace Pratt (1789-1863). Robson had prepared a paper on these by 8 October 1915, when S.S. Buckman replied sending comments on the paper in a letter to Robson (which Robson later returned to its author in 1923, and which survives in BGS archives 1/1151, letter 11, with a six page MSS Buckman had written to accompany Robson's paper called 'The date of Pratt's species').

Robson's paper was entitled 'An Analysts of Pratt's Types of Ammonites from the Oxford Clay'. It was to have formed number one in a projected series of Bristol Museum Research Papers. In this, which again was never published, Robson recognised nine of the thirteen specimens figured in Pratt's paper as present in the Bristol collections (BRSMG C1796 - C1804) and he also traced a tenth figured specimen, then in the collections of Imperial College, London. Robson redescribed and, for the first time, photographically figured all ten in this paper, on four plates using photographs taken by J.W. Tutcher.

But difficulties arose concerning the publication of this paper during World War I (probably again of a financial nature) despite its being nearly ready for the press and it was laid aside. Later, in 1923, Robson passed the original typed version (which survives in the Buckman archive in the British Museum (Natural History)) to Buckman for publication as far as possible in *Type Ammonites'* (Buckman 1909-1930, vol. 5, pt. xlv (1924), p. 6). Of the material from Robson's paper subsequently used by Buckman, two new species published by Buckman, *Hecticoceras rursicostatum* (pl. 501) and *Kosmoceras acutistriatum* (pl. 486A, B), should be credited to Robson's authorship 'in Buckman' according to Recommendation 51B of the *International Code of Zoological Nomenclature* (1985) and not to Buckman alone, as all subsequent authors have done (e.g. Kennedy and Cobban 1976, pl. 1)

Robson had arrived in London to work for the Admiralty late in 1916. In March 1917 he wrote to Buckman from Putney

Curator Turned Astrologer

about how hunting for digs in London and colitis had both been troubling him, but that he liked the work at the Admiralty and was getting on well with it. He then added 'what will happen after the war I don't know possibly I may stay on but I rather doubt it. I expect I shall drift back into Geology in some form or other though not at Bristol' where he said Bolton had spread the tale of his departure. Palaeontology, he noted, he had dropped entirely. The Admiralty work under such war-time conditions was undoubtedly hard and in another letter of 23 December 1917 he noted that he had then been working late into the evenings at the Admiralty for some months.

ROBSON'S LATER CAREER

The end of Robson's work as a geological curator and as a geologist was finally signalled early in 1921 when he resigned as a Fellow of the Geological Society and suddenly became a journalist and professional writer, on the subject of astrology. One could hardly find a more remarkable career change for any geologist. I have not felt it worthwhile to investigate Robson's career as an astrologer in great detail but the first date I have found Robson active in this field is 1919. This is the date of publication of a *Life of Alan Leo* (1860-1917) by Leo's widow Bessie (Leo 1919). Alan Leo had been a prolific writer on astrology and had founded the weekly magazine *Modern Astrology* in 1895, whose offices were at 39-41 Imperial Buildings, in Ludgate Circus, London EC4. In this biography there is a horoscope for Alan Leo (pp. 174-203) by Vivian E. Robson, which provides clear evidence of Robson's interest in the subject at this early date.

After his resignation from the Geological Society, Robson seems to have turned full time to the business of astrological journalism. He soon became a joint editor of the magazine *Modern Astrology*, with Leo's widow, and in 1922 the first of his eight separate astrological books and pamphlets was published. *A Student's Text Book of Astrology*. The book's preface is from a Bedford Park, London W4 address and London now becomes

MODERN ASTROLOGY.

The object of this Magazine is thoroughly to purify and re-establish the ancient science of Astrology. Through planetary symbology, it seeks to explain the ONE *universal spirit in its varied manifestations.*

ESTABLISHED 1890.

Founder : THE LATE MR. ALAN LEO.

Joint Editors : BESSIE LEO AND VIVIAN E. ROBSON.

Price 1/- monthly, post free 1/1.

MODERN ASTROLOGY is published on 27th of month previous to date of issue.

Annual Subscription, if prepaid, 13/- post free. *Remittances from abroad should be made by crossed Money Order made payable to* BESSIE LEO, *at the* G.P.O., *and on no account by Postage Stamps.*

CALCULATIONS.

	s.	d.
Chart, to interpret a horoscope from " The Key to Your Own Nativity," when birth map is supplied...	1	0
Map of the Heavens for any place of birth	5	0
Map of the Progressed Horoscope only	5	0
The same with interpretation chart to be used with " The Progressed Horoscope " book ...	6	0
Radical Map, with Progressed Map, for one year (*with interpretation charts*, 2/- *extra*) ...	9	0
Progressed Maps for three years (*with interpretation charts*, 2/6 *extra*)	13	0
Radical Map and Progressed Maps for three years (*including interpretation charts for both*, 3/6 *extra*)	17	0
Book only : " The Key to Your Own Nativity " (for the interpretation of your own horoscope)	15	0
,, ,, " The Progressed Horoscope " (showing future tendencies) ...	15	0

RECTIFICATION OF HOROSCOPES.

	s.	d.
To find time of birth when known within an hour	15	0
,, ,, unknown ...	21	0

214

Fig. 2. An advertisement for <u>Modern Astrology</u> on the last page (p. 214) of Robson, V. E. (ed.). 1929. <u>Alan Leo's Dictionary of Astrology</u>, 214 pp. 'Modern Astrology' Office, London.

his permanent, and final, place of residence. The eight astrological works that he published up to 1937 are listed below, in order of their dates of first publication.

1. *A Student's Text Book of Astrology*. London, 1922.
2. *The Fixed Stars and Constellations in Astrology*. London, 1923.
3. (editor) *Alan Leo's Dictionary of Astrology*. London, 1929.
4. *The Radix System of Astrology*. London, 1930.
5. *A Beginners Guide to Practical Astrology*. London and Philadelphia, 1931.
6. *The Calculation of Sunrise and Sunset*. London, 1932 (privately published by the author).
7. *Electional Astrology*. London and Philadelphia, 1937.
8. *Your Affinity - the Astrological Guide to an Ideal Marriage and to Greater Happiness in Marriages already contracted*. London, 1937.

Copies of all eight of Robson's books are preserved in the British Library, London.

Two points are perhaps worth noting in this astrological output. The first is how the title of the last changes on reprinting, presumably in ever increasing attempts to achieve greater and greater 'market penetration'; becoming progressively *Astrology and Sex* in its 1941 reprint edition, then *Astrology and Human Sex Life* in the 1963 reprint, and finally *An Astrology guide to your Sex Life* in the 1967 reprint!* The second point is the frequency with which nearly all titles have been reprinted since publication. Of the eight titles above, numbers 1, 2, 3, and 5 were all still in print in 1987 and of the remainder, numbers 7 and 8 have been reprinted a number of times in recent years, and thus well after Robson's death. Number 4 on the above list is subtitled *Robson's Astrological Series no. 1*, although no subsequent publication in such a series ever appeared.

One final mystery remains in connection with Robson's geo-

*This is wrong. There is not one word in common between Your Affinity, and Astrology and Sex. I publish one, and have a copy of the other. — *Publisher.*

The Vivian Robson Memorial

logical work. In 1935 his own personal geological collection, by then a general unlabelled collection of fossils, turned up in London. It was purchased by the London dealers Gregory, Bottley and Co. who then sold to the British Museum (Natural History) 63 ammonites, the majority of them from the Robson collection (BRSMG Geology File ROB 1). The neotype of *Hildoceras bifrons* from the Alum Shales of Yorkshire was still present and was later registered BM(NH) C55848 (Phillips 1977, p. 86). But an even bigger surprise was when L.F. Spath (1882-1957), the Museum's ammonitologist, recognised in the Robson collection an unlabeled specimen, bearing only the number 4130, as another of considerable taxonomic and historic significance. This was the long-lost holotype of the American Carboniferous goniatite *Gonioloboceras goniolobum* (Meek) which had been posthumously described by Fielding Bradford Meek (1817-1876) in 1877, in his contribution to the publications of the United States Geological Exploration of the 40th Parallel (Meek 1877). This exploration had been commissioned in 1867 as part of the Congress-sponsored exploration of the American West. Clarence R. King (1842-1901) was the geologist in charge of the geological investigation of a belt of land westwards along the 40th Parallel of latitude in Nevada and Utah (Bartlett 1962; Rabbitt 1979). The type goniatite which was then found to be in the Robson collection must have come originally from New Mexico, to the south east of the survey area, and its recognition was a considerable achievement by Spath in the absence of any labels (Furnish and Glenister 1971, p. 308). It was registered BM(NH) C38093 but is now represented in the British Museum (Natural History) collections merely by a plaster cast since the United States National Museum claimed in 1965 that the original was their property and the BM(NH) Trustees instructed it to be returned (Phillips 1982, p. 24). If it was stolen, the mystery still remains of how it ended up in Robson's personal collection; a mystery not now likely to be solved. Correspondence in 1965 between the British and Bristol Museums (BRSMG Geology File ROB 1) shed no light on this, but T.W. Stanton's earlier connection with

Robson's work on Triassic ammonites in 1914, which might have involved a visit by Robson across the Atlantic, may be highly significant.

The sale of the Robson collection seems likely to have co-incided with relocation of the Robson home in the London area. For in 1936 the electoral registers for Fulham, London recorded V.E. and one Joan Robson living at 56 Talgarth Road, where they remained until 1939. Later in 1939 they moved again to nearby 2A Castletown Road, also in Fulham, W.14 and here Vivian Erwood Robson died on 31 December 1942 at the early age of 52. His death certificate records him as a journalist - a perfectly acceptable description of a man who gained his living by writing on astrology! The local newspapers (the *Fulham Chronicle* and *West London Observer*) make no mention of his death (T. Rix, pers. comm. 21 January 1982), but this was at a time when newsprint was rationed and news thus much restricted. One final intrigue is indicated by the death certificate, which at first gave the informant of his death as 'J. Robson, widow of deceased in attendance' of the same address and who had informed the registrar of his death on 1 January 1943. But nearly four months after this, Joan (now Alldred, otherwise Robson) and Ellen Caroline Winifred McGoun corrected the description of Joan's status as 'widow', to one stating that she 'had merely caused the body to be buried'. This was done by a Statutory Declaration and shows that she had been Robson's common-law wife or mistress. There was no inquest and Robson left no will by which the success, or otherwise, of his journalistic-cum astrological ventures can be judged. The same lack of a will means his intriguing relationship with Joan Alldred cannot be investigated either.

CONCLUDING REMARKS

Readers will have their own views about the relative values, socially, culturally and scientifically, of ammonite studies versus astrology. Ammonite studies have a known and proven value in the search for vital raw materials. But they are, as far as the

The Vivian Robson Memorial

experience of a recent postgraduate applicant to do research in such a field in a British University can demonstrate, completely in the doldrums. Recent press reports, however, do indicate that the Natural Environment Research Council is now aware that classical palaeontological studies have reached near extinction in this country. Of astrology, on the other hand, the prestigious journal *Nature* stated in 1983 (vol 301, p. 184), that it is 'sheer superstition, all the more pernicious because so many people think otherwise'. But one has only to listen to the television or travel on the London Underground to learn that astrology is thriving in 1987. The problem is that, in Paul Johnson's 'enterprise culture' of today, decisions over what is worth support are not likely to be made in terms of such subtleties, but on the basis of the numbers who will support any particular decision. Clearly all remaining ammonite workers should retrain as astrologers!

ACKNOWLEDGMENTS

I am grateful to the following for their help in uncovering Robson's remarkable careers: Dr. B.S. Benedikz (Special Collections Librarian, Birmingham University), C.A. Boardman (Foundation Archivist to King Edward the Sixth School, Birmingham), Dr. Michael Crane (Bristol) and Dr. Peter Crowther (Bristol City Museum), T.J. Rix (Hammersmith and Fulham Borough Librarian) and John Thackray (Geological Museum, London). The library staff of the British Geological Survey at Keyworth kindly helped locate material from their Buckman archives in the midst of the library's traumatic move from London. This research has been supported from the author's personal 'enterprise culture' - his salary! Relevant research notes have been deposited in the Geology Department of Bristol City Museum (BRSMG Geology File ROB 2).

REFERENCES

Anon. 1907. List of Patrons, Officers and Members of the Birmingham University Society of Mining Students. J. Brit. fed. Soc. Min. Students, 1., 23-28.

————1918. Review of Yorkshire Type Ammonites, edited by S.S. Buckman. Part xvi. Geol. Mag., dec. 6, 5, 547-548.

Bartlett, R.A. 1962. Great Surveys of the American West. University of Oklahoma Press. Norman, 408 pp.

Bolton, H. 1911. Report of the Museum and Art Gallery Committee, Bristol for the year ending 30 September 1911. Arrowsmith, Bristol, 50 pp.

——————1913. Ibid., for the year ending 30 September 1913. Hemmons, Bristol, 33 pp.

——————1914. Ibid., for the year ending 30 September 1914. Hemmons, Bristol. 32 pp.

——————1916. Ibid., for the year ending 30 September 1916. [no printer named], Bristol, 32pp.

——————1917. Ibid., for the year ending 30 September 1917. Ford, Bristol, 23 pp.

Buckman, S.S. 1909-1930. Yorkshire Type Ammonites, vols. 1-2 (1909-1919), continued as Type Ammonites, vols. 3-7 (1919-1930). Wesley, and Wheldon and Wesley for the author, London.

——————1918. Jurassic Chronology, I - Lias. Q. Jl geol. Soc. Lond. 73, 257-327.

Furnish, W.M. and Glenister, B.F. 1971. Permian Gonioloboceratidae (Ammonoidea). Smithson. Contr. Paleobiol. 3, 301-312.

International Commission on Zoological Nomenclature. 1985. International Code on Zoological Nomenclature (Third Edition). ICZN, London and University of California Press, Berkeley, 338 pp.

Kennedy, W.J. and Cobban, W.A. 1976. Aspects of ammonite biology. Spec. Pap. Palaeont. 17, 94 pp.

Lang, W.D. 1956. Stanley Smith - obituary. Proc. geol. Soc. Lond. 1541, 142-143.

Leo, B. 1919. Life and work of Alan Leo. Modern Astrology, London, 210 pp.

Meek, F.B. 1877. Part 1. Paleontology. In United States Geological Exploration of the Fortieth Parallel. Reports, Vol. 4. Government Printing Office, Washington, 197pp.

Phillips, D. 1977. Catalogue of the type and figured specimens of Mesozoic Ammonoides in the British Museum (Natural History). BM(NH), London, 220 pp.

——————1982. Catalogue of the type and figured specimens of fossil Cephalopoda in the British Museum (Natural History). BM(NH), London, 94 pp.

Pooler, H.W. 1948. My life in General Practice. Johnson, London, 193 pp.

Pratt, S.P. 1841. Description of some new species of Ammonites found in the Oxford Clay on the line of the Great Western Railway near Christian Malford. Ann. Mag. nat. Hist. 8, 161-165, pls. 3-6.

Pugh, W.J.. 1967. Owen Thomas Jones, 1878-1967. Biogr. Mem. Fellows R. Soc. 13, 223-243.

Rabbitt, M.C. 1979. Minerals, lands and geology for the common defence and general welfare. Vol. 1. Before 1879. United States Government Printing

The Vivian Robson Memorial

Office, Washington, 331 pp.

Strachan, I. 1979. Birmingham University Geological Museum. <u>Newsl. geol. Curators Gp.</u> 2, 309-321.

Hugh Torrens
LowermillCottage
Furnace Lane
Madeley
Crewe CW3 9EU

Typescript received 3 August 1987
Revised typescript received 20 October 1987

From <u>Astrologers' Quarterly</u>, March, 1943. *Supplied by Philip Graves:*

OBITUARY

British astrology has suffered a severe loss in the death on December 31st, of Mr. Vivian E. Robson.

His horoscope was published in Modern Astrology for June 1919; he was at that time co-editor of that periodical. He was born at Birmingham at 11.56 a.m. L.M.T., on May 26, 1890, and I regret that lack of space prohibits my printing his nativity.

However, those who erect it will find that he was a strongly Mercurial type and that he had serious afflictions with which to contend. His health was never robust and he was also averse to publicity and seldom appeared on the platform. Nor did he exactly "suffer fools gladly".

But in private conversation he would talk for hours on the science of which he was a master. Indeed, his knowledge, not only of astrology but of many other sciences, was phenomenal; and few who enjoyed his conversation could fail to go away with an enhanced knowledge of whatever subject had been under discussion.

He will be remembered best by his two chief books, <u>A Student's Text-book of Astrology</u> and <u>The Fixed Stars and Constellations in Astrology</u>. Of these the former is deservedly popular and the latter is a classic, containing as it does a mass of information dating from the days of Greek mythology up to modern times.

The only criticism I can make of his books is that, whilst he was full of original ideas in familiar discourse, his works were rather of the nature of compendia of what others, often far and away inferior to him intellectually, had compiled. Much of this – and I refer particularly to the writings of the Arabs on the fixed stars – might better have been left in the astrological lumber-room.

I have had no time properly to examine his directions, but at the winter ingress Mars was in close opposition to his natal Sun, which had recently felt the impact of Saturn and Uranus by transit; and by the measure of death Saturn was square radical Mars, exact to the minute.

C. E. O. CARTER

From Astrologers' Quarterly, June, 1943. *Supplied by Philip Graves:*

De mortuis:

Many readers will have felt deep regret at the loss the astrological world has suffered in the passing of Mr. V. E. Robson. I did not know him personally, but in the correspondence I had with him from time to time always found him most helpful. Apparently his end was quite unexpected for he thought he would reach the age of 63 if not 68 or 70. I do not know on what data he based this prognosis, but like many other astrologers he made no use of converse directions, and therefore did not foresee the intensity of stress to which he was subject last year. It was not that he disbelieved in converse progression, but merely considered forward directions were sufficiently comprehensive for the purpose of prediction.

The possibility of a sudden death was clearly shown in his map, for Mars, ruler of the 8th, was in opposition with the Sun and Mercury (his ruler) and in square with the risen Moon and ascendant, at the same time being close to the cusp of the 4th, and by converse secondary progression it had moved to the exact square with the radical ascendant and opposition Mercury at the time of his demise. As readers know, I hold no brief for transits, but as Mars was so obviously the anareta, I must record that on the day of death it was transiting its converse place. Death occurred through heart failure, typical of Mars afflicting the Sun.

In the radix the effect of 5°N latitude was to bring Luna in close mundane contact with Saturn, and this was evidently a pointer to one of the contributory causes of death, for a few months previously when consulting a doctor due to a chill on the liver and stomach trouble, extraction of the teeth was advised, as they were poisoning the system, a condition which was confirmed at the post-mortem, which revealed that the arteries were corroded by the poison.

Whether death could have been avoided had these factors been foreseen is a moot point, for Destiny so often blinds us that her own ends may be served.

GEORGE H. BAILEY

Vivian Robson, An Appreciation, by Dorothy Ryan.

First published in Charles Carter's "Astrologers' Quarterly" *July 1943. Reprinted in* American Astrology, *November, 1943. Supplied by Philip Graves.*

Astrology has indeed suffered a great loss in the death of Vivian E. Robson. This must be sadly clear to all students, but those who knew him only through his books could not fully appreciate the real man. In his books he showed more of the precise, scholarly and pedantic Virgo side than anything else. One missed something of his Geminian wit and talent, and something of his profound wisdom and understanding. Through his books he set himself out to undertake a good, sound job of practical instruction, and he performed that task with all the Virgo accuracy, competency and close attention to detail, withholding other qualities which he probably considered extraneous to that particular side of his work for astrology.

To know V. E. R. personally and to see him in his private life was to contact a character of great range and talent, and no one who knew him well could fail to accord to him a great measure of respect and affection.

With four elevated planets in Gemini he naturally possessed all the amazing intellectual versatility of that gifted and clever sign. I have heard him converse knowledgeably on a dozen and one different subjects. I really believe he knew something about everything, but so far as astrology was concerned his versatility showed forth in a phenomenal knowledge of his subject. To converse on astrology with him, even if only for one short hour, was inevitably to gain something new and valuable in the way of experience and information. In his conversation he allowed himself more scope for speculation and theory than in his books.

273

The Vivian Robson Memorial

Yet his theorising was always based on the foundation of years of practical experience. It has been suggested that he concentrated too much on medieval astrology, but I think it should be remembered that medieval rules (so rigid and didactic to the casual eye) suggested infinitely wider ideas and possibilities to his brilliant intellect than would be suggested to some.

I always found it a joy to study his astrological judgment. It was so quick, so sure and poised, always impeccable in its principles, and frequently unerringly accurate. In the early days of our friendship I recall that I was struggling with the task of rectifying my husband's map, and that I began to discuss it with him over the tea-table. He produced a piece of paper, pushed the tea-cups aside, and in five minutes had worked out directions for salient events, handing the result back to me with the remark that he thought I would find this the correct birth hour. I afterwards laid his calculations aside and completed the work independently. Our results tallied, but where I had taken 3-4 hours, he had completed his calculations in less than ten minutes. The difference, of course, was that where I was forced to use the slower method of gradual elimination, his wise and experienced eye could instantly single out the true directions for the specified events. In his first glance at any map he seemed to have the knack of segregating instantly the really potent factors and of seeing the horoscope in its true perspective. Nor have I ever met anyone who could spot vital transits more quickly than he.

One very endearing characteristic was his Virgo modesty. Although he had a quiet confidence in his intellectual gifts, he never paraded his cleverness. In speaking of astrology he, whose knowledge excelled that of so many others, was always the first to admit that he had much to learn, and he truly said that we were only on the fringe of a vast realm of undiscovered knowledge.

Moon conjunct Saturn also made him extremely shy and retiring. This conjunction was also the means of bringing phases of severe depression, although he never complained of these, and only spoke of them with the philosophic detachment that he brought to all other human weaknesses. Fortunately the natural

274

An Appreciation, by Dorothy Ryan

buoyancy of Sun-Jupiter trine in Air usually came to his rescue in these moods of depression.

Maybe he never suffered fools gladly. He certainly had little patience with the "crankiness" that our Uranian study sometimes produces. At the same time I always found him ready to give help and encouragement to the less experienced student, provided that he was first assured that their interest in astrology was sincere and sensible. When I first met him in the early days of *Weekly Horoscope*, I was a young and inexperienced student, all too dismally conscious of that crude inexperience. V.E.R. quickly sensed all this nervous uncertainty and took pains to give me the encouragement so badly needed. He did this with such quiet and thoughtful sympathy and with so much tact and delicacy that I can never hope to express the gratitude I felt towards him. I was never able to pay the debt I owed him during his lifetime. Now I can only hope that some day I may be able to repay it, as it were vicariously, by helping students less experienced than myself. I believe I was not the only member of *Weekly Horoscope* who benefited by his help, although he never spoke of his efforts for others.

Naturally, with the Mercurial signs so prominent in his map he was profoundly intellectual and completely lacking in sentimentality. Being an emotional Water type myself, this was sometimes a friendly bone of contention between us. He certainty had no patience with over-emotionalism, but the elevated Sun-Neptune conjunction trine Jupiter in Aquarius gave him great understanding, and he had much Neptunian tolerance of human frailty. One felt that although he could view the varying phases of human activity and endeavor with complete unemotional detachment and exclusion of the purely personal, yet he also saw them with great wisdom and a compassionate understanding.

Virgo rising made him a meticulously accurate astrologer. He fussed about seconds as well as minutes, and on one occasion I recall that he lectured me for failing to calculate the Moon's position with sufficient accuracy.

He was an accomplished mathematician, and at our last meeting he showed me a weighty folio of mathematical tables which he had just completed. He had been doing this in his spare time, after the day's work was over. When asked if he did not find it tiring, he assured me that he found it a soothing and restful task. Truly, the active Gemini brain could never be at rest. Physically he was lazy—he would not walk a few hundred yards if he could find a bus or train to take him to his destination—but into his mental life he packed sufficient activity to fill a dozen life-times.

One wishes that all students could take an example from his Virgo neatness. Even his rough maps were beautifully clear, and his finished work was perfection. The mathematical tables I have just referred to would have to be seen for their clarity and sym-metry to be credited. The desk at which he worked reflected the same exquisite neatness, with its orderly rows of pens, and pen-cils of different colours.

He was the proud possessor of the most comprehensive as-trological library I have ever seen. It contained, I believe, prac-tically every astrological book (ancient and modern) ever pub-lished. When I visited him I always used to look forward to the moment when he would begin to ramble around his beloved book-shelves, picking out a volume here and a volume there to show me something of interest. Apart from the pleasure it gave me, I de-lighted in the equal pleasure it brought to him. I think these brows-ings among his books gave him some of his happiest moments.

Aside from astrology, one of his chief pleasures lay in the enjoyment of music. He had an enormous collection of gramo-phone records, and although these reflected something of the Geminian versatility of taste, he was true connoisseur of great music. He was very fond of Wagner's music—naturally enough, since Wagner himself was a Geminian. Strangely enough, he also had great fondness for Tschaikovsky. I say "strangely enough" because Tschaikovsky's music is so predominantly emo-tional. However, I believe that Tschaikovsky's gift of suggest-ing in his music all the sorrows and struggles of tragic humanity must have appealed to his strongly Neptunian side.

An Appreciation, by Dorothy Ryan

His active Gemini brain made him a great lover of tricks and puzzles of all kinds. He had collected quite a number of these. I particularly admired an exquisite Chinese jigsaw in delicately carved ivory. He also liked detective stories—naturally preferring the problems of pure deduction, but also having a weakness for thrillers. He was, of course, extremely quick and ingenious in solving puzzles, but I recall one occasion when my husband sent him a brain-twister which all but defeated him. We learned afterward from Mrs. Robson that he had been unable to concentrate on his work throughout the day, and that he had been awake during the night twisting possible solutions over in his mind. However, the next day came a letter from him containing an accurate solution setting out all the logical stages of his reasoning, and ending with a triumphant Q.E.D.! I may say that this particular teaser had completely baffled a dozen or more puzzle experts at my husband's place of business, and when they declared that it was impossible to solve I backed V.E.R. to do the trick—and he did.

In connection with this liking for tricks and puzzles I must mention that he was a skilful exponent of sleight-of-hand. I still cherish the memory of delightful evening when, in lighter mood, he broke off a serious discourse on astrology to show me a series of conjuring and card tricks. Under his hand the cards literally took wing and disappeared with magicianly skill.

I seem to have strayed away from Robson's astrological life. If so it has been because I wanted to give a picture of the man as a personality as well as an astrologer. Although I cannot hope to present a complete picture, I hope I have been able to touch upon same of the traits that will endear his memory to others, as it is endeared to me. Although I cannot help but feel the most profound regret at his passing, I shall always feel happy in the memory of having enjoyed his friendship. I wish that those students who had never met him could have had the same opportunity. No one could fail to be enriched by the experience, for Robson was not only one of the truly great souls, but also a great astrologer.

The Vivian Robson Memorial

EDITORIAL NOTE - We feel that the above Appreciation is not only a fitting tribute to a leading astrologer, but also an instructive character study. As stated in our March issue, Mr. Robson died on December 31, 1942, and was born at Birmingham at 11:56 a.m. L.M.T., May 26, 1890. See also observations in the June number in Mr. G. H. Bailey's "Q" on page 52.

A list of articles by Vivian Robson, as published in <u>The Weekly Horoscope</u>. (This list may not be complete):

1937:

    13 November: First Steps in Astrology
    20 November: Be Your Own Astrologer
    27 November: Astrology Simplified
     4 December: First Steps in Astrology
    11 December: How to Understand Your Ephemeris
    18 December: How to Calculate the Cusps
    25 December: Our Special Course in Astrology

1938:

    1 January: How to Erect a Horoscope
    8 January: Now You Have Learnt the Worst!
    15 January: Astrology for the Beginner
    22 January: How to Cast a Horoscope
    29 January: How to Become Your Own Astrologer
    5 February: Astrology for the Beginner
    12 February: Astrology for the Beginner
    19 February: Calculating a Horoscope for a Foreign Birth
    26 February: This Completes the Casting of the Horoscope!
    5 March: Vivian E. Robson Sums Up!
    12 March: Calculating the Aspects
    19 March: On Calculating the Aspects

How To Read Your Horoscope, a new series:—

    26 March: How to Read Your Horoscope
    2 April: The Judgment of the Horoscope
    9 April: The Influence of the Moon and Mercury
    16 April: How the Planets Influence Us
    23 April: How the Planets Jupiter and Saturn Influence Us
    30 April: How Uranus and Neptune Influence Us
    7 May: The Houses of the Horoscope
    14 May: The Rulership of the Houses
    21 May: [missing from Mr. Graves' collection]
    28 May: [No title: On other classifications of signs]

— *Thanks to Philip Graves*

Afterword, by David R. Roell, publisher
revised, 13 October 2010: Joan Robson / Alldred

In publishing this book I set myself the task of finding a picture of the mysterious Mr. Robson. At the Astrologer's Memorial, it said he had been a curator at the British Museum. I emailed and was told they had no record, but that I should try the Natural History Museum, in South Kensington. I did, but they had no record, either.

On further investigation, the British Museum found and emailed a scan of Vivian Robson's application for a Reader's Ticket, dated 1 May 1917. He signed himself *Vivian Robson B.Sc. F.G.S.* Which is, *Fellow, Geological Society.*

So I went to the website of the Geological Society, where I found a list of obituaries. Vivian Robson's name was not among them, which did not surprise me, as I presumed he had resigned or lost his membership decades before his death in 1942.

But I emailed them anyway. And the very next day was stunned to receive Prof. Hugh Torrens' biography, from 1989. Seven pages of two-column text, more information than we had ever imagined possible. I emailed to ask for permission to reprint, and was even more surprised when Prof. Torrens himself replied the very next day. A week later he graciously sent me a photocopy of Mr. Robson's Death Certificate, which I have reproduced. It is legal sized, measuring nearly 15 x 6 inches.

Prof. Hugh S. Torrens is the Emeritus Professor of History of Science and Technology at Keele University, Staffordshire, UK. He has specialized in the history of early geologists, among them, Mr. Robson. It should be noted that Charles Lapworth, who wrote a letter of recommendation for the young Vivian Robson, as well as sponsoring his candidacy to the Society, was the leading geologist of his day.

Prof. Torrens frames his essay in economic terms. Robson left his post at Bristol presumably because they failed to honor the salary terms in his contract. I have thought about this and regret I must disagree.

While I agree that money was an issue, I do not think it was a decisive one. In his letter of recommendation, Lapworth describes Robson as, "*a man of quiet, gentlemanly bearing . . .*" Someone – presumably the recipient, in Bristol – underlined these very words. Which were in keeping with the report from the King Edward VI School, that Vivian Robson's time there "[*was*] *mainly negative; in that he was not a member of a sports team, not active in the literary society or debating society, and not a prefect.*"

Vivian Robson, in other words, seems to have been the quiet scholarly type. He does not appear to have been sociable, he was not a "joiner." It seems he was happy sitting in a corner with his books and his work. It may also be that he lacked the physical stamina necessary for boisterous activities, such as sports.

Sheer study is, after all, a large part of a curator's job. But the curator is also the museum's public face. While in Bristol, Vivian Robson gave a series of public lectures. Prof. Torrens kindly supplied me with a news account of such a lecture, given on May 2, 1914 (Folk Lore in Fossils, Times and Mirror, Bristol, May 4, 1914). It may well be that the "extra funds" the museum's director, Herbert Bolton, promised to Robson were contingent upon Robson's successful interaction with the museum's donators. Prof. Torrens presumes Robson's departure was the result of the market at work. It might just as well be that Robson failed to woo the museum's sponsors!

Robson resigned from Bristol in November 1916. Prof. Torrens reports that Robson "*had been offered a position in the Admiralty on War Work and . . . was needed immediately,*" which was probably how Robson presented it in his letter of resignation. But it was unlikely the Admiralty would have solicited Robson, who was, after all, a newly installed curator of geology.

In March of 1917, Robson wrote Buckman. According to Prof. Torrens, "*he liked the work at the Admiralty and was getting on with it.*" What work could this be? The British Navy in

Afterword

World War I was not in need of geologists. Lapworth's letter cited Robson's skills as a draftsman. A navy, especially in wartime, has need of draftsmen. In the same letter Robson adds, "*I expect I shall drift back into Geology in some form or other though not at Bristol.*" Drifting is not a ringing endorsement of his area of expertise. Robson is clearly happier at the Admiralty, but is unable to see a future, either there, or in geology.

Mr. Philip Graves, of Kilsmo, Sweden, is in possession of Alan Leo's <u>Modern Astrology</u> for this period. He reports that, according to the magazine, Vivian Robson began Alan Leo's Astrological Correspondence Lessons about this time. According to an advertisement placed in the 1929 edition of Alan Leo's <u>Dictionary of Astrology</u> (itself edited by Robson), each of the nine lessons cost £1 1s each, which cannot be described as cheap. Robson's progress seems to have been rapid, as by the end of 1918 he was jointly (with Bessie Leo) editing <u>Modern Astrology</u>. As those of us who have attempted to learn this arcane discipline can appreciate, this was no small accomplishment.

The question is, why? Why would a trained research scientist, with experience going back to his boyhood days, blithely give it all up for the whimsey of astrology? It cannot merely be the result of a bad time in Bristol, nor is it likely that Bessie seduced him (32 years his senior). It wasn't money, it wasn't the war. Robson had already shown a love of geology that would, or should, have overwhelmed such trivial concerns. Yet while in London, Robson chanced upon astrology and then gave himself to it, completely and utterly, and with amazing speed.

As astrologers, we are tempted to look at Robson's birth chart, to see if we can find easy answers there. Vivian Robson had a stellium of planets in Gemini in his 10th house, among them, Neptune at 4°, the MC at 5°, the Sun at 5°, Pluto at 6°, Mercury retrograde at 10°, the north node at 24°, and Venus at 29°. Opposing them was Mars at 6° Sagittarius. (See the chart on page ii.)

In May, 1913, transiting Saturn conjuncted his Neptune, MC Sun and Pluto. It opposed Mars. Saturn conjuncted Mercury in

The Vivian Robson Memorial

June, 1913, before making a station at 17° Gemini in October, retreating to 11° in February, 1914. Direct, Saturn reached the north node in July (25°), and then conjuncted Robson's Venus (29°) in August, before quickly disappearing into Cancer. It passed over Venus again, retrograde, in December, and for a final time, direct, in May of 1915.

As astrologers know, this is a difficult set of transits to live through. Years later Robson would have seen it through the prism of solar arcs: In 1930, he took an idea from Sepharial and spun it into a small book, The Radix System, where all natal planets are advanced by 59' 08" per year, termed a Solar Arc, or SA. Advancing them to Robson's 24th year, May of 1914, gives an arc of 23° 39'. I note the following:

SA Pluto is conjunct natal Venus. SA Mars is opposed to natal Venus, as well as SA Pluto. Three months later, SA Pluto was sextile Robson's natal Moon, while SA Mars was trine. SA Jupiter was inconjunct Robson's natal Sun and MC.

A further aggravating factor was transiting Pluto, which conjuncted natal Venus in June, 1913, made a station directly over it in January, 1914, before finally clearing it in March. Add in trivial aspects from transiting Mars (conjunct Venus, mid-September 1913, square in August 1914, opposed in December), and you have an horrific nightmare. I would expect that Mr. Robson was engaged to be married (this is what transits to Venus signify in a young man's chart), and that the engagement was broken. There were probably other problems as well.

Such were Robson's circumstances before and during his stay in Bristol (December 1913–November 1916). If he hoped to bury himself in his work, he was not successful. Such transits leave permanent scars. It is customary that one seek answers for such a prolonged experience, indeed, many of us took up the study of astrology and ultimately became astrologers from similar experiences. Those who scoff at the subject are invited to study their own worst times and see if there are not simple and direct astrological answers that will explain their miseries.

Truthfully, there are other systems that attempt answers.

282

Afterword

There are psychics and clairvoyants who offer help, there are those who cast spells and consult with the dead, or who will bless you in the name of Christ Our Savior, but for those who are intellectually driven, like Robson, nothing surpasses astrology in providing precise, concrete answers.

And here I cannot but point out that scientific hostility to astrology is not to the benefit of science, so far as Vivian Robson's professional career was concerned. If there was an astrological flimflam artist, like me, on every street corner, if the ABC's of astrology were commonly known, Robson could well have stumbled into his neighborhood Astrological Office and have been reassured that, as awful as it was, that there was a reason, that, although hard and cruel, it would end, that better days would dawn. A sort of, "Cheer up old boy, England thinks you're a wonderful chap, of course you will make it, of that there is no doubt whatsoever." Which, as I think of it, was the sort of attitude that Alan Leo (1860–1917) tried so hard to promote.

Thus reassured, Vivian Robson might have returned to geology. Judging by his subsequent astrological writings (some of the finest ever penned), Geology lost one of its very best. Science has made peace with religion, to the profit of both. It should do the same with Astrology. Astrology is, after all, older than modern science, older than Christianity. While it has had its ups and downs, Astrology cannot be extinguished. It will survive both science and Christianity. Call it whatever names you like.

Robson's decision to quit geology and embrace astrology was definitive. He resigned from the Geological Society in 1921. As this would not be received kindly by his sponsors, readmission would likely have been difficult. From 1918 to 1929 he edited <u>Modern Astrology</u>. His co-editor, Bessie Leo, was the widow of the magazine's founder, Alan Leo. Charles Carter's opinion of Bessie was scathing, "*Bearing in mind that she had little education, she was a fluent, if rather superficial writer and lecturer . . .*" (as quoted in <u>Astrological Pioneers of America</u>, by James H. Holden and Robert Hughes, AFA, 1988). Holden and

The Vivian Robson Memorial

Hughes go on to quote Ellic Howe, that while her husband was alive, she was largely inactive. Carter says this changed upon his death, and goes on to say, "[*Vivian*] *Robson tried to continue with* Modern Astrology *but could not tolerate her constant interference...*" (Ibid) This would seem to be belied by Robson's eleven years as co-editor, in contrast to his three years in Bristol.

Carter, like Robson, was professionally trained (B.A., admitted to the legal profession in 1913) and, like Robson, abandoned his profession for astrology. He was early on associated with both Alan and Bessie Leo. In the years following Leo's death it would seem that he was outmaneuvered by the upstart Robson for the prize of editing Modern Astrology.

Perhaps as a result, in 1920 Carter became president of Leo's Astrological Lodge, which was part of the Theosophical Society. In 1926 he founded the Astrologer's Quarterly as the Lodge's magazine, which he edited until 1959. Reading both Robson's and Carter's books closely, I can, from time to time, see Carter sniping at someone. For example, in An Encyclopaedia of Psychological Astrology (1924), under Gout, Carter says, "*Rules are given by recent authors, copied from Lilly and Gadbury, but they are hardly satisfactory.*" Who might the recent author have been? In A Student's Text-Book of Astrology, published in 1922, Robson had written of Gout on pg. 106. On pg. 107 of the same book Robson delineated accidents, which Carter would attempt a decade later, and not as satisfactorily (Astrology of Accidents, 1932). Careful readers will find other examples.

Robson's work at Modern Astrology came to an abrupt end with the October 1929 issue. In that issue Bessie Leo made the following statement:

> With this issue the work of Mr. Robson for MODERN ASTROLOGY terminates. He is neither on the Office Staff, nor Co-Editor of the magazine, therefore all communications must in future be addressed to Mrs. Alan Leo, "Modern Astrology" Office, 40, Imperial Build-

Afterword

ings, Ludgate Circus, E.C. 4, or to her private address,
Dollis Lodge, Church End, Finchley, N. 3. (quoted by
Philip Graves, private communication to me)

This bolt from the blue needs context. Starting with Charles
Leadbeater's discovery of Jiddu Krishnamurti in Adyar in 1909,
the Theosophical Society, of which both Alan and Bessie Leo
were life-long members, had become totally absorbed in pro-
moting him as the World Teacher, as the Second Coming of Jesus
Christ. This mission was imposed on the young Krishnamurti,
who lived from 1895 to 1986. It intensified in the 1920's, and by
1929, The Order of the Star was a world-wide organization with
tens of thousands of members. Regrettably, the Society left Krishnamurti to manage the Order on his own, and by the mid 1920's,
it was overrun with frauds and cheats. Krishnamurti put up with
it for the sake of his "mission", but on Saturday, August 3, 1929,
he had had enough. In front of a crowd of 3000, he renounced
his mission, dissolved the Order of the Star, and promised to
return all donated property to its original owners. He said,

> "I maintain that truth is a pathless land, and you cannot
> approach it by any path whatsoever, by any religion, by
> any sect. That is my point of view, and I adhere to that
> absolutely and unconditionally. Truth, being limitless,
> unconditioned, unapproachable by any path whatsoever,
> cannot be organized; nor should any organization be
> formed to lead or coerce people along a particular path."

And also:

> "This is no magnificent deed, because I do not want
> followers, and I mean this. The moment you follow
> someone you cease to follow Truth. I am not concerned
> whether you pay attention to what I say or not. I want
> to do a certain thing in the world and I am going to do it
> with unwavering concentration. I am concerning my-

self with only one essential thing: to set man free. I desire to free him from all cages, from all fears, and not to found religions, new sects, nor to establish new theories and new philosophies." (Both quotes from Wiki, as taken from The International Star Bulletin. For more, see Mary Lutyens' Krishnamurti The Years of Awakening, 1975, numerous publishers.)

The immediate response, as one might expect, was the Theosophists reaffirmed Krishnamurti's rejected mission. They tried to smother over the differences, pretend it didn't happen, and attempted to carry on as before. This, more than their leader's renunciation, shattered the Theosophists, they have not recovered to this day.

It quickly played out in a thousand ways throughout the Society. At the Modern Astrology offices, run by the very Theosophical Bessie Leo, it was a defining moment. In his Student's Text-Book of Astrology (1922), Robson had included a chapter on Esoteric Astrology, but it was the weakest chapter in the book and one in which he clearly had little interest. I regret I do not know if Vivian Robson was ever a member of the Theosophical Society. Judging by chapter 14 of A Student's Text-Book, he was not enthusiastic.

So how did the August explosion end up in the October issue? This has to do with how magazines are produced. Modern Astrology appeared on the 27th of the preceding month. The October issue was therefore scheduled to appear on the 27th of September. To do this, the magazine needed at least one full month, possibly a little more, at the printing plant. Which meant the deadline for submission of materials for the October issue was no later than the middle of August.

When Krishnamurti renounced his mission (and in the process, destroyed his own career), he brutally exposed the corruption at the heart of the Theosophical Society. In the October issue of Modern Astrology, Bessie Leo had not the space for a detailed statement, most of the issue having already been finalized. She did the following month, November:

'In closing this year which is the fortieth year since publication, it will be as well to offer a few remarks that
may come as a surprise to many readers. The amount
of opposition and frustration brought to bear against
our efforts during the past has been exceptional, but
those who were so foolish as to think we could be in-
jured when our intentions were to help and uplift the
world have yet to understand how mighty is the power
behind. It is not our intention to comment upon the
past, but we wish most emphatically and honestly to
assure all our supporters that while we have life we will
try to spread true Astrology, and that Astrology is based
upon actual experience, and is not merely the result of
many different authors' opinions. Forty years constant
practice in connection with this magazine has given us
a unique experience, to which we are daily adding. We
are quite convinced that a knowledge of Astrology will
help and not hinder the world's evolution, and where
knowledge abounds there is no room for error and ig-
norance. What is wanted is a philosophical and esoteric Astrology; no system of Astrology can be of any
value until it can show a reason for its laws. We might
go on quoting Ptolemy, Ramsey [sic], and all the authors of the past until the end of time, but this would not
illustrate why we come under planetary law, and why
we are joyful or sad. Life is not the problem it was now
the inner side of Astrology is demonstrated; but it must
be admitted that until MODERN ASTROLOGY appeared upon the scene, now forty years ago, the science
was open to scoffs and jeers, simply because there was
no astrologer who would or could, give his reasons for
the assertions he made, and there is not one person
amongst the many who study this profound subject who
can deny that a light has now been thrown upon astro-

logical problems which has never appeared since the days of ancient Babylon.' (Philip Graves, ibid.)

The reference to Ptolemy and Ramesey was a direct swipe at Robson, who championed the old astrologers, which Leo had rarely done. I presume that upon hearing Krishnamurti's announcement, Robson quit in disgust, but it really makes no difference, either way, if he quit or was fired. Both Carter and Ryan have stated that Robson would not suffer fools.

Robson replied on page 113 of A Beginner's Guide to Practical Astrology (1931):

There is too great a tendency nowadays to float about in a comfortable haze of so-called esotericism. The first need of Astrology is accuracy and definition, not pseudo-religious speculation, and it is only by concentrating on the practical and scientific side that we can really make Astrology of service, and obtain for it the recognition it deserves.

As it turns out, 1929 was to be the high point of Vivian Robson's life. He thereafter sank slowly into obscurity. Charles Carter, by contrast, ducked. Gracious and good-humored, he stayed on as the head of the Astrological Lodge until 1952, when, aged 65, he retired. He died in 1968.

Sepharial (Walter Gorn Old) passed away in December, 1929. For a number of years he had edited the Kaleidoscope section of the British Journal of Astrology. Robson took it over but was gone by 1935 (to me, from Philip Graves, who has a partial collection of issues). In moving from Modern Astrology to the British Journal, Vivian Robson thought he was moving ahead. In October 1930, Robson published The Radix System, which was subtitled, Robson's Astrological Series—1. In it, he boldly wrote,

Afterword

This series of astrological manuals, of which this is the first, is designed to cover the whole field of Astrology in volumes of a convenient size, each self-contained and dealing exhaustively with one special aspect of the science. . . The second volume will deal with Electional Astrology, and will appear early next year. (pg. v.)

This series would appear to have been a sequel, and an update, to Alan Leo's well-known Pocket Manuals, some 15 inexpensive books that had first appeared some thirty years before.

Robson's plans did not succeed. There was to be no second volume, and Electional Astrology would not be published until 1937. He was presumably unable to attract the supporters he needed to make his plans a reality. The economic difficulties of the period may have been a factor.

Instead, 1931 saw the publication of A Beginner's Guide to Practical Astrology. Here, Robson attempted to reach a broader audience, but despite the title, the Beginner's Guide is one of the fiercest beginner's books ever written.

1932 saw the publication of The Calculation of Sunrise and Sunset, a privately published monograph. In 1935, his private collection of ammonites, some 63 specimens, turned up for sale in London. I do not know what Robson might have gotten for them, but the fact that it was noted by dealers at the time is significant, as well as the fact it ended up in the British Museum.

According to Prof. Torrens, in 1936, the electorial registers in Fulham (a borough in SW London) recorded a V.E. and Joan Robson as living at 56 Talgarth Road.

1937 saw the publication of Electional Astrology, as well as Your Affinity, a "kabalistic" work intended for a mass audience. In it, Robson divided the zodiac into five degree segments (known as "faces"), related these to days of the year, and offered interpretations for those whose birthdays fell during those days. Your Affinity was published by Foulsham. Robson presumably received an advance for it. To my knowledge, it has never been reprinted.

The Vivian Robson Memorial

1937 also saw the start of The Weekly Horoscope, a 28 page magazine. Cover price was 3d. It was published by W. H. Burt, at Link House, 300-304 Gray's Inn Road, London WC1, who published numerous books and popular magazines. The Weekly Horoscope was edited by "Orion", a man whose identity is unknown. (Mr. Graves and I are in agreement that "Orion" was unlikely to have been Robson.) The pseudonym would seem to be a throwback to Orion's Prophetic Almanac, which had been in publication from 1841 up to World War I, though perhaps not continually. (These details from Philip Graves.)

The Weekly Horoscope first appeared on Saturday, September 11, 1937. It sought to capitalize on the astrology fad of the 1930's, which had been kicked off a few years earlier by the development of early "sun-sign" columns by R.H. Naylor, Edward Lyndoe, William Tucker and others. (See Kim Farnell's Flirting With the Zodiac, Wessex Astrologer, 2007, for more.) The date of The Weekly Horoscope's last issue is not known at this time. Vivian Robson wrote a weekly column starting no later than the November 13th issue, continuing through at least May 28, 1938, which is where Philip Graves's collection ends.

Dorothy Ryan was a fellow contributor to the magazine. It seems that Robson met her at this time, an association which presumably ended when Robson's column ended, or when the magazine folded. The Weekly Horoscope featured a coupon. Clip and return it and the magazine would answer your astrological query. Graves tells me that by May 1938, there were on the order of 100 personal replies per issue. The task of answering was presumably shared by the editor and his staff. With the books, the weekly column and perhaps a share of the coupons, Vivian Robson seems to have been busy.

By 1939 the Robsons had moved to 2A Castletown Road, also in Fulham, where Robson wrote his final book, Astrology and Sex, 1941. In it, Robson gives thanks to Harry and Ella Elliott-Ball for housing him during its writing. Those who have read the dedication commonly presume the Elliott-Balls to have

Afterword

resided in a country manor and that Mr. Robson and his wife were honored guests (à la Masterpiece Theatre, or the short stories of Saki), but the reality seems different. The "A" in the address presumably refers to the basement flat. Such flats, which are common in London, have their own entrance, which is reached by an exterior flight of stairs, descending from the street itself.

It is unknown why Robson moved. A basement flat, which is damp and prone to flooding, is not a good place for the antiquarian books or gramophone records which Ryan noted. That Robson was a guest implies either financial hardship or, if George Bailey's obituary is correct, medical necessity, or perhaps both.

Vivian Robson died at 2A Castletown Road, Fulham, on December 31, 1942. A strict reading of the Death Certificate turns up several surprises.

In the space given for the signature of the next of kin, the name J. Robson is written in the same hand as that of the rest of the document. Which would presumably be that of W. James, the acting Registrar. Which means that Joan Robson was not present at the time. Robson's body was presumably discovered by the Elliott-Balls, who phoned the coroner, and who then gave Joan's name as the next of kin.

Joan arrived sometime later to take care of the remains. We deduce this from the marginal notation on the Death Certificate, in which she denies she was his wife.

According to Prof. Torrens, Robson left no will. As Robson seemed to have only Joan as his heir, his possessions presumably passed to her upon his death, making a formal will unnecessary.

So who was Joan? If Robson had been married, a record of it would have turned up in Kew, where all English records are kept. If he had a child, it would have been in Kew. If he had a will, it would have been in Kew. Robson's own parents can be traced in this way.

As a part of his research, Prof. Torrens attempted to trace Mrs. Robson, who, in the marginal notation on the Death Certificate, gave her name as Alldred. Prof. Torrens wrote to me,

The Vivian Robson Memorial

Also re: Joan Alldred. There are Births recorded in June 1920 quarter as Alldred Joan M. to a mother née Woodhams at Romsey and June 1922 as Alldred Joan to a Highton at Wigan which might be her? Then a Marriage in Sep 1947 of an Alldred Joan to one Baird at Southport, which may explain what became of her...

There are problems with this. The Joan which Prof. Torrens has found is thirty (or 32) years Robson's junior and, if related to him, would presumably be his child. Robson himself mentions his wife in this very book (pg. vi), which was written in 1922. I suspect the Professor was misled as he seems to have not looked at any of Robson's books. Mrs. Robson is again mentioned by Dorothy Ryan, in her account of Robson's life in 1937-8.

If we combine Robson's change of address c. 1939 with Joan Alldred's statement in 1943, that she was not his wife, we speculate that in 1938 or '39, Vivian and Joan split. Robson presumably moved to the basement flat, while Joan eventually moved in with friends, as the electoral register showed both of them at Castletown Road.

If Joan's association with Robson was as a common law wife, then there would be no marriage certificate and no divorce papers, hence, no records. If we further presume Robson never told the Elliott-Balls of his current status, it implies his personal circumstances in the last years of his life were not of his choosing. This also explains Joan's statement on the Death Certificate, since, legally, the two were never married, and, by 1943, she had presumably wed a Mr. Alldred. It seems to me that, either by birth or by association, Joan was likely to have been as meticulous as Vivian. I have questions about Vivian Robson's death, but regret I do not have the means to investigate.

My goal was not to make a memorial edition, but to find a picture. After two months looking hither and yon, I understand why it has been so hard. Vivian Robson may have spent the 1930's as a recluse. It certainly seems he ended his life that way.

Afterword

Casual snapshots are therefore unlikely. In his life he may have sat for one or two formal portraits, but copies are likely to be few, and in the possession of friends who have long since disappeared. I considered the <u>Modern Astrology</u> archives (wherever they may be) might have a photograph of its one-time editor, but then remembered that of all my employers, the only ones who have my photograph are the ones who issued photo IDs. There may be one or two photos of the young Robson among the sources Prof. Torrens consulted, but those sources are now two decades older.

In passing I note the belief that Vivian Robson was a librarian seems to be in error. If Robson was ever a librarian, it would have been as a casual job sometime in the 1930's, perhaps simply as a means of paying the rent.

With the astrological revival of the last twenty years, it seems that Vivian Robson was born 50 years too soon. Astrology is much in need of his medieval expertise. As publisher, I am honored to present his books to the world, anew.

David R. Roell
September 3, 2010

your way to granting me a Reader's Ticket, or inform me what steps I should take to obtain one.

Thanking you in anticipation I am, dear Sir, Yours faithfully, V. E. Robson. (B.Sc, F.G.S.)

The Director, British Museum Bloomsbury.

1, Ruvigny Garden, Putney, SW 15.

BRITISH MUSEUM 2 MAY 1917 No. 2467

Dear Sir,

Being temporarily employed at the Admiralty, I am anxious to avail myself of the opportunity of consulting certain scientific books in the British Museum Library.

I should therefore esteem it a great favour if you could see

Vivian Robson's application to the British Museum for a Reader's Ticket, dated May 1, 1917. The original is in faded blue ink. Robson's request was granted on the 4th.

Transcription:

1, Ruvigny Garden
   Putney, SW 15
     1/5/17

Dear Sir,

   Being temporarily employed at the Admiralty, I am anxious to avail myself of the opportunity of consulting certain scientific books in the British Museum Library.

   I should therefore esteem it a great favour if you could see your way to granting me a Reader's Ticket, or inform me what steps I should take to obtain one.

   Thanking you in anticipation,

           I am, dear sir
             Yours faithfully
               V.E. Robson (B.Sc, F.G.S.)

      The Director
       British Museum
       Bloomsbury

Vivian Robson's Death Certificate, dated January 1, 1943

Transcription, by column numbers:

1. When and where:
Thirty-first December 1942, 2A Castletown Road

2. Name and surname:
Vivian Erwood Robson

3. Sex: Male

4. Age: 52 years

5. Occupation: Journalist

6. Cause of death:
Synapse Cardiac Infarction Coronary Athe-?
Certified by H.N. Stafford Coroner for County of London after P.M. without inquest.

7. Signature, description and residence of informant:
J. Robson
Widow of deceased in attendance 2A Castletown Road W14

8. When registered:
First January 1943

9. Signature of registrar:
W. James Acting Registrar

Marginal note:
In entry no.56 Cancel for 'Widow of deceased in attendance' and 'causing the body to be buried.' Corrected on the 20th of April 1943 by me, W. James, Acting Registrar, on production of a Statutory Declaration made by Joan Alldred otherwise Robson and Ellen Caroline Winifred McGoun.

295

Form A504 D.L. 8264216 25M 1/81 Mer(2016)

DA 749608

DEATH in the Sub-district of _Fulham East_ in the _Metropolitan Borough of Fulham_

REGISTRATION DISTRICT _Fulham_

Application Number _157 G_

No.	When and where died	Name and surname	Sex	Age	Occupation	Cause of death	Signature, description, and residence of informant	When registered	Signature of registrar
56	Thirty First December 1942 2A Castletown Road Fulham	Vivian Erwood Robson	Male	52 years	Journalist	Synapse Cardiac Infarction Coronary Atheroma Certified by H.N. Stafford Coroner for County of London after P.M. without Inquest.	J. Robson Widow of deceased in attendance 2A Castletown Road W 14	First January 1943	W. James Acting Registrar

CERTIFIED to be a true copy of an entry in the certified copy of a Register of Deaths in the District above mentioned.
Given at the GENERAL REGISTER OFFICE, LONDON, under the Seal of the said Office, the _7th_ day of _December_ 19_61_.

This certificate is issued in pursuance of the Births and Deaths Registration Act 1953. Section 34 provides that any certified copy of an entry purporting to be sealed or stamped with the seal of the General Register Office shall be received as evidence of the birth or death to which it relates without any further or other proof of the entry, and no certified copy purporting to have been given in the said Office shall be of any force or effect unless it is sealed or stamped as aforesaid.
CAUTION:—Any person who (1) falsifies any of the particulars on this certificate, or (2) uses a falsified certificate as true, knowing it to be false, is liable to prosecution.

In entry no 56 Cancel for 'Widow of deceased in attendance' and 'causing the body to be buried.' Corrected on the 20th April 1943 by me W. James, Acting Registrar, in production of a Statutory Declaration made by Joan Alldred otherwise Robson and Ellen Caroline Winifred McGoun

Better books make better astrologers.
Here are some of our other titles:

AstroAmerica's Daily Ephemeris, 2010-2020
AstroAmerica's Daily Ephemeris, 2000-2020
   - both for Midnight. Compiled & formatted by David R. Roell

Al Biruni
**The Book of Instructions in the Elements of the Art of
   Astrology**, *1029 AD, translated by R. Ramsay Wright*

Derek Appleby
Horary Astrology: The Art of Astrological Divination

E. H. Bailey
The Prenatal Epoch

Joseph Blagrave
Astrological Practice of Physick

C.E.O. Carter
The Astrology of Accidents
An Encyclopaedia of Psychological Astrology
Essays on the Foundations of Astrology
The Principles of Astrology, *Intermediate no. 1*
Some Principles of Horoscopic Delineation, *Intermediate no.
   2*
Symbolic Directions in Modern Astrology
The Zodiac and the Soul

Charubel & Sepharial
Degrees of the Zodiac Symbolized, *1898*

Nicholas Culpeper
**Astrological Judgement of Diseases from the Decumbiture
   of the Sick**, *1655, and,* **Urinalia**, *1658*

Dorotheus of Sidon
Carmen Astrologicum, *c. 50 AD, translated by David Pingree*

Nicholas deVore
Encyclopedia of Astrology

Firmicus Maternus
Ancient Astrology Theory & Practice: Matheseos Libri VIII,
c. 350 AD, translated by Jean Rhys Bram

William Lilly
Christian Astrology, books 1 & 2, *1647*
   The Introduction to Astrology, Resolution of all manner of questions.
Christian Astrology, book 3, *1647*
   Easie and plaine method teaching how to judge upon nativities.

Alan Leo
The Progressed Horoscope, *1905*

Jean-Baptiste Morin
The Cabal of the Twelve Houses Astrological, *translated by*
George Wharton, edited by D.R. Roell

Claudius Ptolemy
Tetrabiblos, *c. 140 AD, translated by J.M. Ashmand*
The great book, in the classic translation.

Vivian Robson
Astrology and Sex
Electional Astrology
Fixed Stars & Constellations in Astrology
A Beginner's Guide to Practical Astrology

Diana Roche
The Sabian Symbols, A Screen of Prophecy

Richard Saunders
The Astrological Judgement and Practice of Physick, *1677*
By the Richard who inspired Ben Franklin's famous Almanac.

Sepharial
Primary Directions, a definitive study
A complete, detailed guide.

Sepharial On Money. *For the first time in one volume, complete texts:*

- **Law of Values**
- **Silver Key**
- **Arcana, or Stock and Share Key** — *first time in print!*

James Wilson, Esq.
Dictionary of Astrology
From 1820. Quirky, opinionated, a fascinating read.

H.S. Green, Raphael & C.E.O. Carter
Mundane Astrology: *3 Books, complete in one volume.*
A comprehensive guide to political astrology

If not available from your local bookseller, order directly from:
The Astrology Center of America
207 Victory Lane
Bel Air, MD 21014

on the web at:
http://www.astroamerica.com

Printed in the USA
CPSIA information can be obtained
at www.ICGtesting.com
LVHW041258151023
761121LV00001BB/175